Published in the United States by Random House, an imprint and
division of Penguin Random House LLC, New York.

RANDOM HOUSE and the HOUSE colophon are registered
trademarks of Penguin Random House LLC.

Library of Congress Cataloging-in-Publication Data
Names: Abdurraqib, Hanif.
Title: There's always this year: on basketball and ascension /
Hanif Abdurraqib.
Description: First edition. | New York: Random House, [2024] |
Includes index.
Identifiers: LCCN 2023025673 (print) | LCCN 2023025674 (ebook) |
ISBN 9780593448793 (hardback: acid-free paper) |
ISBN 9780593448816 (ebook)
Subjects: LCSH: Abdurraqib, Hanif, 1983– | Basketball—Ohio—
History. | Basketball fans—Ohio. | Ohio—History.
Classification: LCC GV885.72.O3 A43 2024 (print) | LCC
GV885.72.O3 (ebook) | DDC 796.32309771—dc23/eng/20231215
LC record available at lccn.loc.gov/2023025673
LC ebook record available at lccn.loc.gov/2023025674

Printed in the United States of America on acid-free paper

randomhousebooks.com

6 8 9 7 5

Contents

FOURTH QUARTER: CITY AS ITS FALSE SELF
237

ACKNOWLEDGMENTS
323

INDEX
325

Wanna fly, you got to give up the shit

that weighs you down.

—TONI MORRISON

Well it must be close to the Armageddon,

Lord you know that I won't fly by that lesson you taught me

—BIZZY BONE

5:00

You will surely forgive me if I begin this brief time we have together by talking about our enemies. I say *our* enemies and know that in the many worlds beyond these pages, we are not beholden to each other in whatever rage we do or do not share, but if you will, please, imagine with me. You are putting your hand into my open palm, and I am resting one free hand atop yours, and I am saying to you that I would like to commiserate, here and now, about our enemies. And you will know, then, that at least for the next few pages, my enemies are your enemies.

But there's another reality: to talk about our enemies is also to talk about our beloveds. To take a windowless room and paint a single window, through which the width and breadth of affection can be observed. To walk to that window, together, if you will allow it, and say to each other *How could anyone cast any ill on this.* And we will know then, collectively, that anyone who does is one of our enemies. And so I've already led us astray. You will surely forgive me if I promised we would talk about our enemies when what I meant was that I want to begin this brief time we have together by talking about love, and you will surely forgive me if an enemy stumbles their way into the architecture of affection from time to time. It is inevitable, after all. But we know our enemies by how foolishly they trample upon what we know as affection. How quickly they find another language for what they cannot translate as love.

4:25

Our enemies believe the twisting of fingers to be a nefarious act, depending on what hands are doing the twisting and what music is echoing in the background and upon which street the music rattles windows. Yet there is a lexicon that exists within the hands I knew, and still know. One that does not translate to our enemies, and probably for the better. Some by strict code, some by sheer invention, but I know enough to know that the right hand fashioned in the right way is a signifier—an unspoken vocabulary. Let us, together, consider any neighborhood or any collective or any group of people who might otherwise be neglected in the elsewheres they must traverse for survival, be it school or work or the inside of a cage. Let us consider, again, what it means to have a place as reprieve, a people as reprieve, somewhere the survival comes easy. Should there not be a language for that? A signifier not only for who is to be let in but also who absolutely gotta stay the fuck out?

There are a lot of things our enemies get wrong, to be clear. But one thing they most certainly get wrong is the impulse that they should be in on anything, and that which they aren't in on is the result of some kind of evil. But please believe me and my boys made up handshakes that were just ours, ones where we would slap hands and then make new, shared designs out of our bent fingers, pulled back and punctuated with a snap. We would break them out before parting ways at the bus stop to go to our separate schools, and break them out again upon our return at the end of the day. The series of moves was quick, but still slow enough to linger. Rarely are these motions talked about as the motions of love, and since we are talking about our loves over our enemies, lord knows I will take whatever I can to be in the presence of my people. To have a secret that is just ours, played out through some quiet and invented choreography. A touch between us that lingers just long enough to know we've put some work into our love for each other. We've made something that no one outside can get through. I do not waste time or language on our enemies, beloveds. But if I ever did, I would tell them that there is a river between what they see and what they know. And they don't have the heart to cross it.

4:10

And since we know our affections well, we also know the granular differences between their movements—the moment when an existing sweetness is heightened, carried to a holier place, particularly when orchestrated by someone we know that we love. For example:

3:55

The difference between enjoying food and enjoying a meal. I believe there is a sliver of difference between being naked and being bare; I believe that difference also exists between those who enjoy food and those who enjoy a meal. A meal is the whole universe that food exists within—a universe that deserves its own type of ritual and honoring before getting into the containers of it. As a boy, I got into the habit of watching my father eat. At dinner, our table was circular, and on the nights when it was all of us, four kids and two parents, my mother and father would sit in the two chairs on one side of the table. I would sit directly across from them, along the other side. I loved being an audience to my father's pleasures, a man who did indeed have a deep well of pleasures to pull from, but a man who was also kept from them far too long, for far too many days, working a job he didn't love but needed. Of the many possible ways to do close readings of pleasure, among my favorite is being a witness to people I love taking great care with rituals some might consider to be quotidian. And my father was a man who enjoyed a meal. Our dinner table was mostly silent, save for the pocket-sized symphony of metal forks or spoons and among them, my father, the lone vocalist, mumbling or moaning through bites weaving in and out of the otherwise mechanical noise with sounds of his present living. But even before a meal, my father would prepare, slowly: blessing the food in Arabic, seasoning it, stretching a napkin wide. There was a point I always loved watching, when he first set upon his plate, deciding exactly what he was going to allow himself to enjoy first. The moment never lasted more than a few seconds, but it was always a delight. To know that even he was at odds with his own patience, wanting to measure his ability to sprint and his ability to savor.

My father is a man who has no hair atop his head. I've never seen my father with hair, save for a few old photos from before I was born or shortly after where, even then, his head is covered by a kufi—only revealing that there is hair underneath by some small black sparks of it fighting their way out of the sides or down the back. It is because of one of these photos that I know my father had hair when I was a baby, too young to remember anything tactile about my living. In the photo his head is covered and he is holding me, but there is, unmistakably, hair in this photo. There is no way to tell how abundant it is or isn't, no way to tell if it was ever robust enough for me to have run a small and curious hand through it while resting in his arms and fighting off sleep.

But in my conscious years, I never knew my father to have hair, which is, in part, why watching him eat was such a singular delight. No matter the level of seasoning that was or wasn't on his food, small beads of sweat would begin to congregate atop his head. A few small ones at first, and then those small ones would depart, tumbling down his forehead or toward his ears to make way for a newer, more robust set of beads. This process would continue until, every now and then, my father would pull a handkerchief from what seemed like out of the air itself, dabbing his head furiously with one hand while still eating with the other. The sweat, I believed, was a signifier. This is how I knew my father was somewhere beyond. Blown past the doorstep of pleasure and well into a tour of its many-roomed home, an elsewhere that only he could touch. One that required such labor to arrive at, what else but sweat could there be as evidence?

I never saw the old photos of my father with hair until I was in my teenage years. I don't remember when it was that I realized that the bald black men I loved had hair once. Or that they put in work to keep their heads clean, to stave off whatever remnants of hair might try to fight their way back to the surface. My father and grandfather both had clean heads. And they both had thick, coarse beards that they cared for rigorously. The scent of my father's beard oil arrived in rooms before he did, lingered long after he left. He approached his beard care with a precision and tenderness—his fingers shuffling through his beard when he spoke or listened intently, a beard comb peeking out of his front pocket at almost all times, hungry to once again tumble through the forest of thick hair, be fed by whatever remnants clung to the teeth on the way down.

Because I came into the world loving men who had no hair on their heads but cared for what hair they did have—bursting from their cheeks, or curved around their upper lips like two beckoning arms—it seemed that this was a kind of sacrifice made in the name of loving well, of having something that a small child could bury their hands in, something closer to the ground those hands might be reaching up from.

If my father worked in the backyard washing his car or hauling some wayward tree branches, his bald mound laid out for the birds to circle around in song, I could see the sunlight find a spot to kick its feet up, right at the crown of his head. I was so young, and so foolish, and knew so little of mirrors. I imagined that if I crawled high enough, on the right day, I could look down from above and see my own face reflected back to me from atop my father's shining dome. And nothing felt more like love to me than imagining this. A man whose face I hadn't grown into yet, wielding an immovable mirror which is, always, a sort of promise which, through your staring, might whisper to you *Yes, this is what you have now. Yes, the future has its arms open, waiting for you to run.*

3:50

I have told you all of this because I found a love for the black bald head early, and I pity those who might not appreciate it. Even "pity" might be too generous a word, but I am working on generosity toward our enemies, if it might get me closer to any heaven my beloveds are furnishing.

3:45

It was James Brown who once said *Sometimes, you like to let your hair do the talking,* and I do not know what he looked like at the exact time he said it, but I would love for us to imagine him tenderly touching his palms to the sides of an absolute monument of a pompadour, the way he looks in one of my favorite photos of him, backstage and staring into a mirror with a look of both concern and determination, the sleeves on his robe puffing out around his wrists, one of which is adorned with a gold watch and then, slightly farther up, a gold ring on his pinky. And I would love for us to imagine that James Brown said this and then said nothing. Allowed the room to be silent while he made the necessary adjustments. When you performed the way James Brown performed, some nights it would be a miracle to have your hair stay in place. There were no promises of what might happen when the spirit took hold of the body, and so the first time the crowd saw the hair, it had to be perfect. It had to be its own song, its own conversation. This idea that what is atop the head or not atop the head or what is temporarily masking the head is all a language, a code. That at the highest point of the body, there is still a point that can be made to ascend higher, by some invention of whatever God has given us to design with, or even whatever wasn't given, or what was given once and taken away.

In returning to the Gospel of James, the hair (or even lack thereof) does do the talking, and it has been true for me that black hair talks in a language that is entirely its own, and a language that not all hair can achieve—even among the multitudes of black folks, some hair can speak in a manner that other hair might not be afforded. Even among kin, even among siblings. But when it speaks well, there is nothing else that needs to be said to it or about it, although if I know my folks, I will say that many of us don't mind heaping praise upon someone who knows they look good, even if they already know it.

If there is a discomfort that registers, perhaps it is in the realization that, once again, there is a lock that our enemies cannot pick. There is a code that they cannot decipher, no matter their desire to. No matter how many times they have fallen into dreams of our language, our enemies wake up with the same tongues, reaching but falling short. What else to do, then, but to imagine every gesture toward flyness as an affront to their own monochromatic living?

3:40

I don't recall when I first heard of the five black boys who made their way to Ann Arbor in 1991, but I know I heard of them before I saw them. This is a miracle of the past—one that many young folks might not have the opportunity to indulge in now. Hearing word of something, someone, some brewing storm. Hearing before seeing, building up the myth before confirming it. I am from Columbus, Ohio, which means that even when I was a kid of eight years old, I knew wasn't nobody in my city fucking with that school in Ann Arbor, but I knew the Fab Five had people around me shook. You might hear about them on the schoolyard courts, watching the older kids play, fetching the ball for them when one careened off of a foot and out of bounds. Some would say they'd seen them play, or they'd played against a couple of them in some tournament or whatever. This was the time then. Information would crawl through an ever-evolving game of telephone on corners, on porches, on cracked courts. It was miraculous, a gift for the imagination. It beckoned us to see without actually seeing.

And yet I do recall when I first *saw* the Fab Five, both in stillness and in motion. First, in stillness:

before the 1991 season starts, there are photos in *Sports Illustrated* and the *Detroit Free Press*. Two different ones. In the first one, the one taking up most of a page in the magazine, the five freshmen are sitting on the floor of University of Michigan's Crisler Arena. Jalen Rose, Juwan Howard, Jimmy King,

Ray Jackson, and Chris Webber. At the center of them is Michigan coach Steve Fisher. Their poses are textbook. Looking at the photo now, I can almost hear the photographer shouting out directions the way photographers shouted at me and my teammates when we took our high school sports photos. One player on one knee, arm draped over the bent knee. Anyone in the front, stretch your legs across the floor. The smiles, fluorescent as they are, also seem trained. The only player breaking decorum slightly is Webber, who rests his head on King's arm, slightly thrown back like he's either entering or exiting a large laugh. For the uninitiated, for those not on the playgrounds or in the streets or privy to the whispers in locker rooms about how big and bad the storm descending on Ann Arbor was, this photo is a photo of reassurance. The one that calms those who might think they were going to be subjected to years of towering swagger that might disrupt the precious landscape of college basketball.

And then there is the other photo. The five freshmen form a half crescent in their white Michigan uniforms. King and Howard on one side, Rose and Jackson on the other. In the center, Webber sits on a lowered basketball hoop, cradling a basketball against his thigh with one hand. His other hand is across his chest, angled toward his heart, stretched into what would be a distinct "5" if not for his index finger and middle finger twisting together into what looks like could be a single, winding, and interconnected finger. At a second glance, they are all making this same motion with their hands, all twisting together the same finger. There is no Steve Fisher in this photo. Absent also are the smiles which could have placated some of those who were witness to the first photo. Yet here they do not look bereft of joy. They look mostly like teenagers. Certain of their own invincibility because no one has come correct enough with anything to make them uncertain. Each of them glaring into the camera, except for Webber, atop the rim, looking somewhere slightly above—not quite heavenward, but his eyes appear to be at least curious about the doorway to the angels.

3:25

And then, in motion:

When they came back for their sophomore season, the Fab Five had chosen to evolve their style. Their sneakers were all black. So were their socks. Both going against the tradition of uniform that Michigan wore, and also going against the style of their teammates at the time. They were a team within a team. But it wasn't only the black socks and kicks—Chris Webber and Jalen Rose also sported freshly shaved heads. In their freshman season, Webber and Rose both flirted with baldness but usually kept a tight fade. Low, but still just high enough to let people know there was, in fact, hair present, its abundance stifled with intention. In their sophomore season, the two left no doubt. Clean-shaven, shorts so baggy that the fabric trailed behind them like a herd of horses during a fast break—and there were many fast breaks.

Let it be known that the Fab Five were always what some would consider brash, which is to say they came through talking shit from the word go. Talking shit to anyone who happened to be within earshot, and that sometimes meant talking shit to each other. You can always tell who did or didn't grow up playing the dozens by who clutches their pearls when they see some black folks talking shit to each other, to their competition, to the world. All kinds of affection tucked underneath the talking of shit. Jalen Rose used to study his opponents, do real-time research on motherfuckers—in the no-internet early 1990s, no less. Just so he would have some shit to say to make sure a nigga was shook. And listen, ain't that a *kind* of love? To say *You are worthy of the time it takes to dismantle you.* Yes, do not waste language on our enemies, but an enemy, to me, implies a permanence. A thorn that cannot be removed. An opponent is different than an enemy, even if you see that opponent twice a year. If you know you're good, an opponent is a temporary roadblock, something to be taken apart and moved out of your way. Before the Fab Five knew this, Ali knew this. Even in the years before Ali knew this, black folks who couldn't talk shit to their bosses or whoever presided over their lives knew this, because they'd run home and talk their shit to anyone who would listen. Shit talking is a right, a gift, a mercy with a lineage all its own.

If you were to go back now and look at or listen to some of the commentary from white college basketball experts and announcers going into the sophomore season of the Fab Five, you will find the occasional odd fixation on baldness as something menacing. It was often looped in with the black socks and the black shoes and the baggy uniforms, all as a way of saying that there was something troubling about the team's presentation and therefore something troubling about their approach to the game. *These* weren't the people who were supposed to make it. Not this far, not this fast. Announcers, shaking their heads, decrying how much time the five freshmen spent in the ears of their opponents, particularly Rose and Webber, who were artists at squeezing everything they could out of a small moment of excellence. There was an unspoken (and sometimes loudly spoken) glee when the Fab Five would lose. And this, of course, is where I came to love them more. With an intensity that led me to understand that anyone who did not love this team was my enemy. Anyone who might wish to pull apart their brilliance, to tame or temper their flourish, was my enemy.

3:15

So much of the machinery of race- and/or culture-driven fear relies on who is willing to be convinced of what. How easy it is to manufacture weaponry out of someone else's living if the emphasis is placed on the right or wrong word, or if that word is repeated enough, perhaps in a hushed tone. The early '90s—like the majority of American eras before it—had no shortage of panicked people who already feared young black folks, simply looking for anyone, anywhere to dress those fears up in an attire that the panicked might consider to be more publicly palatable than the boring racism humming underneath the dressing up of haphazardly assembled fears. But the targets of the panic know better.

I do not spend time in the caverns of fear our enemies have built for themselves, and I especially did not do this when I was young. When all of my heroes either had long hair that looked like it would send any and all devils back to their smoldering misery, or no hair at all. Afros or glistening curls cascading from the backs of LA Raiders hats or hats with a red, black, and green "X" directly at the center. And I know, this began by talking about an *absence*

3:00

of hair, and we absolutely will return there, if you will allow me just one more moment to say that I never believed any of my beloveds to be villains. I don't need to say that here, to you, but I do adore the way it looks on the page, so I will preach it while I still have you. Back then, when there were those who might strip my beloveds of the fluorescent accessories of their living, I never once thought they were the villains in the story. Not the ones who tucked colorful bandanas into their back pockets and slowly unfurled them once they got the fuck off school grounds, not the ones who sat in principals' offices because they had just left the salon or the barbershop and looked too damn good to cater to anyone's comfort but their own. Not the ones who wore jean jackets with thick, puffy letters airbrushed onto them—the names of who was once among us but no longer, the name of a block you refuse to leave behind even for a few meager hours per day. If I had any heroes at all, I know none of them gave a fuck about the targets being stitched to their immaculate garments. The first way I felt myself operating on the other side of America's fear was being young and idolizing the people America was trying to convince me to be afraid of.

This is what propelled my love for the Fab Five most in their sophomore season. In the fall of 1992 and early 1993, when announcers sometimes talked about their black socks and baggy uniforms and bald heads and trash talk and the music they listened to and the clothes they wore before and after games and the way they walked into arenas, with a lean and a slight dip, and isn't it funny the lengths our enemies go to in order to say *I am afraid I am being left behind, and then who will love me?*

2:29

But since we are talking about an absence of hair, let it be known that by the time Chris Webber and Jalen Rose were swaggering through Ann Arbor with their bald heads, having a bald head wasn't exactly something that was decried, particularly not in the sports world. This was 1992, and MJ sure enough didn't have a single hair on his head when he won those titles and smiled in those commercials and wore a gold medal for his country. It was Jordan, also, who first had longer shorts made for him in 1989, which moved the Fab Five to do the same two years later.

In 1992, Michael Jordan was a *bad* man, but he wasn't a Bad Man. Feared on the court, but mostly beloved in the world outside of it. Wasn't a hustler but could sell damn near anything. Smiled for every camera once the game ended. Only had enemies between the lines, or at least it was easy to believe that for a little while.

Athletes had been bald before Jordan, but his baldness was a signature, in part because he had the perfect head to pull off such a show of nakedness. Aerodynamic, some might say. Made it easier for him to be cradled in a tunnel of air when he stretched himself skyward, made it easier to believe oneself as impenetrable cool, even as you pulled strands of exhausted hair from your scalp during showers or woke up to dark hair on a white pillow. It's okay, was part of MJ's promise. There is a way to be cool on the other side of whatever befalls your scalp. Which is funny to me, because Mike was never as cool

2:23

as he was in '85, when he showed up to the dunk contest with thick, tightly coiled patches of hair making up a hairline that was fighting for what little life it had left, if you look closely. If you are the type who has loved or known a black person whose hair has begun to retreat along their dome. Mike would shave all that shit off in '89, but at the dunk contest in '85, he had yet to cross the threshold that would define him. I propose that the difference between being naked and being bare is that in a state of nakedness, the end can be seen even if it hasn't arrived yet. It has less to do with what one is or isn't wearing or showing, and more to do with how poorly one keeps the inevitable hidden or how long a person can hold back the undoing (pleasureful or less so) that awaits them.

But in '85, it wasn't the hair, and it wasn't even the fact that Mike lost the contest. It is the photo of him soaring toward the basket, his arm cradling the rock with ill intentions, eyeing the rim like prey, like he's already seen its demise. And Mike took flight in a pair of kicks the NBA had banned and the gold—yes, the gold—stretching up along his neck, almost angling toward his open mouth while he was in the air. Some might say that in any consideration of flight, one must also consider the excess weight of anything that might render you closer to the earth than to the sky, but one must also consider that you don't show up with gold if you only plan to take it off. There are those who demand to be buried with all their gold on. To reach heaven, perhaps, still wrapped in the arms of their earthly jewels. Mike was never as cool as he was when he climbed toward the sky with two gold chains around his neck, ascending, too, so there could be no mistake about that miraculous air that refused to let MJ down. I believe no gold to be subtle. I believe nothing to be subtle when it can be snatched from a neck in order to feed a family. But Mike said, again, you're going to have to catch me. You are going to have to climb, and I know you want no parts of the world from this high up. Find the point where you are unkillable and jump toward it if you can. Mike was never as cool as he was in '85, when he hadn't yet begun to take a blade to his scalp. When he started at one end of Market Square Arena in Indianapolis and ran, catapulting himself from the free-throw line (yes, the *actual* free-throw line!) and remaining, suspended and extended, for what feels, even now, like a glorious hour. Your finest hour. The hour you've dreamed of living again ever since the final grains of it kissed the mountain of sand at the bottom of the hourglass. Have you ever been in the air so long that your feet begin to fall in love with the new familiar, walking along some invisible surface that is surely there, that must be, as there is no other way to describe what miracle keeps you afloat? How long have you been suspended in a place that loves you with the same ferocity and freedom as the ground might, as the grave might, as a heaven that lets you walk in drowning in gold might?

When Mike finally came back down to earth, gold in the exact same place it was when he took flight, he simply pumped his fist, clapped his hands a little bit. Mike was never as cool as he was right then, in the moment directly after his singular defiance of the routines of both flight and flyness. Smiling to himself like he was awaking from a dream—a good dream, a dream of invincibility, a dream where no one can kill you but you. Even now, I wish to touch the hem of that type of cool. To ascend and then return, knowing the world has been altered before I landed. And there is no reason for me to be longing for this now except for the fact that I am looking up at the sky and thinking, again, of the most cartoon version of heaven—a place overcrowded with people whose names I have brought back to life, whose names I have scrubbed the dirt off of after long winters have weighed their headstones down with the treachery of the season. A place where the dead have nothing else to do but watch the living they loved and still love, watching all of the sweetness lurking around the corners we ourselves cannot see, shaking their heads as we deny ourselves our waiting miracles. This is a self-indulgent way to imagine the life after this life, but I have massaged all other meaning I can out of the sky, out of the shapes of clouds and the oranges and reds that fight their way through those clouds while the sun laughs its way to surrender.

I have led us astray again, I know. I meant to talk about gold—which is both a color and a state of being—though definitely a color, one I have seen knocking tenderly on the glass of a window in an airplane in the early moments of descent, right after waking and sliding open the plastic lid temporarily quieting the shining empire of light, which—if you are lucky— greets you at just the right distance, where you can see where you are going and see what is carrying you there. Which means, if you are coming back to Columbus, as I do always, you can see the yawning mouths of stadiums bursting with green and you can see the familiar buildings, the ones you might take for granted if you live in a place long enough and forget to look skyward all that often. And yes, with the plane tilting at the right hour, the gold from the sky can make its way across your newly awakened eyes, the color itself, two hands nudging you home. And this is why I must believe that there are my people, beyond the clouds, draped in some exquisite shit, untucking the shine just as a reminder. And Michael Jordan was coolest when he was close to them, alone, statuesque and still but for the stadium lights dancing along the gold around his neck, sending a signal to someone, somewhere. Yes, my beloveds, it is all this talk of gold and skies that makes me want to jump toward you, even with my sturdy head of hair and my legs not having as much to give as they used to. My god, how I miss you all. My god, how I pray to be buried in whatever decoration will allow me to arrive to your arms, new again. Clean.

1:49

Today, Chris Webber's hair piles in neat and even knots atop his head. Jalen Rose's hair is the source of awe and jokes on the internet. His hairline, so precise that if I look at it for too long my vision begins to blur, trying to figure out the math of it all. The two friends don't talk much anymore. The intensity of their years-long feud waxes and wanes, sometimes punctuated by a brief, awkward interaction. It feels important for me to be honest about this here—this insurmountable rupture between the two. I am reminded, again, of Chris Webber in 2015, on *The Dan Patrick Show*, lamenting Jalen and his other four team-mates for cashing in on the legacy of the Fab Five, doing documentaries and putting out merch.

"No one ever loved the Fab Five," Webber says, seemingly exasperated. "So why would you use us to tell stories to get that fake love now?"

1:48

I loved you // I'm sorry // I loved you.

1:30

If you didn't have the money for the barbershop, someone in the crib damn well better know how to cut hair. And not just a little bit. Surgical with the Wahl, someone who learned how to fade their own shit by holding a mirror in one hand, slightly angled to pick up the reflection from another mirror, looking both into it and behind them—assessing both their present self and the potential for their future self—with the clippers, stretched toward the back of their head, thrusting upward in small shouts, but never too high.

It is probably best if this someone is a someone who also carries your last name, or some kinship, so that there is just a touch of extra incentive to not fuck your head up. Any good barber takes pride in their work, but that pride increases depending on how easily the results of it can be traced back to their doorstep. And so, in my house, that someone was my oldest brother, who cut my hair from my first haircut and almost every haircut I got after, into my early teenage years. Even when he went off to college, I would let my hair grow until he visited for a weekend, when I could convince him to take care of my head. I believe he enjoyed being of service to his younger brothers in this way, even if he didn't show it. He would sigh, jerk our heads around and tightly hold them in place. But there was also a sense of care that came through when he caught a good groove within the cut. When he was proud of his work, or even fascinated by it, you could tell. His pace slowed down, his grip on the back of my head would loosen a little bit. It was a strange pleasure, getting to act as his sometimes-unruly canvas.

Through almost every year I was in school, I wore a kufi. Not just in school—I also pulled one on to go to the store, to run errands with my parents. Bright, colorful designs were stitched into them by way of my mother's hands, working at a loud, vibrating sewing machine that could be heard echoing throughout the house in the evenings.

Because of this, my hair was covered for most hours I spent outside of the house. There was no real reason to spend much time on my hair at all. People would be able to see the faint lines of a fade beginning, if anything at all. But my brother took to the cutting of our hair with the knowledge that we didn't have yet. To keep a part of oneself covered sparks a fiery curiosity within others, particularly if those others have to remove whatever hats they have on when they enter a school building and you don't. This isn't to say that I was the target of excessive bullying or that my elementary and middle school experiences were significantly more tortured than anyone else I knew—the specifics of my tortures, at least, were more rooted in the fact that I was both small and a little too eager to talk my shit than they were in whatever was worn on my head.

It is, instead, to say that my hair and what it did or didn't look like became a source of wonder for the people around me. I took a youthful and foolish pleasure in holding on to that kind of power. Having a secret that, almost every day, I knew someone would want revealed.

I was never good at cutting my own hair, and I knew I would never be good at cutting my own hair. My oldest brother passed down his knowledge to my next oldest brother, but I didn't take to it as easily myself. Part of this was due to lack of care or investment. Sure, when I took to the basketball courts across the street from my house, my head was uncovered. But in pretty much every other corner of my life, no one saw my hair anyway. The other reality, of course, was that I knew I wasn't good at it. And to learn to be good at it meant fucking up hair on my own head. I was the youngest. The lineage of home-taught barbers ended with me, and so there was no one to practice on but myself. Even if no one else saw much of it, I would have to live with a reminder of the damage I'd inflicted on myself in my attempts to learn. It is a challenge for someone, even with the steadiest of hands, to be confronted with themselves in the mirror while pulling a humming blade across the front of their head, trying to adhere to a strict line. A line that is predetermined for some, but not nearly precise. The widow's peak that pushed its way to the front of my mother's forehead, rising slightly out of her afro, had descended upon my own hairline, which always caused me to stumble through my already shaky attempts to line my hair up to the point of unmistakable precision. I would start by cutting off the small mountaintop at the front of my hairline, almost resetting what I believed to be the natural starting point. But then, wait, what of the curves as the line makes its way around the head? What of the stopping point? Not going too far into the hair itself, or too far back? It might have served me best to imagine the hairline as a border, a clear interruption between two interconnected but distinctly different expressions of black. I didn't see it then.

During most of these attempts, one of my brothers would come, frustrated, to get me in order again. Repairing the damage.

1:15

I don't remember when my first crush was, but I remember the first *real* crush I had, which means the first crush that sped me toward the cliffs of all things irrational. In seventh grade, I wanted someone who didn't notice me to notice me and I figured the way to do it was to show up to school, finally, with my head entirely uncovered. To be the talk of the hallways, even for a few hours, and go from there. So many of my childhood impulses relied on the logic of taking to the air and then figuring out a plan on the way down. This plan, of course, involved coming to school with a fresh haircut. One that *I* would be the architect of. I would be the only one to be under the hood of my romantic destiny, I thought. And so, in the bathroom, with the door closed, I unfurled my brother's clipper set and went to work. The hairline would be done last. I had learned that much, at least. Get the hair to a desired length. What I didn't learn as clearly was about the guards that needed to be placed over the clipper blades to get the desired length, or the sound the old clipper blades would make when they ran over a patch of hair the wrong way, a sort of growl emerging from the otherwise constant hum.

When it was all said and done, what I had inflicted upon myself was beyond repair at the hands of anyone who lived under my roof. My parents, too amused to be annoyed, gave me a little bit of money and told me to walk to the barbershop down the street. It was just enough money to get the most basic remedy for my affliction: a bald cut. A baptism of sorts. The hair will grow back, I was told. And then it can become anything.

In the mirror the next morning, I looked at my own bald head and thought about the men I loved who had worn theirs so well. The men who wore it so well, I thought their heads were never graced with any hair. My own baldness was jarring, in the face of what I knew. The light wasn't beckoned toward it. The top of my head, instead, was shadowed, hiding from its own luminescence. It isn't the uninterrupted blackness I was ashamed of, it was how we arrived there together.

1:00

I have been better than I have wanted to be at giving in to the foolishness that allows us to sometimes mistake the desire to not be lonely for love. Perhaps I am averse to my own baldness because of what it signals to my often fragile interior: another language for loneliness, having to carry a version of myself that is at least a little bit more empty than the version before it.

I was best at giving in to this foolishness in my teenage years, and so, after school let out, I would go to Leslie's house. Her father worked second shift and her mother's name was carved into one of the headstones in a field a mile west of the school, just a few miles north of the field where I'd buried my mother two years earlier. In the fall and winter months, there would be a small break between the end of the school day and the start of whatever practices I had to get to: soccer, or basketball, or drama club. I had no car until my senior year and lived too far away from the school to bus home and then make my

way back, and Leslie lived a few short blocks away from the soccer field. Convenience is also mistaken for something a little
bit like love, or a lot like love, depending on what is at stake,
and what part of a life is being made easier.

Leslie and I didn't talk in school. We'd pass each other in the
hallways, tucked into our respective groups of friends, and not
make eye contact. Within the loose social hierarchy of our high
school, it wouldn't have mattered or been all that surprising if
we did interact, but it was an unspoken choice. It made the
seeking of each other outside the confines of the building feel
more forbidden and also more transactional. If we don't talk
about what we do beyond the frantic moments of what we do,
then we can convince ourselves that there is a newness to each
clumsy encounter. That we're mostly strangers, drifting toward
each other, desiring only touch and nothing else. And in the
hour that is our hour, a window opens and we can breathe out
all the sad stuff. Find a closet for our tapestry of aches. Both of
our mothers had died, which might bond us in another world,
if we were considering falling in love and not simply pouring
ourselves into what would otherwise be vast, lonely gaps of
living.

Above her bed, Leslie had a promo poster for Meshell Ndegeocello's 1999 album *Bitter*. If you were buying records in the
'90s and early 2000s or any time before, you will know that
some record stores would keep such posters on hand, hang
them in the windows in the lead-up to an album's release. And
if you were smart and looking for a free (or at worst cheap) way
to adorn the bare walls of an otherwise unbearable childhood
room, you could go into the record store on the week before
the album's release and have your name and phone number
scrawled on the back of the promo poster. And when the store
was done with it, the poster was yours.

The poster, a large reproduction of the album cover, was stunning. Ndegeocello is lying upon gold-colored bedsheets. She is slightly out of focus in the photo but is also being generously gripped by sunlight, slanting in from an unseen mirror, clarifying the unmistakable position of the artist, resting on her side, one arm propping her up and one ring on the hand of that arm. Ndegeocello's head is the star of the album cover. Bald and half-awash with that eager sunlight, glowing, a clear, expansive dark brown.

In the small moments when Leslie and I did talk, she would obsess over the poster, over the album cover. She would show me pictures of bald black women in magazines and ask if I thought they were beautiful. She would sometimes run a hand through her dark curls with a look of surprise, as if she'd dreamed them away and couldn't believe they had the nerve to reappear.

One day toward the end of the school year, it rained, delaying some spring practice I was supposed to get to. Leslie and I sat together on her bed, weaving in between the silence that we both came to understand as us telling each other *Not today, the world is too much.*

She told me she'd borrowed hair clippers from one of the boys on the football team. She was ready, she said, to cut all of her hair off. It grows back, after all. That's the miracle of hair. It allows us our mistakes and still returns to us, potentially ready to endure more.

She wanted me to do the cutting of the hair. It was easier that way, and she knew that I at least had some limited and clumsy experience in the cutting of hair, enough to know how to work my way around cutting hair off of someone's head evenly, leaving no remnants of what was. We laid a bedsheet down and then placed a chair atop it, as I'd seen my brothers do before. I wrapped Leslie in a blanket as she sat. It escaped me then, the tenderness of the moment, something far beyond what we'd experienced even in our most heightened pursuits of physical affection. During those pursuits, we were never scared. There was never anything at stake except for a stumble toward the ecstatic, which was easy to stumble toward at that age, at that level of physical curiosity. Here, alone in a house with a chair and a head full of hair that required removal, we were both scared. Of separate things, I am sure. Fear is one thing that can carry an unassuming heart to the gates of love, or at least gates that might be in the same neighborhood as the gates of love. Something that has been denied until it is undeniable, like a slightly out-of-focus photo colliding with a bath of irresistible sunlight, which says *What you have imagined seeing has always been real.*

The short, sparse title track of Meshell Ndegeocello's *Bitter* ends with the lyric "For us there will be no more / and now my eyes, they look at you / bitterly / bitterly / bitterly." And though I understood this to be about a beloved making a permanent exit, I used to think it would be better if I understood it as the present version of a self pushing a past version away. The past version who loved someone, and then buried someone, and then was never the same after.

I knew Leslie's mother wore wigs. I saw the open closet once when I had to slip into her older brother's room—he was then well off to college—to steal another one of his old condoms. In all the time I spent with Leslie, our mothers never entered the room. We never spoke of what ailed them, what took them from us. I never asked about the wigs, and I never asked about the cancer. I never asked about the old coat of her mother's that never seemed to leave the coat rack by the front door. I knew what it was like to keep something close, just in case there was some error in the universe. The people we love deserve to return to the places they left with the things they love intact.

In the makeshift chair at the center of the makeshift barbershop, I moved Leslie's head into the best lighting in the room, the way my brothers had done with me a hundred times, trying to find the best place to start. When I turned on the clippers, Leslie squirmed, and so I turned them off. I turned them back on and she slid down in the chair a little bit, and so I unplugged them. I moved to the front of the chair and sat down on the floor. When we looked at each other, her face contorted as though she had just considered something immense for the first time.

"What if I've got, like, a fucking *weird*-shaped head??" she asked me, her nose upturned slightly.

After a pause to do the math of such an outcome, our laughter began small—hiccups of snorting and snickering and then outright shouts that sent both of us rolling on the floor, knocking the chair over with our temporary madness. And yes, laughter and crying both tumble out of the body's orchestra at a similar tune, and so who is to say, really, when one became the other, or if they were ever disparate devices of pleasure at all on that afternoon, the rain percussive against the windows, keeping time with our reckless unfurling. The two of us, laughing and crying ourselves to sleep, wondering if there would ever be a time when we might find ourselves unleashed from the kingdom of vanity.

0:30

There is, though, a strange sort of honor in pulling up to the court with a rock that has worn itself down, with no grip, no traction to speak of. A rock that some might call *bald* on the street where the games are played, and never played with that worn-down ball you rolled up with. But still, on my block, the hoopers everyone thought were the realest either showed up with a brand-new ball or showed up with a ball that looked like it had been through hell. Whatever brand or logo beaten off of it, the black rubber lining the seams cracked and waving down, signaling surrender. And yes, none of the raised rubber along the surface that might offer grip, or the comfort of stability while shooting.

There is a reality of loving ball in a place where people don't have money. A place where sacrifices are made to keep the lights on, to keep food on the table. Sacrifices that, sometimes, don't have your desires at the end of them. Hardly anyone I grew up around could play for the high-profile traveling teams, and so the training ground for the offseason was the neighborhood court. And because people from all over the neighborhood converged in the same place at the same time, one of the negotiations of the game, and of the court, revolved around which ball could be played with for the real, serious, full-court runs. There wasn't judgment in these assessments as much as a kind of science. Players passing a ball around, squeezing it, turning it over gently in their hands. It was here I learned the difference between an indoor ball and an outdoor ball and a ball that served well for both purposes, depending on how well the outdoor surface was cared for, and on my block it was never cared for, but we knew how to navigate the aftermath of neglect. Which side of the court dipped slightly and which crack in the surface might send the rock careening toward the baseball diamond, which, depending on the day, might be housing a little league game and a throng of concerned parents who never made it to our side of town, eyeing the players on the basketball court with their loud, echoing foul language and the music sometimes spilling out of a small boombox at the court's edge.

But it was also here that I learned that there is nobility in a basketball that has faded, that has gone bald. And there is nobility in the person who carries it to the court. The shooter who has learned to shoot at a deficit, with a ball that slides around in their hand, or the dribbler who made a way with a ball that had endured seasons of being battered against the concrete.

Your ball is your ball, and depending on how you and your folks are livin', you might not see a new one for a while. And so, of course, praise to the person who made a way with a bald rock, and a little path of concrete that was their concrete, and a rusted rim with no net. Those be the noblest of hoopers. The ones who, back then, you had to keep an eye on. Cuz they've done all the hard shit already. Once they get a little bit of a grip on something new, it's lights out.

0:20

Islands of gray have begun to form on the beard of LeBron James, and have started to grow toward each other, uninterrupted, reaching toward each other through the once-black hair. You can notice it best in the offseason, depending on the light he's in or how long it has been since he's gotten a beard trim, how long the grays have had permission to flourish without bowing to the sharp edges of a blade.

In a clip that circulates on Instagram, LeBron is standing on the sideline at his son Bronny's game, shouting out instructions, lovingly. His beard is long, and the lighting in the arena is dancing upon it in a way that highlights the patches of gray that are harder to spot when he's in-season, seemingly more aware of the fact that he's on television more often than most people.

It is a strange miracle to be able to trace your own aging, your own mortality through someone who is living alongside you, someone who has survived eras at the same time as you have, in some of the same places. LeBron's face was as bare as my own when I first heard his name. It is impossible to believe that any of us ever looked like children. I understand, of course, that we *were* once children. The cloak of time has yet to grow so long that I have surrendered my childhood. My shouts thrown into air like knives, just to hear my own symphony cutting through the night sky and returned to me in small slivers of echo. The lightning bugs who surrendered, lazily, to my open palms for a few moments before flickering their bodies on and off and then flying away again. The tree branches that sighed against the fresh arrival of my weight but still did their best to hold me. I believe that I was a child once because I am afraid today. There are parts of me that might die soon, parts of my memory that might drift to a distance too far for me to get back, and because I know myself to be afraid of this, that is all I need to believe that I was once a child. But it is hard to believe that we ever looked like children. Even when the people I love, fresh from a trip back home, excitedly pull me close to unfurl photos of themselves when they were babies, or preteens, or even disaffected high school goths or punks or jocks or drama kids. Even when my best friend shows me a video of her toddler making the same exhausted and delightfully scolding face that I have seen her mother make many times, through many years, clearly a transference of the divine, it is still hard for me to believe that anyone I know now was ever physically not who they are. I do not say this to submit the aesthetics of childhood—specifically black childhood—to a nefarious algorithm. I am not suggesting that I do not see children as children. When the black boys on my block zip through the streets on their bikes, I can't resist shouting some concerned correctives at them the way elders did for me growing up. I'm talking, instead, about our past selves. The way romantics have failed my own clear memory. I remember LeBron James as a fourteen-year-old, skinny and seemingly poured into an oversized basketball uniform that always suggested it was one quick move away from evicting him. But even with what I know, even in photos, his face blurs into the face it is now, the face that ages alongside my own.

Conventional wisdom says that we look to our elders to find the footprints leading us toward what we ourselves might look like as elders. I last sat down to dinner with my father five years ago. The meal wasn't spicy, but it was a meal he loved, and so I watched the sweat begin to congregate at the crown of his head, and I watched him wipe it away tenderly, as he did when I was young. I also watched how sincerely and intently he spoke with his hands, the way they would slice through the air. The way they would sometimes make the shape of the word, cup themselves toward the sky and make the shape of a bowl, well before my father finished describing what once held a soup he missed tasting. His hands always moved while he spoke, seeking to animate the language of a story, or lesson, or monologue. I hadn't noticed this about him until I noticed it about myself, that it was something I would find myself apologizing for. I am sorry for what has been passed down to me without my knowing, what has just shown up on the doorstep and found its way in.

My father and I also probably have the same smile, though it would be hard for me to know, because I don't smile enough to trace it through any kind of consistency. One thing that is for sure is that my father and I have two different hairlines, mine (gracefully! thankfully!) still intact, and I pray to whatever gods oversee such matters of self-indulgence to keep it intact for at least a little while longer.

But it is true that small clusters of gray stars have begun to make their way through my otherwise dark solar system. When the light shines down on me from above, in the bathroom mirror, I notice them, slightly peeking through the top of my head. In the rearview mirror while driving, I look up, and there is a small curved gray hair unmistakably hanging down from the edge of my hairline. At first it was jarring. Something I believed was happening *to* me. Even though the grays have not yet overrun my head and beard, I still found myself wondering how to remove them, pick them out one by one, even against the advice of my beloved barber at the time, who was an old black man with a head covered in gray, who I went to because he cherished the hair on his head, and you must find a barber who cherishes the hair on their own head slowly, thoughtfully, and carefully, so that they might (if you are lucky) extend that kindness toward yours. And this barber told me never to pull the gray weeds from the dark garden, for they might simply grow back with a newfound ferocity. An anger at their removal, he told me. *You don't want to make an enemy out of the grays,* he told me one day, while lining me up. *Best to just thank them for showin' up to the party. Lucky you got a party for them to show up to.*

There has been much made about the fading of LeBron James's hair. All largely uninteresting jokes, or at the very least jokes that are immensely predictable. LeBron himself doesn't acknowledge it much in any explicit manner, which is probably for the best. Even in the early points of his NBA career, anyone who knew hairlines well enough, who stood under good lighting and checked their own for signs of vulnerability, knew that LeBron's hair wasn't long for its more youthful state. There have been moments in his career when he's seemed to try to revive his hair, to mask the portions of it fading along the top and back of his head. There are those who have, in their incessant joking, insisted that LeBron just go bald, give in to what the hair itself seems to be demanding.

There are ways that LeBron James does seem to be concerned with the project of vanity, though perhaps this is not among those ways. Most of those ways seem aligned with how he is perceived as a full, expansive person with a legacy to uphold in a sports ecosystem that—during the time of his initial NBA ascension—became more hands-on, more rigorous in not only how players were critiqued but how easily and how often players could hear from fans. The vanity of LeBron James seems to be the vanity of legacy first, and I might be apologizing for my Ohio brethren for the first of many times in these pages, but I believe there to be far worse vanity projects to pursue than that of legacy.

But enough, enough.

If you are someone who is from a place not everyone made it out of, or if you have been to enough funerals where parents or grandparents weep over the caskets of their babies and grandbabies, if you know *forever* is a hand dealt by an uncertain dealer, you may wear the signs of your aging like thick, heavy gold, weighing the body down, but still stunning—unavoidable in its shine. Lord, the clouds atop the fields of my life are so thin now, the sky is bare and pummeling all that rests below. Lord, the gray won't stop coming, and for once, my arms are open to it. Lord, I have lived long enough to look like my father, though I might fight it. I have lived long enough to cut through the air with my hands, to trim the long hair of the Midwest wind, to make the shape of a bowl when telling a story about something sweet I once held, and can still taste. Lord, release me from whatever might make me wish for the way I looked as a child, which I can hardly remember through this beautiful fog of mortality, this slow march to the kingdom. Lord, when Tyler left us, his hair was so long and dark, I would still find tiny ropes of it around my apartment for months after the funeral. When the judge sentenced Brandon, with not a single line yet woven into his furrowed, boyish brow, to thirty years in a cage and his mother whispered *He'll be so old when he gets out,* I know what was unspoken on the other side of that was *And what will become of me in the meantime?* Yes, Lord, I come to you today pleading for all of the aches of age, all of the permanent and immovable damage you have to offer. Yes, there are moments I have spent and will continue to spend in a mirror, massaging products onto my skin and slowly washing them off, if not to delay the very things I am now welcoming, at least to make them as luminous as possible. Do not be fooled by the weapons I refuse to lay down. I come to you today with gratitude in knowing the fight cannot be won. Let the hair turn its drab colors and, perhaps, slowly begin to depart down the drain. Let the pain in the knee linger as a reminder that movement might one day come with a price, if I am lucky enough to make it that long. Yes, Lord, I am thankful today again for every reminder of how I have outlived my worst imagination. I will walk slowly through the garden of all that could have killed me but didn't.

0:10

When the world has grown weary with indulging our selfish living, I hope to not be alive for whichever apocalypse is the one that ends humanity. But if I am alive for it, I hope that it takes me out early. I do not wish to be alive in the aftermath of the world ending. The movies and television shows don't make it look appealing, what with all of the scavenging and the hard surfaces and the need to be proficient with multiple forms of weaponry and alert at all times. Survival, sure, but when the world suggests it may be done with us, I have no interest in pouring myself into rebuilding it.

But one thing I would crave is the silence. The emptiness of it all. In the spring of 2020, when I thought the world was doing a dress rehearsal for the apocalypse, the only thing that comforted me was the silence. Knowing that the city would otherwise be flooded with shouts and sounds and yet was forced to restrain itself was strangely calming for me.

There was a window of time in this moment, when people were still too stunned to spend any time outdoors and before the parks decided to take the basketball hoops down and lock the gates and barricade the playgrounds. In that window of time, I would grab a ball and go to the court alone. I loved most when the world felt newly bald. If you have ever gone from having hair one day to waking up without it the next day, you might be familiar with the gestures of disbelief: the repeated touching, the returns throughout an hour or a day, the shock when a breeze first plants soft kisses upon your new nakedness. The world felt like that to me then. I would walk into it, tentatively, astonished by the quiet until I let it envelop me.

On the basketball courts, alone, there was nothing to contain the shattering echo of the ball's dance with the concrete. I love a sport where even when I am alone, I am not alone. And I am a little bit ashamed to say that I also love basketball for the violence of its sounds. The way a ball sounds when it ricochets off of a metal hoop that has been worn down by the seasons. The way that a ball, when it rips through a net, might sound the way a thin leather belt sounds being lashed across a child's bare skin by a parent who might sometimes have been one of our enemies, but only sometimes.

This was how I came back to what I considered might be the end of life as I knew it. Alone on a court at the arrival of spring, while the world was locked indoors. Until one day, the rims vanished. Not just at my most beloved park but at all of the parks. I drove around the city frantically, ball in the passenger seat, looking for anywhere that might still have a rim fastened to a backboard. They were all gone, overnight. In a place where suddenly so few people were surviving well, I was asking myself, again, how I might survive.

And I know, it might seem like this has all been about absence. But do you see it now? Absence, maybe, but absence requires an understanding of what *should* be. What was once. It has always been impermanence, beloveds. Impermanence was the altar I was leading us to this entire time. The altar that right now we are kneeling before. My hand on your shoulder, as it has always been. A promise is a foolish thing to make, but here is one, again:

We will leave our enemies behind here and never turn to face them again. But this is not a story about heroes, either. Not everyone will die. No one will live forever.

0:00

"To leave a place . . . you'd best leave everything behind;
all your possessions, including memory. Traveling's not as easy
as it's made out to be."

—VIRGINIA HAMILTON

12:00

Three days after Christmas in 2002, a white pair of kicks, clean enough to still be worn, swings from the telephone lines a few blocks outside of Value City Arena in Columbus, Ohio. Jordan 7s. White and blue. The pair that had just dropped two weeks earlier. If one looks long enough, the thin wires blend into the dark sky and the shoes emerge as though they are swinging from nothing, ornaments at the mercy of clouds. There are a greater number of older white people than usual in this neighborhood today, a cluster of them walking ahead of me, nervously trying to make sense out of the mythology of the sneakers swinging from phone lines, rattling through rumors they'd heard from their kids or things they'd read on the corners of the still-young internet. Drugs, they decided. People sell drugs here.

Tourists believe the hood is a monolith, not an ecosystem that can function differently from block to block, from corner to corner. And so, when someone speaks in hushed tones and says *Bad things happen here*, they don't necessarily need to define the *here* in order to get an affirmative response from the types of folks who only walk through an area because it was the closest place they could park to get to the basketball game that drew the attention of the entire state, most of it in that glowing haze that exists in the days after Christmas but before the new year. Akron St. Vincent–St. Mary was coming to town to face Columbus's own Brookhaven Wildcats, state champs last season. In 2002, SVSM was otherworldly, unfuckwithable to an astonishing degree. But Brookhaven were our guys. Columbus City League kids, and if you came up watching Columbus City League ball, you know ain't no one in there afraid of shit. Keep the rankings, keep the decoration, keep the magazine covers. You come to Columbus, you gotta be able to scrap it out. Even blocks away from the arena, old heads waved signs suggesting that they needed tickets. For weeks leading up to the game, my boys and I hatched a plan to sneak in before reluctantly shelling out the bread for seats, fearing the increased security. And here we were, on the long walk to the arena, in a cluster of white men, already fantasizing about the danger they believed they were traversing just to watch the chosen one, descended from Akron.

I didn't know the kid who was shot a few blocks south of here on Christmas Eve. I knew he was younger than me, and he could hoop. I'd seen him at the park in my old neighborhood once or twice. Quick first step, never passed but could get to the rim anytime he wanted. The bullet that hit him wasn't meant for him, but the bullet doesn't apologize and isn't especially discerning. The bullet only knows what is in front of it. I don't trust people who don't love a place to understand how that place remembers its dead. The living who throw an item the dead once cherished toward heaven, wrap it around the highest wire. So high that it looks like the shoes are swinging from the sky itself. Like two legs are hanging down from the edge of a cloud.

11:40

And don't get it twisted, this wasn't some underdog story of some City League kids lucky to get a little on-court time with the teenage messiah. Going into the game, Brookhaven was ranked sixth in the country, Akron SVSM was ranked ninth. More people packed into the Arena that Saturday night than

there were earlier in the day, when Ohio State played an afternoon game there. Even they knew to surrender prime time to
the pulsating radiance of this matchup, which, in the moment,
felt once-in-a-lifetime. I tricked you there, not long ago. Not all
of you, of course. Not anyone who is from a place that gets
talked about a certain kind of way, or anyone who has had to
fight their way into, out of, or through the merciless yawn of
neglect that growls over the beloved corners of a city. I could
never trick those of you who already know that what an underdog is or isn't has little to do with what small number rests next
to your name in a newspaper. Brookhaven were underdogs because they weren't on magazine covers, they weren't on ESPN.
They didn't have anyone who was going to leap straight to the
league. They were underdogs because the streets loved them,
and the streets can determine who is chosen and who isn't
because the streets are where underdogs flourish—niggas who
quit something or dropped out of somewhere but still ain't
gonna be taken for no fools when it comes to getting to the
money a whole lotta folks said they wouldn't ever get to. I propose that above all, you are a reflection of who loves you. And
look, I ain't from Akron and so I can't call it. I'm sure the streets
were teeming with affection for LeBron and his mighty crew,
and I love those who love the streets and are beloved in the
streets, which means it would be treasonous for me to try and
strip whatever reality existed for Akron SVSM in their north-
eastern corner of Ohio. But I'm from East Columbus and I
know what I know, and I know Brookhaven must have been
underdogs because people who didn't have the money for tickets found the money. Because kids who didn't have cash for a
fit or a clean pair of kicks to show up to the game in made some
shit shake, blew all their Christmas cash and then some, for
one night. Underdogs because they required people to show up

to a place in whatever made them feel singularly limitless, even if the paychecks and the bank accounts didn't have it, even if the hustles dried up for the winter and the shoeboxes under the bed were running low. I ask you to arrive here, for one night, and never consider the possibility of losing anything or anyone.

11:15

In the end, Brookhaven's star point guard, Andrew Lavender, uncharacteristically missed two free throws. The game was frantic, bogged down at points by referees who didn't seem equipped to handle the pace or the stakes of the matchup. St. Vincent–St. Mary overwhelmed Brookhaven in the first half, but in the second half, Brookhaven stormed out and returned the favor, setting off a second-half rally that involved a flourish of fast-break basketball led by the dazzling and ever-calculated Lavender, diminutive at five-foot-seven and yet still the best player on almost every floor he stepped on, even this one, with LeBron James, who would often step out to the perimeter to hover over Lavender, bending down low in a defensive stance that still had him taller than his opponent. And time after time, Lavender would blow by LeBron, get to the rim, and push a floater toward the basket, over the late-arriving outstretched arm of LeBron. The floater, the most romantic shot in the game when done right, guided toward the rim with a heave and a wish, how the follow-through after the ball leaves the hand can look like an overeager wave, like saying goodbye to a person you never wanted to leave. The floater is beautiful for how it relies on height, how the shot itself turns the ball into a bit of a show-off, obsessed with drama, almost pausing in the air to make sure you get its good side before it begins to twirl downward. If you were a small, quick guard, you probably learned to get good at the floater. And if you were Andrew Lavender, you learned to become lethal with it.

But after Lavender led a ferocious second-half comeback, with the score tied 59–59 with ten seconds left, he was intentionally fouled by Sian Cotton. Two shots *and* the ball for Brookhaven. There was a section of us, city kids, the ones who spent our paltry paychecks to get into this hot, crowded gym and sat through most of the first half thinking about the cash we parted with, who were too stunned to celebrate in the moment of the foul and Andrew Lavender, the best player in the city, going to the line for two. All he had to do was make one, and then Brookhaven just had to inbound the ball, make another free throw or two, and get the fuck outta here with a win.

An entire half of the court was empty, save for Andrew Lavender at the free-throw line. The free-throw line can feel like an island when the lanes are clogged and crowded with limbs trying to carve out an inch of space, an elbow aiming for the softest spot in a torso. Without its accessories, the line can feel like a broken-off piece of metal one clings to while floating in the center of an ocean that seems endless, the kind where it is difficult to say where sky ends and water begins. Lavender's first shot was short, and the crowd—even those who were neutral— let out a collective groan. Lavender walked away, mumbling to the hardwood as he paced just beyond the three-point line and then readjusted himself at the foul stripe. The second shot was just as short, if not shorter, hitting the front edge of the rim, and careening back toward where Lavender stood, his hands on his knees in disbelief, the ball bouncing slowly, a mockery of sorts. It was fine, someone behind me said. A few seconds left, Brookhaven gets the ball back. Lavender catches the ball on the baseline and gets a step on LeBron, same way he'd been doing all damn night, and he throws up that reliably potent floater, which looked good for just a split second, the way a ball that flies toward a rim can look good before it descends and touches nothing but air on the other side.

If you've played enough basketball, or watched enough basketball, you know there are some games that are over when they make it to overtime. You can see it in how the two teams carry themselves. The team that wasn't supposed to be in the game at all, who got within a murmur of victory and couldn't finish the job, walking to the bench, dejected, while the presumed victors bounce on their toes, grinning as if they already know the end of the movie and can't wait to see your face while you watch.

11:00

When I say Brookhaven were our guys, I mean that in a vague, overarching sense, though it is also indicative of how basketball worked, how it came to life in a city like Columbus during the heyday of the City League, which began, most prominently, when East High School won the first state championship for Columbus back in 1951, and then won three more in the '60s.

One miracle of Columbus City League basketball, which is not a miracle unique to Columbus, is the geography of the city and the hard borders drawn around the public school districts. It is hard to call this a *miracle,* since there were, of course, nefarious intentions undergirding the decision-making process, intentions that restricted access to city kids, structures to keep them in their place, both literally and in any other sense one can imagine. But it means that schools are clustered in the city's four primary geographical corners, defined by neighborhoods and all that neighborhoods are sometimes defined by— pride, territory, lineage, history. But also, everywhere was easy to get to. Any school you wanted to be at was a bus ride away.

For this, the Columbus City League was susceptible to seemingly fleeting dynastic eras, passed from school to school, depending on what player or coach ended up where and who chose to follow them. The league was also susceptible to heated competition, because most everyone playing knew everyone else, with varying degrees of intimacy. AAU circuit aside, there were only so many parks in the city where *real* hoopers played, and it didn't matter what side of town you were from: if you could play, you'd find your way there. Scores that bloomed from the cracks of some neighborhood's blacktop in the heat of summer were settled in City League high school gyms. The stakes of every game ventured into the intersections of pride, respect, a weekend of immortality on the block for someone who got especially hot from three or worked a crossover at just the right moment to send someone flailing backward, like a ghost of their future self latched on to their jersey to get them the fuck out the way of whatever was coming.

The Brookhaven Era began in earnest in 1992, when Coach Bruce Howard took over the program. Brookhaven was, by that point, a school that dominated in football, sometimes baseball. When Howard came to the school, he sold a simple, three-pronged principle: family, academics, and basketball. Players were required to take all three equally seriously. Howard had played for Mifflin in 1977, when they were runners-up for the state title, and he coached both the boys' and girls' basketball teams at Crestview Middle School before being handed the keys at Brookhaven. Most importantly, Howard was respected. Players wanted to play for him. When he asked them to prioritize family, what he lived was the reality that he might have to be a family member to the players who lacked that closeness elsewhere. In Howard's first season, Brookhaven made it to the City League title game, where they lost to Marion-Franklin by one point. In 1996, they won their first city title. In 1998, they captured the district crown. And by the early 2000s, they were reveling in their dominance. Many of the city's best players flowed into the Brookhaven pipeline, even if they could have gotten more run at other schools. Sixth man with more Division I letters than most other City League schools' star players. Seventh and eighth guys getting ten minutes a game at Brookhaven even though they could have been the best players—by far—elsewhere. You went not only because you wanted to win but because if you played for Brookhaven, people came to watch you. Not just college coaches but the whole city.

They were brash and thrilling, dunks punctuated by a player swinging on the rim like a gleeful metronome, and then coming back down to the floor and throwing up the dynasty sign: palms extended, both thumbs and index fingers touching, making the shape of a diamond. And even if you envied them or hated losing to them or knew you couldn't hang with them even though you desperately wanted to, it was still difficult to ignore how special the moment was, especially because no matter what happened when encased in the game's whistles, they were still a group of kids from the city, like all of us. Their ascension meant something, even for those of us who were residue in the midst of their greatness.

And the real thing about Bruce Howard that I will always remember is that he never forgot

10:52

a face. It didn't matter if you played for him or not. It didn't matter if you even played varsity or played basketball at all. If he saw you enough times, he remembered you. Might not have been great with names, but he'd remember what you looked like. If you played during a junior varsity game that he half-watched one time while waiting for his team to take the floor, or if you came to a few Brookhaven games and pushed your hand through a crowd to congratulate him on a victory, making a fleeting moment of eye contact. You'd run into him in the mall or at the grocery store, and he'd look to you again, and you could watch him, slowly but desperately, attempt to do the math, to bring himself back to where he saw you first, but then giving up, realizing that all that matters is the fact that he's seen you before, which would be more than enough to propel him toward you, offer up his hand, and ask how you were doing, if you were staying out of trouble. If you caught him out on a Saturday morning, after the Friday night game, and complimented him on the win, he might nod a little, smile knowingly, and turn the attention back on you. He was rare in this way, how broadly his affections extended beyond not only his players but also beyond the young people who were students at Brookhaven. It was a salve in a sometimes vicious place, to have a respected adult, a pillar of greatness, look at you and remember your face enough to want to say hi, to ask if you were staying out of trouble. To, in so many words, say *I will not let you move through this city and be forgotten.*

10:27

When Bruce Howard was hospitalized in late January of 2003, just a few weeks after Brookhaven's near-victory at Value City Arena, everyone I knew who wasn't close to him, or close to those who knew him, loved him, or played for him, figured he'd be out and back on the sidelines by the next game. His ailment, initially, was unknown. During a tournament in Orlando, Howard choked up a few pints of blood on a locker room floor and was rushed to the emergency room. Even with the alarming nature of this, there were those who still downplayed what could or couldn't be happening. Stress, most likely. He'd coached long seasons, with deep tournament runs and little time off in between, also coaching AAU basketball during the high school offseason. He was so dedicated to his team, his players, his family; he did nothing as a half-measure. He just needs some time to rest. As the days went on, there was little word other than a sort of citywide whisper network that mostly found itself trafficking in theories and half-prayers. A mantra of "he'll be okay, he's going to miss the next game, and then he'll be right back," repeated as one game fell from the calendar, and then another, and then another. Tuesday nights and Friday nights peeling off and receding into air. At a Brookhaven game during this stretch, before tip-off, an announcer asked people to say a prayer for Howard. No one knew exactly what they were praying for, exactly. It had been two weeks since he was hospitalized, and the concerns about whether or not he'd coach again had turned into concerns about whether or not he'd make it out of the hospital alive at all. And still, in Brookhaven's gym, house of miracles, under a state championship banner less than a year old, a crowd descended into a choir of disparate murmurs. Hushed prayers climbing atop other hushed prayers, some mouths moving but no sound coming out, fitted caps removed and resting inside clasped hands, cats who I knew hadn't been back inside a church since they emerged, screaming, from the waters of baptism nervously reaching back toward God. I propose, once again, that you are, in part, who loves you. Who might step outside of themselves to find whatever will heal you, return you to a place where you are loved. I prayed, too, though I don't recall who I prayed to or what I asked for. I just remember that I looked around, nervously, and an older man behind me placed a hand on my shoulder, gold orbiting three knuckles. *It's going to be okay,* he said, and for the first time, I considered that it might not be. It is one thing to experience death and another to understand it to be possible on its own terms. To grasp the certainty of its arrival but still cling to a hope for that certainty to come in a very specific way, at a very specific time, after a life has fulfilled all of its promise. Death, ushering a person toward an upturned beam of light after they've thrown up their hands and said *Thank you, my life has been good, I want to see the people I miss.* And yes, my mother did not want to go, and yes, there are caskets smaller and shorter than a loud, twisting cry pitched along the wooden walls of a church. I should know better. I don't remember what I prayed for, but I might have prayed to be freed of my own foolishness.

10:25

It's about sacrifice, I'd heard coaches say my whole life. Nothing you do is about you anymore. There's a greater good, and I promise, even if you can't see it, it is there. And just like that, we are back to our allegiance to the unseen glory. It is harder to catch the ghosts that aren't people.

10:21

I didn't know anyone who knew what cirrhosis was, let alone *advanced* cirrhosis. And it was better to not find out, it was decided. Bruce Howard left the hospital in February and said he'd maybe be back by the time the state tournament rolled around, as long as Brookhaven got there and got far enough. This could have been his own optimism, or it could have been him wanting to deliver a message of optimism to the city, or it could have been him doing one final trick of motivation, telling his team *If you make it, I'll be there,* but it was likely an intersection of all three of those impulses. And it seemed possible. Of course it did. There were those of us who could see the story unfolding, fit for the screen, some sweet gospel song laid over the scene. Brookhaven winning the state title and their coach right there, back on the sidelines like he promised, tired but not yet gone. The fantasy was enough to hold on to for a little while.

Bruce Howard died of liver failure less than a month later. Brookhaven lost in the state championship game, though I don't think anyone could blame them. The heart doesn't break all at once. It would be easier that way, cleaner. The process of breaking begins somewhere many of us can't even recall. It accelerates in bursts throughout a life; sometimes it hums along at its steady pace. But with the accumulation of enough pain and the promise of more to come, we can only carry ourselves so far. The joyous weight of trophies and medals is nothing when compared to what the heart must endure, how it shields us from what it can, for a little while, before falling to its knees.

10:15

Science tells us that the brain remembers more faces than we know it does, but it can't create new ones. In our dreams, faces appear on a whim. In my dreams, they exist in a sort of in-between haze. I know the person I should be seeing, but I can't explain how I know it. Their face is a series of shapes that seem familiar, but they could be anyone. They could be everyone. I wake, and I know in my heart who I saw, but I know it by what they were doing, by the sound of their voice, distorted even in the chaotic echoes of dreaming, but still clear enough to know who haunts my sleeping hours. The nature of this is fascinating and a little bit frightening. The brain stores a backlog of faces, even if you've only seen a face once or twice, but because it cannot alter or re-create any portion of it, you only see the face as you saw it last, despite how a person has aged or changed. Despite however many years they've been gone. When the dead visit us in dreams, they could look like the last good version of themselves that we'd ever seen. They could look like themselves as children, if our history with them goes back that far. Everyone I love appears to me in my dreams as they might have looked as a child, if I have loved them for long enough. I can't make sense of their features, but I know they are younger in my dreams than they are now, than they were when I carried their caskets. Everyone arrives to me this way, and when I wake, I cannot remember their faces.

10:00

Geography and pride and rivalries aside, what also made City League basketball special was that it was an expression of lineage. Take the Lavenders, for example. Drew Lavender was the third Lavender brother to play for Brookhaven. Anthony played in 1996, when Brookhaven got its first City League title under Bruce Howard. Antwain Lavender played in 1998, when Brookhaven won the district. But that was just a small example of the phenomenon, which isn't really a phenomenon at all beyond the fact that folks stay where they stay and the game gets passed down to little brothers who watch from the sideline until they can hang on the big courts, that gift coming for some of us sooner than for others. There were the Turner brothers who played at Mifflin, the Gibbs brothers at East High, right in my own neighborhood there was Andre and Kenny Gregory, both playing at Independence.

Within this, there was always the understanding that the younger sibling was the *real* talent. The one to watch out for, no matter how vast the accomplishments of the elder siblings were. The whispers would flood through playgrounds and postgame parking lots. When Antwain Lavender was guiding Brookhaven through the district playoffs, dazzling crowds with his ballhandling and his quick-release jumper that always looked like it was going in, even when it wasn't, people would point to his little brother Andrew in the stands, studying the game like an eager hawk, and they'd mumble *He's the one. He's going to be* special.

I always loved this part the most, even if the mythology of the always-emerging younger sibling didn't come to fruition every time (though, admittedly, it did bear fruit more times than not). I simply liked knowing that there was someone else arriving behind the someone I already knew. That there was another person to admire, a gentle toss away. A kind of magic in saying *I am not sorry, there are more of us, you haven't seen anything yet.* A kind of magic in staying, too. In building a tiny kingdom in a corner of a city that some folk talk on but don't have the heart to ride through. It is a gift to resemble someone who has already done something memorable. If not physical resemblance, to at least carry their name or at least carry some shadow of their game. A crossover practiced in a narrow hallway, a jump shot perfected with a roll of socks and an open laundry basket, a rim generously lowered so that a younger sibling might feel the thrill of a dunk, the hands calloused from grasping the rim's metal and swinging.

But let's speak plain, for a moment, before all this talk of lineage becomes too abstract. What I love is the unspoken message, what those who know need not say, but it's good to get it on the record just once: there are more of us, always. There is no corner of this jagged city that can take us all.

9:30

I don't remember when the place I lived first got referred to as a "war zone" or who said it. At the earliest point in my life that I can remember, my family lived out near the Greenbrier Houses, far east Columbus. It's gone now, or at least it isn't how I remember it. But few things are. The city is no longer the city from my childhood.

On the news, the neighborhood we lived in and lived adjacent to was called Uzi Alley. Of course, no one in the neighborhood itself gave it this nickname. It was given the nickname by Columbus police, who suggested that the violence that took place in this neighborhood was of a special sort. Violence so robust that even they, heroes of this wretched city, wouldn't set foot in the hood. They'll have to police themselves over there, they said.

This happens, of course. It happens everywhere, all of the time, in tight-knit communities that wouldn't rely on the cops even if they trusted the cops in the first place. All it takes is a couple of times calling those who are supposed to save you and have them not show up until it is too late, or not show up at all. A community learns how to manage on its own. Gangs also exist to keep a neighborhood safe from outside threats, after all. That has always been a part of their history. There are codes to be followed and punishments for not following them. The hood becomes its own city, governed by no one, governed by everyone.

And still, there is material impact to these declarations, that a place is unfit for anyone to enter. That it is so violent that it might as well be left to collapse on itself. It doesn't matter what magic exists inside the borders of a place neglected by those in power. They wouldn't be able to recognize it even if they could walk through the hood without fear, which they couldn't. It's all part of a larger mission. When a city names a place unlivable, it suggests that there is something wrong or damaged about the people who *do* live there. It suggests that their lives are expendable, down to the homes or apartments they live in. And just like that, the lens turns toward property, toward land. Toward the value of vacancy. Don't play like you haven't heard this one before. When you create the conditions of war, you get to name the places it happens.

9:20

The Mobb Deep song "Survival of the Fittest" opens with a spacious, haunting piano. The song is built around a sample from the Barry Harris Trio's 1976 rendition of "Skylark." And, while it must be said that few producers in music history have been able to directly translate beauty into a type of terror like Mobb Deep's Havoc, the beat is only a small segment of why we are here. The song's opening line, delivered by Prodigy, twenty years old at the time: *There's a war going on outside no man is safe from.* It's one of the most enduring lines of an era of '90s hip-hop that was defined, in part, by young black men attempting to retranslate the idea that had been pushed upon them that they were all living in war zones, destined to be casualties, that it was either death or prison. It wasn't so much subversion, I think. It was an acceptance, forced through a lens of glamour and sold back to record labels, to fashion brands, to vehicle companies.

As I approached my teenage years, army fatigues began more aggressively sprouting up in the hood, in music videos, on magazine covers. Some rappers and collectives—like the Boot Camp Clik—kept it traditional, cloaking themselves in dog tags and fatigues that looked as though they could have been issued directly from the military. But there were others, particularly as the '90s went on, who decided to go a more colorful route. Red fatigues, yellow fatigues, bright pink fatigue pants. No one around me took the fluorescent fatigues seriously. The standard greens and browns and blacks did the trick just fine. They signaled that you were a soldier in your own universe. Surviving something that a great many others wouldn't have the heart for. In 1997, the rappers Capone-N-Noreaga released *The War Report,* an album that was, among other things, an ode to staying in a place and knowing it might kill you. Staying in a place when the people you love are locked up, some of them not coming home from a bid for years, if at all.

The people I trust most understand a love like that, understand it even if the money from the record deal got them out of a place, or if ball got them out of a place. Call it war, call it whatever you want. You wouldn't know what to do with your face turned toward the blaring dawn, having survived another handful of hours that someone didn't want you to. There is no language I can find for the affection of repeated survival. To know you haven't been caught just yet. That with some luck, you never will be.

9:00

The space between what you can get and what people think you deserve to have is sometimes a crack, but sometimes a canyon.

It depends on where you're from or what you look like. It can depend on what your parents do for a living or if your parents are still living at all. Depends on your stride, your slang, the way developers do or don't eye the blocks you came up on, licking their lips with money swelling their pockets. If you know, you know, and if you don't, then you've never had to answer a set of questions that begin with a tone of curiosity and then gradually become more accusatory as they unfold.

By the time '02 and '03 rolled around, I knew what I had and what people believed I was supposed to have. The college campus I was on sat in the center of a tight-knit suburb just outside of the Columbus neighborhood I grew up in. Within the borders of a city, there are other, more distinct borders. The suburb was an interesting collision of circumstances: people with old money, some of whom had been living there for generations. People who knew what to look out for, if you understand what I'm saying, which you might if you've ever walked down a street and seen a curtain briefly flicker open, or heard a door lock. No one would ever claim that war unfolded here.

In high school, it was always so much easier for me to understand the word "classmate" as something communal, beyond a plain understanding of a shared world. In my high school, like in many high schools, most of the peers who were alongside me for four years came from miniature worlds around the city that were either mine or close to mine. We had similar concerns, even if we didn't have immense bonds. And material conditions also aligned, give or take a few aesthetic choices. The student parking lot was lined with used cars, none of them from the decade we were living in. Even if someone did have a clean pair of kicks, it was one of one, or at best one of a few. There was a shared language not of struggle, not of

survival, but of pleasure. Reveling in what we did have, knowing that we could have so much less.

When I got to college, the idea of "classmate" was stripped
down to its base form. A vague collection of people who understand the geography of a place and time, but certainly don't
understand it in the same way. This makes sense, of course.
The pool of people was wider, pulled from broader areas. Most
of the people were from Ohio, sure. But in Ohio, like so many
other places I've known, the definition of who you are and how
you're seen can shift every ten miles. As a result, most of the
people I was supposed to be close to were not my people. Beyond understanding this simply by the number of black people
on campus, I understood it most by the material conditions
and material concerns of the people around me. The campus,
the neighborhood. The way the student parking lot was lined
with towering SUVs and slick sports cars, and by the way that
my fellow freshmen could afford a spot in that lot, with its
prices at a premium.

I felt more curious than inadequate, even as I drove slow
circles around the outer blocks of the suburb some nights,
music down, searching the street for parking, preparing for the
long walk back to my dorm. It was this that would get me in
trouble, more than anything. I wasn't pushing any wheels that
those white folks peering through their curtains would have
found suspicious during the daytime. I had the kinda whip
those people would have expected me to be in. Early '90s Nis-
san, a hideous shade of brown. Its muffler loud, but its stereo
system louder. That part, of course, an intentional choice. In
my neighborhood, most everyone only had so much money for
a car, and then they only had so much money to take care of
that car when it inevitably began to fail them. But a sound sys-

tem was coveted. A way to reclaim some small bit of glory amidst the loudly coughing exhaust, or the passenger door that won't open from the outside, or the window that won't roll down all the way. Subwoofers encased in a box, weighing down the trunk, a kingdom of sound. People able to hear you coming in more ways than one. I had a homie who knew how to tint windows. Did it right in his driveway as long as you showed up with the tint yourself. And so halfway through my first year of school, my windows were dark. Too dark to see inside of. Some shit that would get me pulled over if the cops in the burbs were bored enough, and they sometimes were. The way I figured it was that I didn't need to be seen by anyone most likely doing the looking, and everyone I wanted to be seen by would know my car by its sound, its shape. How they, too, perhaps attempted to fashion some beauty out of the hand they were dealt.

Driving through the residential streets looking for parking during my first year of college was when my car transformed into something else. Forgettable in the sunlight, sinister in the darkness. Even when I turned my music down so that my trunk didn't ping and rattle. There was something, I imagine, about the combination of slow driving and occasional starts and stops that had rotating police lights flashing into my windows on a semi-regular basis. Regular enough that at a certain point in the year, I just started parking in lots on campus, even though I couldn't afford the permits. Parking violations piled up, but they could never tow me. I knew that if I moved my car at the right time, I could escape a ticket some mornings. If I got up early enough or ran out in between classes.

The whole setup was another border between what I could afford and what everyone else could afford. I couldn't afford to park on campus, so I had to find another place, and in the process of that finding, I was in the clutches of the cops, of the "concerned" neighborhood.

My old college wanted me to come back and speak to the graduates this year. In exchange, I jokingly asked if they would release my transcripts. I was told that my parking debt was in the thousands, even nearly two decades later. I'd have to pay it first. Everything has a cost.

And since we are speaking of cost and of what gets driven to school,

8:30

2003 was the year of LeBron James driving a Hummer H2 to high school and all of Ohio being pulled to the edges of their seats, some in awe, some in anger. By this point, The LeBron Show was immense. Even if people hadn't tuned in for the first two seasons, they were definitely tuned in now. LeBron was a figure of national interest. He was an Ohioan, someone people here still counted as one of their own, despite the national and global spotlight that had swept him up. LeBron's movements were now news well outside of Akron, and well outside of the state. St. Vincent–St. Mary had become something of a touring company during LeBron's senior season. They traveled around the country to play other high-profile basketball schools; they played on ESPN. And the team was good. They were especially juggernauts in LeBron's senior year, led by him and his childhood pals Dru Joyce and Romeo Travis. The Irish were steamrolling teams through the end of 2002. And then, in January of his senior year, LeBron James showed up to school driving a brand-new $50,000 SUV.

His senior season was still in full swing; there were competing investments around getting to the bottom of how the vehi-

cle was acquired. James and his mother, Gloria, had a simple
explanation: Gloria had taken out a loan against her son's future earnings to secure the money for purchase. This made
sense even to me, then just nineteen years old and fairly finan-
cially illiterate. LeBron was one of the most surefire #1 overall
picks of a generation, even in an NBA draft that was loaded
with talent at the top. Teams were torpedoing their seasons just
to have a better chance at ending up in the top of the draft lottery to pick him. There are some players who transcend risk,
and LeBron was one of them. Even if he'd suffered some cata-
strophic injury in his senior season, as long as it wasn't career-
ending, a team would still take a chance on him. Fifty thousand
dollars was a drop in the bucket against his future—a future
that was just months away.

The Ohio High School Athletic Association saw things differently. As did basketball fans spread out across the state,
eager for an opportunity to halt Akron SVSM's inevitable
dominance, and also, whether it was explicit or implied, to put
LeBron James in his place.

There was, as it turned out, a reality and a so-called problem
born out of that reality. The reality was that LeBron James and
his mother were not wealthy. They did not come from wealth,
or live in an area flooded with wealth. White sports fans love
this narrative, and so do white recruiters. White journalists
salivate over it. The singular, once-in-a-generation black athlete
who is born into struggle, playing to make a better life for
themselves or their loved ones. It was the way the black athlete
was most commonly portrayed, by that point. Someone who
had to traverse a bad neighborhood somewhere in order to arrive to a gym, to a classroom, somewhere deemed "better."

The problem was that, to those narrative-makers, LeBron
James had skipped the line. The athlete is supposed to work for

a better life but make the struggle visible. With no struggle for the comfortable viewer to revel in, there's no pity to balance out the envy. There's nothing left to hold up the narrative. I have sat at the feet of poets who told me that there is power in withholding. In not offering the parts of yourself that people are most eager to see. In the high school career of LeBron James, there was access to his dominance, but not always access to whatever struggles he might have been pushing through. And it proved hard for people to stay fascinated with dominance, especially if they were on the losing side of it, especially in consideration of who was doing the dominating.

8:15

And then there is the fantasy, not only the way America can sell war but also how eagerly it can sell the aesthetics of war back to people who have been convinced they live in so-called war zones. Believe they are in places not all that different from the places that America bombs, runs over with tanks. America has bombed its own neighborhoods, too. It's taken whole blocks apart. Children have been killed in places of worship here, police have blown apart homes. The powerful call things "war" because it's hard to sell the plain horrors of terror, but it is not nearly as hard to sell the materials.

The H2 was a luxury vehicle modeled after a war machine. Humvees were first used in the U.S. invasion of Panama in 1989, initially for transport. By the early 2000s, they were flooding Afghanistan. Armed and capable of traversing mountainous terrain. The Hummer H1 hit the civilian market in 1992 and it found an audience, sometimes among rap stars. Lil' Kim rapped about them; Tupac had a custom one. But there was something about the Hummer H2 release in 2002 that

collided with another cultural shift in excess. The H2 was easily customizable, its wheel wells suited for larger tires and
therefore larger rims. The interior was spacious enough to be
modified. And its size wasn't as overwhelming as the H1, but
still large enough to mean something when it was seen on a
residential street. Professional athletes looked cool flinging the
doors open and emerging, hardly having to step down at all. Its
boxy look was slightly removed from the original Humvee, but
not so removed that one might forget that it was a descendant
of a vehicle roaming other countries in the name of empire.

There were those who suggested that the vehicle lost value
when the "streets" got ahold of it. When it became the latest
canvas for overwhelming modifications. When, in short, black
people began driving and designing it to meet their desires.

And I can't think back on any of this without also thinking of
the fatigue jacket my oldest brother coveted and then finally got
in the mid-'90s and began to wear everywhere. Or the fatigue
pants older heads roamed my block with. Same ones that
showed up on rap album covers. In criticisms, steps are always
skipped. America relies on making the soldier both an inspira-
tion and an aspiration. It relies on making war and surviving
war a part of the American fabric by making the aesthetics of
war cool. And then makes those aesthetics available for the
public to buy. And it is one thing to map those aesthetics onto
the suburbs, a Hummer parked in a garage with an American
flag affixed to a wall or swinging from a post in the front yard.
It is one thing for people to romanticize the violence of sports
and compare game to war. It is another for athletes to call
themselves soldiers. It is one thing to create conditions under
which survival seems unattainable for some, but it is certainly
another thing for hood niggas who have never enlisted in any-

LONNIE CARMON, COLUMBUS, OHIO (1901–1955)

& the hood called him the junk man, would throw him all sorts
of their undesirables—cartons & metals & cardboards right here
in columbus & wouldn't you know Lonnie built a plane outta what his people
didn't want in their homes & on their porches & they shoulda never
let him get his hands on that motorcycle engine cuz that was all he needed
& before you knew it, Lonnie was flying his plane over his neighborhood
on weekends, the people on his block running outside & pointing at him
in the sky, their old trash now cradled by endless blue & Lonnie had no training
which is maybe why port columbus authority never gave him a gig
even though he tried & today Lonnie got himself a monument in that same airport
& in the photo he is wearing his helmet & his glasses & he is next to the plane
he made from whatever the people he loved showed up to his doorstep with &
I tell my homies I am not superstitious but here I am touching the photo of Lonnie
again while I walk to the security line before getting on a plane, before forcing
    myself
to forget about the mechanics of flight & all the ways it could fail & I think about
    Lonnie
in the sky, kept safe by his people & the small but useful things that outlasted their
    dreams
again while I walk to the security line before getting on a plane, before forcing
    myself
to forget about the mechanics of flight & all the ways it could fail & I think about
    Lonnie
in the sky, kept safe by his people & the small but useful things that outlasted their
    dreams

JOHN GLENN, CAMBRIDGE, OHIO (1921–2016)

When he convinced NASA to let him go back it was 1998 & he was 77 & he told a committee that what happens to the body in space is the same as what happens to the body as it ages which means that he had already begun to live the familiar undoing & wanted to sit at the edge of the dark & vast cavern of stars again & he hadn't been back up there in 36 years & the country swore he couldn't go back because they needed him to be a politician & a war hero & I wonder what his dreams must have been like in the years between ascension & I'm saying that once you've seen the impossible how can you ever stay earthbound for 36 years knowing what's up there & it is true that none of us will live forever & the mere existence of that knowledge suggests we all have to pick a thing we might die for if the opportunity arose & one time before he pushed past the atmosphere once more in 1998, John Glenn visited my middle school & when I reached my hand out firm & rigid to shake his the way my father taught me John Glenn took my small hand in both of his hands & I asked him if he was ever afraid & he looked somewhere above my head somewhere beyond even the ceiling & he said I've never been more afraid than I have been curious

My crew and I were never embarrassed, making the road trip
north to be an audience to some kid who was close to our age,
a high school student just like we were. During his sophomore
year, before SUV controversies and a little bit before the national media began to fully descend upon Akron, you could
sometimes still catch Akron SVSM playing in their home gym,
like a normal high school team, with a phenom who still felt
like he was ours, an Ohioan for an audience of Ohioans. And
so it didn't matter if the only one of us who had a license during
our junior year would pile some of the crew into a car on the
days our school didn't have a game and Akron SVSM did.

Akron St. Vincent–St. Mary sits inconspicuously behind
Dominic's Automotive Services. The building itself is unim-
pressive, except for the towering white bleachers of the football
stadium arching behind the building's brick. But for those of
us who are from a certain era of Ohio, the place is unmistakable. The thing is, making this pilgrimage never felt strange for
me and my crew, because LeBron James never felt like he was
in high school, even when he was in high school. It's hard to
understand this unless you were there and also in high school
yourself. If you were in high school in Ohio but in a different
city than Akron and made it to Friday night with enough gas in
your car and a little change in your pocket. If you drove a couple
of hours north through some inevitably shit weather, in winter,
to stand in a line or hover outside a gym's flung-open doors to
get a small glimpse of He Who Would Be King, climbing end-

lessly on the air during warmups, or flinging passes through
impossible slivers of unoccupied space. To people who weren't
from Ohio, it all seemed too good to be true. That he was here
and not anywhere else. That he didn't start sprinting down the
court on a fast break and then keep running.

7:00

Kenny Gregory didn't have an expensive SUV to his name, some
shit that his peers would envy and his enemies would plot on.
Kenny Gregory drove an early '90s Honda Accord and didn't
even bother to tint the windows. Didn't put any of the cheap
hubcaps over the tires, the type dudes on the block got before
they could afford real rims, the type that would lose their shine
at the end of summer but if you caught them in June the beams
of sunlight or moonlight or any light would sprint off of them,
reflecting one hundred new illuminating vessels, sometimes
splitting into a chorus of color, and so no one really cared that
they weren't *real* rims—what is real and not real is sometimes
simply a matter of who is witnessing the miracle and who can
be tricked into a suspension of disbelief at the altar of light.

Kenny Gregory drove a normal-ass car on the Eastside of
Columbus in the mid-'90s, in an era when what you drove sig-
nified how you got by. The whip tells a tale about who has been
hustled and who is willing to hustle. It tells a tale of the once-
promising star who didn't make it in the way their parents
prayed they would, and so they had to make it another way.
Didn't matter if you lived a block away from the court at
Scottwood Elementary School. Didn't matter if you could walk
your ass across the street to ball like everyone else. If your car
was fly enough, you pull it out of the driveway, pull that shit up
on the playground, right next to the court itself. Break off a little

bit of bread to have the young kids watch it, retrieve any way-ward ball that might careen in its direction after spinning awk-wardly off the rim.

To flex in a place where not everyone has the means to flex is vanity, but it is not only vanity. We are all trying to stunt on someone, after all. I am not above it now and was certainly not above it then. Even with no food in the cabinets and no clothes in my closet, I knew I could piece together something that might hold the attention of someone on the block who had less than I did. To stunt on those you live in close proximity to is also a type of intimacy. It requires a level of knowing—I know the heights that you cannot reach, the ones that I can barely ascend to, but can still ascend to, at least today. And I love you for your limits, I love all of us for what we do and don't have in this beautifully unbearable container of heat, of sirens, of bike chains popping and black sneakers that have seen better days. The borders between the stunt and being stunted on are flimsy when the come-up happens in small, barely noticeable incre-ments, until it doesn't. I love the stunt, for how it opens the gates to dreaming, and I love anything that pushes against the door of reality and offers an elsewhere. I don't need the else-where to be better, I just need it to be somewhere else. And I remember, at the courts, when the dealer with the mean handle but no jump shot to speak of let me sit in the passenger seat of his '96 Mustang, if only for a moment, if only to run a hand along the leather, if only to watch the lights flickering across the stereo in the center console, if only to sink back into the seats and feel like I was being swallowed by a newer, darker universe. And it was only when the Mustang stopped coming around, and it was only when he stopped showing up to the courts altogether, that I learned the other lesson. The lesson that begins

6:45

with loss and nothing else. There is so much to lose, and even more to be taken. To stunt is also to know what you have, which is also to know what everyone else doesn't have, which is also to know what can be lost. What can be taken. I don't know how someone decides what they'll kill for, or what they'll spend years locked up in the name of. At night, a man wanders the empty courts and sings a Stevie Wonder song so loud it snakes through the open windows of the whole neighborhood, but no one shouts him to silence. No one curses his name. He's lost something and he's trying to find it in the silent hours, in the sinning hours. Good morn' or evening, friends. Here's your friendly announcer. The sun sets after a funeral and someone with a taste for revenge loses their nerve, loses the combination to a safe where a gun rests inside. Someone who gets out after a short bid comes back to the court and hops in a run where he misses four shots in a row and the sideline weighs in *This nigga got locked up and lost his jumper!* There was hair on my father's head once, remember? I told you of it though I never saw it for myself, with my own eyes. But it was there once, before it, too, was lost. To shave away the patches on a scalp is to accelerate loss, to embrace it.

Look, I love you

6:30

and so I must tell you that anything that can be taken, will be taken. You are lucky if it is sudden. You are lucky if you survive the forest of reaching hands. The open window and the aching voice that floods a room and holds you firm to the night, thinking of all you have that might be gone upon your waking.

I'm sorry, I've pulled us away again, away from one of the greatest basketball players the Eastside of Columbus has ever seen, and his normal-ass car, its dull tan, its boxy frame. Kenny Gregory did, at least, drop a subwoofer in the trunk, as was customary. If you had a car, and you had a way to get speakers, you didn't think twice about dropping some heavy box in the back of that thing in the name of suffocating the block with distorted basslines, married to the rattling metal of the trunk, indecipherable but for an announcement, an entrance. Elders on their porches shaking their heads, wondering how anyone in the car could even hear anything. But all of their stunts were from a different era, when being loud meant something other than being loud. It ain't about what you can hear on the inside, it's about what motherfuckers can hear on the outside, and how far away they can hear it from, and how long the song lingers once the car passes, the way the air chops and screws whatever faint vocals might be fighting beneath the swell of deep bass, how the voice might sound like it is descending under water as the car inches farther beyond the block.

My crew and I would sometimes chase Kenny's car down the block on our bikes, to get to him just as he was pulling into his driveway and stepping out the driver's-side door, sometimes fresh from basketball practice, sometimes with a girl on his arm. And no matter the scenario, we'd launch questions at him while he shuffled around us to get his gym bag out of the back seat or nervously looked at his date while patiently trying to wade through the cacophony of disparate inquiries: *How many points you gonna score on Friday? What sneakers are you gonna wear? Are you gonna win state?*

Depending on the week, the questions would get more specific. For example, in the week before Kenny's Independence High School played against West High, the questions all revolved around his rivalry with West High's Michael Redd, a player who was equally as feared and respected as Gregory was in the city, but not on the Eastside. On the Eastside, Kenny was our guy. Michael Redd never made his way out to the Scottwood courts, where no one cared about your all-state credentials or the envelopes from college recruiters piling up on your mother's table.

There is more than one way to make yourself a legend in the hood. Kenny would lean against his unspectacular car and answer most of our questions whenever we caught him outside. If he especially wanted to dispense with us, if he did have a girl on his arm a mere hour or so before his mom returned home, he would break us off a couple of dollars from his pocket and tell us to grab some candy for ourselves down at the corner store.

One might grow up loving Michael Jordan or Allen Iverson or whoever else would come along. But none of us could ever touch those players. We could fantasize ourselves into their worlds, into their league. But they weren't one of us. There isn't a Michael Jordan in every neighborhood, but I had the Michael Jordan of East Columbus just four doors down from my house, sometimes with his car pulled up on the grass of his front yard, shining up the fading beige exterior, drowning the block in warbled bass.

On the day before he left to attend the McDonald's All-American Game, Kenny was there, lingering on his front porch, cleaning a pair of sneakers. My pal Josh and I hovered for a bit before ambling over. Word had gotten out that he was going to participate in the dunk contest, something that had been hit or miss earlier in the week. Independence, favorites to win the state championship, were upset by Zanesville in the regional round, led by their lightning-quick, tenacious point guard, Travis Young.

Kenny had laid relatively low since the loss, preparing for life in Kansas, where he'd signed to play college ball. On his porch, as he was cleaning a pair of Jordan 12s with a toothbrush, I asked him what he was going to do in the dunk contest. If he was going to jump from the free-throw line, like I'd seen him do before at the court over at Scottwood. He looked up from his shoes, looked across the street toward Scottwood as if he were seeing it for the first time.

"I don't know, man," he began. "Free-throw line over there is a little bit shorter than regulation." And then, perhaps noticing the slightly discouraged look on my face: "I'll try it. You gotta find somewhere to watch. It's on ESPN."

And who did or didn't have cable in those days was an inconsistent roll of the dice, but sure enough, someone did. Someone let half of the hood into their home, packed into a basement or a living room. I remember nothing of the night except for Kenny Gregory, walking to a far corner of Clune Arena in Colorado Springs, palming a basketball in one hand, his arms outstretched to the crowd, urging them to rise to their feet for what would be the grand finale in a dunk contest that it appeared Kenny had already won and just needed to bring home. His opponents in the contest, including Baron Davis and Ron Artest, were impressive, but not nearly as electrifying as Kenny, who came out in the second round and threw the ball off of the very top of the backboard, casually ascending to meet it as it floated back to him, his head well above the rim.

Before 1997, there had only been one player from the Columbus area to play in the McDonald's All-American Game. Martin Nessley, a massive seven-foot-two center from Whitehall, made the squad back in 1983, before the exhibition was steeped in as much fanfare as it was by the time the late '90s rolled around. At home, it was the first time any of us could turn on ESPN and see a kid we'd fetched balls for in the park or hit up for corner store cash. In the first round of the dunk contest, the person doing commentary paused slightly upon reading out Kenny's name and origin, as if surprised: . . . *And here's Kenny Gregory from Independence High School in . . . Columbus, Ohio. . . .*

But by the end of Round 2, Kenny's arms swinging in the air, holding tight to the basketball, he knew he had them. Not just everyone in the arena, not just his opponents, but everyone watching. The entire bench of All-Americans, including the other players he was competing against, rose to their feet and also wildly waved their arms, urging the crowd to do the same. Kenny, from the foul line at the opposite end of the court, politely gestures, asks the kids sitting on the floor if they could move over, just slightly. And the kids, as in awe as I was then, and still am now, shuffled to their left, eyes never leaving Kenny, mouths wide open.

I say praise the miraculous that happens because it must. The miracle that you can see

6:00

coming, its slowly unfolding murmur that matures into a shout and then leaves an echo for an audience to bathe in, not unlike a car dragging down a street, a subwoofer weighing down its trunk on a hot day, giving cause for people to run to their rattling windows or stop upon a tremoring sidewalk to feel the bass in their chest. A dunk contest is where one goes to execute some far-flung dream of what the body is capable of. It is where one goes to fail, often spectacularly. I wish all failure could be as beautiful as the failures that arrive to us midair, a reality setting in that we are incapable and yet still in flight.

And still, there was no way Kenny was going to miss this

dunk. We knew, crowded around a television, palms sweaty even before he took off, sprinting from seventy-five feet out. Even before he launched himself, toe touching *just* above the foul line (though who needs such specifics when miracles are afoot), even before the frozen moment, Kenny with his arm stretched straight up, heavenbound, the basketball an offering to the sky, but only for a moment. When Michael Jordan took off from the foul line in Indiana back in 1985, still with faint traces of hair on his head, all of us boys had been born, but barely. We mostly remembered the dunk in stillness, not in motion. Just like with Mike in '85, a whole life can change if someone is in defiance of gravity for the right amount of time. Even if it isn't happening where you are. Kenny was in the air long enough for everyone crammed in a small East Columbus living room to rise to their feet in anticipation. Long enough for the judges at the dunk contest to rise to their feet in anticipation. Long enough for an entire neighborhood

5:45

to hold its breath, which means that for a moment, the singing stopped and the shouting stopped and the no-good mother-fuckers who might have otherwise been cursing out some weeping beloved just trying to do their damn best held their breath and turned toward a television screen and the cops lurking the corner store stopped following the kids with baggy jeans and pockets wide enough to house a circus of unearned delights and the fist that might have otherwise chipped the tooth of someone who couldn't afford to get their grill fixed recoiled and became an open palm again, and again, and again, collapsing into another open palm, slow applause that beat the hands into a blood-red drumline, and anything on a stove was left long enough to burn but never long enough to catch fire, long enough to fill a corner of a house with puffs of black smoke, the kind that rise in praise of absence, a gentle reminder before the flame, and I know there is a difference between what happens in real time

5:40

and what we are subjected to in the endless replays of a moment, the ones that project into the darkness of closed eyes. But I swear, Kenny Gregory jumped from the damn-near foul line in Colorado, and it seemed like he might never come down. It seemed like he was aiming for something even higher than the rim itself.

He cleared the dunk easily. He could have jumped from a couple of steps before the free-throw line and still cleared it, which I would shout on the court to the envious older kids the next day bemoaning how Kenny didn't *actually* jump from the free-throw line.

By the time he made it back down among mortals, judges already had their 10s in the air, shaking the white cards vigorously. A portion of the bench cleared to embrace Kenny, both arms in the air while his peers threw their arms around him, the announcers beyond words and, for a moment, able to summon only laughter. The contest was over. An easy win. Kenny left the ground as ours and returned as everyone's.

5:20

The thing about 1997 was that there were significantly fewer ways to know who the best high school basketball players in the country were. Before the internet became a widespread phenomenon, it was hard to even know the names of anyone else besides the guys in your city, and sometimes just in your quadrant of the city. I didn't know anyone who knew where Kenny ranked in the grand scheme of players nationally, just that he was the best player in Ohio, winning Mr. Basketball in '97 with relative ease.

And so it felt slightly surprising, then, when Kenny followed up his dunk contest performance by winning MVP in the All-American Game itself. He scored 18 points, almost all of them on spectacular dunks. In the second half, after one such reverse dunk that found him yelling so loud the cameras picked it up, swinging, briefly, on the rim, Kenny landed and began to skip down the court, something he'd do at Independence when he caught a good groove, if he'd get a couple of dunks in a row. Kenny wasn't averse to talking his shit, but his best bit of showing out came in this mode: *I'm having so much fun, this ain't even work.*

His final two points came in the game's dying moments, in his greatest highlight. The cameras landed on Kenny's face with less than a minute left, a seemingly mundane inbound play being prepared. Kenny's eyes dart toward the rim, a mischievous look on his face. And then, a cut, a ball in the air, Kenny rising to meet it.

What I remember, beyond the dunk contest trophy, beyond the MVP trophy, is how Kenny returned home, both of the trophies in the passenger seat of his car. Driving slow down the block once, and then circling the block for good measure, a growing parade of kids on bikes at his back, shouting, opening their arms wide, catching the reflection of his smile in the rearview mirror. And of all the reasons I love the hood,

5:15

the greatest reason is for how we honor our homecomings. The people who will show up to praise your return, simply because it is a return. Doesn't even have to be spectacular, though it often is. A cage opening up and letting a brother or a daughter or a grandson walk free. A child coming home from war, beating the folded flag to the doorstep of their beloveds. And yes, a basketball star who, for a moment, belonged to the quivering air of an arena, thick with sweat. A basketball star so great that on television, the announcers had to pronounce where he was from, every note. I love the homecoming because I have known what it is to leave. I have seen the city I love from the sky just as I have seen the city I love from the cracks in between metal bars. Cherish the homecoming, because you know what lasts forever and what does not.

I love all manner of homecoming, all manner of coming home. I love whatever will send a people into the streets, or whatever will get someone to fire up a grill, even if they don't really know what to do after the fire arrives except stand over it, poke at something with a fork and throw their head back, laughing into the breeze when someone calls them on their inability to get the food moving from the heat to the plate. I love whatever can feel like a good memory, even as it is already unfolding. Yes, for once, your face is in the paper. The good section. The section where no one is dead or divorced. Your name in bold letters, not in the obituaries, not in a crime bulletin. We can cut this one out and put it in a frame. Hang it, lopsided, next to the black Jesus, the gaudy cross. When you cross back into the neighborhood, driving slow with your windows down, the kids will follow you. Running after the red glow of your taillights, all of them holding the paper, pointing at your face, as if it is their own.

5:00

The first photo I remember of a basketball star in the newspaper was in 1993. Estaban Weaver had one hand still on the rim. The ball was halfway to the ground. He was wide-eyed, in the midst of a shout. Estaban was a freshman at Bishop Hartley High School at the time. Hartley was the Catholic school on the Eastside, around the corner from my house. In the early 2000s, my boys and I would sneak into their football games through a hole in the back fence. We would flirt with the girls who thought we were cool, I guess, because we actually *lived* on the Eastside. We didn't pop in for school and then head elsewhere. We went to a city school, we wore what we wanted to in our classes. We were harmless in our corner of the world, dangerous in theirs.

But in 1995, Bishop Hartley was Estaban Weaver's universe. To understand the mythology of Estaban Weaver, one must understand the long arc of how mythology is built within communities already well versed in oral tradition. There were people who saw Estaban play in seventh grade, in eighth grade, at the Gus Macker Tournament in the summers at Franklin Park. People who went and told the story of his game, and so the story of his game grew with each retelling. There were, of course, facts that were nestled in between the exuberant shouts of praise. But this is how it goes: a section of a city opens its collective mouth and from it a sound emerges and echoes, and echoes, and echoes. Who is to say what the sound actually is by the time it arrives to the fifth ear? The seventh? The tenth? The witnesses may be rare, but the storytellers exist in abundance, and I would say it ain't a competition but it damn sure is, and there is always someone ready to jump in, ready to cut off the dull rambling and throw themselves in front of the dry language, someone ready to shout *Can't nobody tell a story like I can.*

And this is how everyone I knew heard about Estaban Weaver, sometimes years before even seeing him play. Not only heard about him but respected him, feared him, admired him. When he was in between his eighth- and ninth-grade seasons, he got invited to the Nike All-American Camp in Chicago, a place only two eighth graders before him had ever been invited. And the legend grew. He took on Allen Iverson, Kevin Garnett, dudes whose posters you might have put up on your wall a few years later. He battled with them all, before he was even in high school. And when it was time for him to pick a high school? Estaban held a whole press conference—as an eighth grader.

He chose Bishop Hartley, where if you tried to get into games at the school during his freshman season, good luck. Hartley was a small school. Tucked between a gas station and a bingo hall, encased by an Eastside neighborhood that wasn't glamorous but got the job done. People would descend on the school hours before tip-off, just to see what Estaban could do. And what he could do was put up 25 per game. First team all-state as a freshman. Twenty-five per game again as a sophomore, but I guess someone was in the mood to humble the kid, and so he took second team all-state that year.

And he was a miracle player. Somehow even better than the best story told from the best yarn-spinner on the hottest block. He could control the entire pace of the game, like he had a remote control attached to his hip. He could get to the rim at will, sure, but he could also fit passes through rapidly collapsing windows of light directly into the hands of someone who would inevitably be wide open, nothing between them and the rim. He had a spin move that was a blur but also somehow simultaneously looked like it was unfolding in slow motion. The rumors of his exploits in the city became concrete fact. Yeah I saw the dunk, yeah I saw the layup where he was in the air for what felt like an entire rapturous hour. Sophomore year, state semifinal game, Estaban scored damn near half of Hartley's points, 28 of the 60. Yeah they lost, I get it. But the performance goes down in history, beyond the box score.

Depending on who you ask, or who knew Estaban and when they knew him, there is a point in his story where the joyful recounting of memories turns into a series of quiet murmurs. Someone may get silent, stare off into the space beyond you, beyond themselves, even. Some might look down and shake their heads. Laugh a little, but not in the way one might laugh when something is *actually* funny—the kind of laugh that keeps a long-forgotten ache at bay.

There were drugs, some would say. Some drinking, sure. He got pulled over once or twice, you'd hear. Coaches would make the trouble disappear, sit him out a game and hope for the best. But Hartley was a *good* school. A holy branch of a bad city, some might say (but certainly not me). Estaban had returned the school to basketball glory, but then the eternal question of *at what cost* lingered over the school, over its administration, its coaches. When Hartley coach Tim Birie was asked to step down, Estaban left the school too. The number one ranked player in his class, out the door. Ungrateful, some might say. He wasn't getting into nothing that every other Eastside kid wasn't getting into. Different standards, I guess, someone will say, their eyes flashing toward that beyond place, the place where Estaban Weaver is on posters, hanging in the homes of Eastside Columbus kids, who idolized him then, who idolize him always.

4:45

Estaban ended up in Maine for his junior year, but he didn't last long. The idea was that he'd go to Maine Central Institute, get his mind right, and focus on ball. MCI had a history of preparing players for the next step in their basketball futures, and for Estaban, going into his junior season, that future seemed limitless. But he was kicked out midseason for violating the school's code of conduct. He came back to Columbus and enrolled at Independence High School to play his senior season alongside Kenny Gregory. Before the 1996 season, *Sports Illustrated* put out a list of high school seniors to watch. Names like Shane Battier, Lamar Odom, Elton Brand, Tracy McGrady, Baron Davis. And then, Kenny Gregory. A few names above Kenny's, Estaban Weaver.

The two central Ohio stars had diverged a bit by that point. Kenny's star had risen while Estaban, once the top player in his class, was an uncertainty. Also an uncertainty was the pairing of the two, sort of friends, sort of once-rivals. Estaban, who would drink before games and stay out late after school, and Kenny, who would make it home on time every night. But Estaban wanted to play with the best player in the state, and so Independence is where he ended up.

But you know how that story ends. Upset in the tournament. They could get out and run you to death, but once a team made them play in the half court, they looked lost, their two stars seeming like they hadn't figured out an effective bond all season, which I suppose happens when everything is a blur of well-earned hype and highlights. Estaban had a good season, though nothing as electric as his first two years. At the end of it, there was no McDonald's All-American Game invite; he wasn't selected for an all-state team. His grades and his so-called reputation had scared away the Division I colleges that risked it all to have a shot at him just two years earlier. At the end of the basketball season, Estaban dropped out of high school.

The other thing about mythology

4:15

is that there is no blueprint for what to make of an entire life when you're a legend by twelve, thirteen years old. When you are good enough at something, anything, that someone might throw some money at you. Might slip a white envelope with some bills into your back pocket during a hug and tell you to get something nice for your moms, put a little food on the table. It is more frightening when everything said about you is true. When you are as good as the streets said you were, or even better. When you are a child but also not a child, also a phenom, also impossible to fathom. Yes, I swear to you, before LeBron James, we had Estaban Weaver, right on the Eastside of Columbus. And so it takes a little bit more to impress us. We've built all the myths already, and we've seen someone breeze past them and then vanish. What else is there to do but walk away while the scent of magic still hangs over you, at least for a little bit longer? Walk away while your present is already being talked about like a distant past, one that no one would believe, even if you told it to them yourself.

4:00

And yes, sometimes it is that unspectacular. The math of who makes it and who doesn't, or what making it even is. All of it, a series of accidents. Who got caught with what, and when. Who did their dirt on the low, so low that it hums, indecipherable beneath the decoration of stardom. Someone catches a bad break, gets injured at the wrong tournament, gets pulled over by the wrong cop before the state tournament. And like that, there's someone else collecting scholarship offers. It might be heartbreaking, but it isn't spectacular. Not if you still get to be above ground. Shit, everyone I love most is from somewhere some niggas could have made it out of but didn't, through circumstances sometimes as arbitrary as the game itself—the unforgiving rim or the pass that slips out of bounds. In my hood, we got a hall of fame that might run the best five from wherever you're from off any court. Pick a decade and I got names you've never heard of, I've got stories you wouldn't believe. I can tell you about guys who didn't hoop to get away from the streets, or to get out of anywhere. Guys who hooped because they wanted to be respected on the streets they loved. They wanted to make themselves infamous in the place that held them, and that, too, is a type of making it. People just looking for a place to feel invincible, for a few hours, in a city that might otherwise swallow them whole. You've got some names, too. You've got some stories from your city, which, for the sake of this exercise, is not unlike my city. Not unlike any city with a flock of clean white nets singing into the breeze at the start of summer, only to be thin strips of surrender by late August. You know someone who was on a court after the sun went down, who slept with a basketball cradled in their arms. The song is a little less sad if everyone knows the words, if everyone sings them together, all at once. If everyone tries to squeeze the same refrain through the crack in a door, right before it closes for good.

3:45

And besides, it might do all of us some good to reconsider what *making it* even means, or at least to honor a world where making it is not defined by the glamorous exit, not only by television cameras, not only by coming back with a pair of trophies riding shotgun. What, after all, do you call it when your name is good on every block you touch, or when kids gather around porches to hear stories of when you were great, even if you haven't held a ball in a meaningful game in decades. When you don't have to pay for a drink, when the guys at the corner store wave you off while you reach into your pockets. What do you call it when players who came after you fight back tears at the mere memory of you, at the mere mention of your life now, the path you made. Someone who ages, thank God. Someone who lives beyond their past selves. But someone who is also bronzed, a monument embedded in the emotional infrastructure of a place. People will remember you, sweat-slicked and twirling through two defenders, splitting the foolish ambitions of your enemies. People will remember you, swinging from a rim with your eyes wide open, as if you can't believe that you got that high and can't believe that you have to come down. People will point to a kid wearing an Allen Iverson throwback jersey or a pair of Kobe Bryant sneakers and shake their heads, and maybe they'll say *Estaban smoked all those fools once*. And that's it, I promise you. Once is all it takes. It takes you, and a ball, and someone between you and the basket. You have won once, a single time, and worn your victory around your neck until it grew rust, and then wore it for years after. Don't talk to me about any version of making it that ends with someone like Estaban Weaver being described as a failure. Not if you weren't here. Not if you don't know what it's like for a city to make you into a savior before you finish ninth grade. Not if, despite that, you survived.

3:00

I don't remember where I was when the news hit that my high school's old point guard was found dead in a car. I don't remember which time I was locked up when I passed my high school's old swingman, who could truly fly, chained at the wrists in a tan jumpsuit, same as I was, the two of us sharing a startled moment of familiarity and then never seeing each other again. I do remember *The Columbus Dispatch* in 1999, where all of them were on the cover, the whole starting five, arms crossed at center court in our school's gym. This band of brothers, who seemed like they might win it all, like they might be immortal, for a little while.

I don't remember when it set in that Kenny Gregory wasn't going to go to the NBA, even though he worked on his jump shot before his senior season at Kansas, even though you could find him in the gym down the street putting up threes in the summer. I don't remember where, in the second round, it set in that the mountain to climb was too high. He was still six-four, he still played like a power forward, obsessed with crashing to the rim, obsessed with the miracle of flight.

I don't remember when Brookhaven High School closed, though I remember wondering what they were going to do with all of the trophies, all of the banners. If they'd just be gone forever. I remember thinking that there is no success that can stop a school from closing, a building from being emptied out, encased by tall, unkempt weeds.

Sometimes there are funerals, and sometimes there is nothing. No portal through which grief can be passed, no house-warming for the new grief that furnishes the ever-growing tower that we carry, that we are responsible for, whether we want to be or not. Both landlords and tenants within our own sadness, and sometimes it just happens. Grows while you sleep. Death isn't the only way to die, though it can be argued that it is the most merciful.

If enough things crumble, if enough things turn to ash, I

cannot convince you that there was anything better here once. You are one of the lucky ones if your name is remembered in a city that is beloved but sometimes unforgiving. If there are no weeds tall enough to eclipse your past, or to reach the heights of your future.

2:30

I must shepherd us back to dreaming, or at least back to untangling faces that appear in dreams. There was a moment of time in my life where I didn't remember any dream except for the ones my mother was in. And even then, I wouldn't remember the dream itself, only the scenes in which she would appear, often an interruption from whatever else was occurring in the dream landscape, no matter how jarring or how violent or how joyful. No way of telling what would surround her appearance, but I would be greeted with her appearance nonetheless. In my dreams, she never spoke, but I would understand the language being passed between us. Every faith has a relationship with the dead

2:00

appearing in dreams. Elders might say *Did you get a visit?* as if a person was popping by for a quick meal or to drop off some flowers at your doorstep, and I do suppose the dream is a doorstep of sorts, and any appearance of someone we can no longer touch in the earthly life is not entirely unlike the flower—breathtaking, but momentary. Fleeting. Forgotten about once the dying sets back in. But in Islam, the appearance means that the dead are in good condition in the afterlife. That Allah has taken care of them, and there is nothing for the living to worry about. I was comforted when I believed

1:45

more faithfully in the trappings of the faith I was raised in, but less so when I found myself asking about all of the dead I did not see. All of the people I loved who never arrived in my dreams in any way that I could remember, until I began to remember all of my dreams. Every moment of them, everyone populating them. The dead and the living, faces of people that were not their faces as I knew them, but were still what I understood to be their faces.

1:30

And the other thing about faces in dreams is that there is nothing stopping the brain from delivering the face of an enemy to you in your sleep. And not only delivering the face of an enemy but also building a world inside of which your enemy might, for a moment, be a lover. Might be someone you would fight for, someone you would die for. Someone who holds your arm tight as you swing from a cliff's edge, and when you look up, there is a face you know. A face you do not love but must love, in that moment. And it is also true that the faces in a dream can be a combination of many faces. The eyes of the dead, gifted to the mouth, the voice of the living. It is easiest to convince myself of something that seems like love when no one looks like anyone. When anyone looks like everyone. When I wake and remember the shape of a mouth, but never the words, sung out over crashing waves, right before my arm was let go.

1:00

My childhood beloveds, my beloved childhood blocks, it is not you, I swear. It is my own memory—memory that I, even now, cannot detach from my dreaming. Which is a more whimsical way of saying that the block doesn't look like the block that I once knew and loved and dribbled basketballs on, dodging the cracks in the sidewalks or the glass, broken tenderly enough to take the shape of a small brown mouth. But I blink,

0:30

and through a blur, my past sparks back to life. I close my eyes and I fall back into the ocean of our past selves. It is a warped image in a bent frame, as all dreams are. But the houses haven't all been torn down yet. They look both familiar and not, in a dream. Halfway between what they were and what they became. The court is filled with people again. The park is not a ghost town. Every moment is a homecoming, cars crawling slow down the street, sounds that warble and bend even more than they would in our waking hours. And you are there, too.

0:15

All of your faces, though not as they were as children. Not as I remember them best, but I know they are your faces, and I know we are young again. Monuments. In my dreams, we are monuments. We get to be somewhere that is ours, forever. A place no other hands can reach.

0:00

Intermission

ON FATHERS, SONS, AND GHOSTS, HOLY OR OTHERWISE:
HE GOT GAME (1998)

Here is where I would like to tell you about the form on my father's jump shot. Or that I learned to shoot from countless hours in a backyard, with a hoop affixed to the top of a garage—holding steady with its rotting wood. And it is true that when we moved from the small Eastside Columbus house to the slightly bigger Eastside Columbus house, my father was most excited about the high garage. From that towering height, the moonlight illuminated the orange halo and the net dangling from it. My two elder siblings were, by then, in high school. Removed from any hoop dreams that might have clouded their heads at a younger age. But my brother and I, not even teenagers yet, still felt like we could be molded into some athletic promise.

Here is where I would say that I ran, breathless, ornamented with beads of sweat, around the narrow concrete of my backyard. Catching passes from my father and tossing high arching jump shots into the night sky while he stayed below the rim to rebound. My pal Josh's dad played that role for him every night, just a door down from where we lived. A basketball hoop rolled into the middle of the street and the pounding of the ball drumming its way along the orchestra of darkness.

The truth, though, is that I saw my father shoot a basketball only one time. It wasn't memorable, beyond the fact that it was someone engaging in an action I'd only heard about them engaging in, sometime in a distant past before I was born. My father's glory days rarely made it into the stories he told. He grew up on the East Coast, in New Jersey and Brooklyn. We knew that he'd played a little ball, but not for any school or rec team. He played ball the way that we knew some of the kids on our block to play ball. There's the court where the serious hoopers play, and then there's the court for if you're just fucking around. Tossing up shots with reckless abandon in hopes to speed up time. It seemed as though my father was the latter, with dreams of being the former.

What we most commonly knew about my father's youth was that he, at some point, got caught up with what he called the wrong crowd. He said it the way parents sometimes say these things: with lament but also with warning. As in: don't you fall in with the wrong crowd. What is rarely said about these people and about these moments in our lives is that sometimes the wrong crowd is simply the crowd that loves you the best. The crowd that sees you the clearest. Their wrongness perhaps not inherent but cultivated through a series of neglects or unresolved pains. But in the midst of that love, the love of the wrong crowd, dirt is sometimes done. And this, we were to understand, is what led my father to steal cars before he could even drive them. He would have been a promising athlete, we'd be told. Who is to say when trouble consumes a life.

The day my father shot a basketball was across the street from our house, at Scottwood Elementary School. It was the place to play in our hood, even though the court itself was uneven, cracked, often littered with broken glass that had to be swept off with a shoe. The courts at Johnson Park Middle School were better, just down the street. The blacktop was more even, painted and repainted with clear, thick white lines on the first day of spring each year. The hoops weren't encircled by a playground, so the more aware players didn't have to watch their language when kids would inevitably be swinging on the monkey bars while a pass slipped just beyond outstretched fingertips.

The problem with J.P., though, was the double rims, fastened too tightly to the backboard. No shooter worth their salt wanted to have to adjust for the unforgiving nature of the double rims. The way the ball could chart a near-perfect trajectory before hitting the stiff rim and spinning out or careening into the fence. Most of us just figured that we'd rather take the chances and play Scottwood. Besides, there was something gritty about the landscape. It made us feel like it was our little slice of streetball heaven, here in the Midwest. If you played hard, you might come home and need someone to pull glass out of your knee. A small map of red where the skin on your palms used to be. You carried the pain of the court with you, often as a source of pride. To show that you cared, even if the games in the middle of the summer meant nothing. Barely even bragging rights, since they were played so often and with such a mixing up of teams that there were never any dynasties.

Also, Scottwood had streetlights that hovered over the court. They never all worked at the same time, but if a couple worked, that was all that would be needed to extend a game until the True Nighttime—not when it got dark but when parents began to circle the park's fence, sometimes with hands on hips and a knowing glance.

On one such night, my father wandered over to the park, more curious than angry. When one of my brothers missed a shot and the ball rolled and knocked against my father's brown work shoes, he picked it up and flung an awkward attempt at the rim, barely jumping. It was all arms, and so it fell short and wide. He called for the ball again, once my brother chased it down. His next shot was long, barely skimming the edge of the rim as it descended from its rainbow arc. His form was strained, almost like he'd never held a basketball before but had watched the game endlessly.

And I know this is small, truly. But the moment was revelatory. Like a mystery revealed in a matter of seconds. My father came up in a city of ball players at a time when the city was buzzing with excitement about the game, but he couldn't make it, so he stole cars. Got locked up for a bit and got out and fought his way toward becoming something better. An American story—the kind people highlight when someone who isn't "supposed" to make it out of somewhere makes it out of somewhere.

I realize now that I don't know how or when I learned how to shoot. Just that I knew I envied the children who played sports with their fathers in backyards or at parks. The fathers who adjusted fingers along the seams of a football or instructed their children which finger should touch the basketball last upon release, for the sake of good rotation. It is a foolish envy, and I am aware of this. My father worked hard at a great many things, and at the end of all that work, there wasn't a lot of time to teach a game he didn't have all that much of a connection to anymore. My envy, while well-worn, never turned into resentment.

The hoop atop our garage didn't make it two summers. When Scottwood was packed, people would come over to play small-sided games, but the allure wore off. Our backyard was too small, bordered by bushes and branches. And the garage itself was aging, requiring a gentleness that was not met by a basketball slamming into it repeatedly. When our pal Lorenzo got tall enough to dunk on the rim, its days were numbered, sighing out-loud squeaks anytime Lorenzo lingered on the rim too long. Until one day it finally snapped, falling to the ground and taking Lorenzo with it. We all laughed. By that point, the hoop—once a selling point for the house itself—had become an afterthought. Once the fantasies of late-night shooting sessions washed away, it stood as a reminder of what it wasn't. We tucked the hoop in the garage. And now, when I think back, I can't remember how long it took my father to acknowledge its absence.

From the unlocked jaws of America's cages, a chain of fathers marches out. Back to their children, who we are to believe were too small to remember them. Who might only know what they look like through a barrier of glass. Back to the women they put their hands on even when they knew better. Back to the corners where they were feared or respected or simply survived. Back to their porches on the fringes of some city and the clouds of smoke they blow above them, a cigarette bummed from some merciful overseer of the night. Back to the bars where the drinks might be free for a while, until the tab starts to run up. But yes, more than anything, back to their children. Their older, more skeptical children. Back to a calendar full of absences. Of first baskets or touchdowns or goals. Of missed days of school or relationships. Back through a door their shadows can barely make it through, weighed down by all of their sins.

The "father returns home from prison" storyline has been baked into so many different shows, and what happens at the end varies. Because of the consistency and ferocity of this trope, one might find oneself rooting for a recently returned father to get a win. A real win, not just a longing gaze from the stands while their estranged child plays in a state championship game.

When the distant father returns from the prison or the war or the streets, one might wish for a tangible victory played out on-screen. Something that shows them as something more than money tucked in a mattress somewhere. The tip of a gun, still hot from being fired. A baggie tucked into a palm.

At the end of *He Got Game,* Jake Shuttlesworth makes his son a deal. Jake is out the joint on a type of temporary work release. His son, Jesus, is the number one high school basketball player in the country, and the prison warden wants Jake to convince Jesus to attend the hilariously fictional Big State University. The warden graduated from there, and the basketball program needs revitalization. If Jake can convince his son to sign with BSU, he will be released from prison—a real gift, since Jake is serving a life sentence. The problem is, Jake went away for accidentally killing his wife, Jesus's mother.

The movie is flawed and stunning, typical Spike Lee melodrama with hoops at the center. Given the background, the story plays out as one might imagine: there is an unresolvable tension between the father and son, only softened briefly during a walk through Coney Island. When Jesus complains about the name he was given and the teasing he endured during the cruelest and most awkward years of his youth, Jake reveals that the name was never biblical. That Jesus was named after Earl Monroe. Monroe, who carried several nicknames with him throughout his life on the court. In Philly, on the playground, he was called Thomas Edison because of his ability to pull new moves seemingly out of thin air. He is most commonly known by another nickname: Earl the Pearl, given to him at Winston-Salem State University when a sportswriter named Jerry McLeese coined his buckets "Earl's Pearls."

But, as Jake explains to his son as they walk below the hovering white birds and ecstatic shouts of the Coney Island Boardwalk, it was when the black folks began to call Earl "Black Jesus" that Jake loved him best. During his final year at Winston-Salem State and in his early NBA days with the Baltimore Bullets, before he went to the Knicks and had to balance his flamboyance alongside the equally flamboyant Walt Frazier. When Earl was still pulling out the moves he learned on the streets of Philly, tiptoeing around defenders as if he were walking on water. The black people gathered in front of TVs in high-rise apartment buildings or in neighborhood bars would shout about the divine—how the man, in that moment, could only be touched by something holy. Black Jesus, dribbling with his back to a defender and then gone in a quick twitch. Black Jesus, lifting a jump shot just above an opponent's outstretched hand, hanging in the air as if being lifted by a choir of angels. In the moment Jake explains this to his son, he cannot control his joy. To give his son the gospel. And for a moment, Jesus Shuttlesworth smiles. But then the scene is over, and the tension between father and son settles back in.

And then there is that ending. On a windy, fenced-in court, Jake determines the terms of the arrangement. He's out of time. He can't wait for forgiveness from his son anymore. He throws down the letter of intent for Big State and says they'll have to play for it. One on one to 11. If Jake wins, Jesus goes to Big State, and Jake walks free. If Jesus wins, Jake walks out of his life and never comes back. The son will have to beat his father with the tools he learned at the elder's feet.

And, oh, how you might root for Jake, even though his loss is clearly inevitable. Jake moves like an old man, worn down by time and ravaged by life inside of a cage. His knees are heavily taped, and he's several inches smaller than his son. But he gets the ball first. In a game to 11, if you get the ball first, you just have to make enough shots to keep getting the ball back. And what Jake lacks in size, in youth, in resentment, he makes up for with clever movements and exquisite footwork. He fakes out his son for an easy layup. He misses a long jumper and Jesus scores two quick layups. After the second, Jesus glides past his father and shouts, "You taught me that!" As the arrangement of strings swells toward almost violence, Jake fires back, "I taught you well. Everything you learned, you learned from me." It represents a tipping point. A father who was beyond seeking forgiveness. A father who knew he was outmatched but certainly wasn't going to let his own son bully him around the court he taught him on. When Jesus misses his next shot, Jake rains in a long jumper over his son's outstretched arm. Before it falls in, he shouts, "I didn't teach you that, though, did I?" as it falls through the net. "That's something you have to learn on your own." This exchange between the two is thrilling. Even now, it pulls me to the front of my chair, despite my knowing the ill-fated outcome. Any competitor knows the heat of this particular moment well, when a competition that was never friendly tilts toward a type of controlled exchanging of punches between two people who know exactly how to push each other's buttons. Where to land the most direct hits during bouts of trash talk. Not just to make someone lose focus but to isolate them from any foolish ideas they might be holding onto about the game being fun, or this clash being done out of affection and not necessity. Jake's next bucket is a smooth finger roll that evades his son's eager reach, and this is Jake's crescendo. There is still music backing the scene, but it almost disappears. Jake's exuberance is the soundtrack. "I think I'll go around again!" he shouts, taking an additional lap around the court while his son, annoyed and exasperated, urges him to get back on the ball.

This is the moment when you are made to feel like Jake

could win the game, could win the freedom being dangled before him. Freedom that it barely feels like he's playing for, anyway. By this point, it is made clear that the disdain Jesus has for Jake wouldn't allow Jesus to attend Big State even if he wanted to. We are made to understand that the game between the two has different stakes than it did when it began. What Jake seems to be playing for is respect—something that is so often denied the father who returns, even a father with as ill of a history to answer for as Jake. But still, there is Jake playing to show his son that he's not yet dead, not yet willing to be vanished into a hole and forgotten. To say *Son, I named you after a heaven-sent hooper, and that's where I learned my game from.* This is the moment, with Jake shouting over the horns and strings of the film's score, that you feel like some holy spirit might guide the father's conquering of the son, just this one time. Jake hits a fadeaway off the glass and shouts, "I feel refreshed!" Jesus, for a moment, looks bewildered, perhaps even proud, but the pride hangs for only a brief moment before it is washed away by renewed anger and determination. And just like that, you know if Jake misses again, the game is over.

And when he does, it is. Jake can barely guard his son, who waltzes past him for an easy dunk. Out of breath, Jake backs off Jesus, who hits the bottom of the net from the top of the key. Even when Jake gets the ball back and banks in an exhausted long jumper through heavy breaths, you are to understand what is coming, punctuated by Jesus telling him that's your last basket with prophetic clarity. And beyond that clarity, there is nothing left. Jake spits blood from his mouth, that appeared there after the arrival of his son's elbow. Jake stops challenging shots altogether. It's 7–5, and then it's 8–5, and then it's 9–5. Jake tells Jesus that he has to earn the last two points, but he's weak, heaving shallow breaths and leaning on his son to stay upright.

There's an awareness that sets in—that Jake is going back to jail, that he's no longer in control. That his son is not interested in mercy. On the final point, Jake is shoved to the ground. Jesus dunks and firmly places the ball on his father's heaving stomach. Jesus taunts his father, who struggles to get up, while gathered bystanders point and laugh.

There is a volta, we are to believe, when Jake stands up to his son and offers final advice, telling him to get the hatred out of his heart, before Jake vanishes into the back seat of a car and heads back to prison.

But I would like to suggest an ending to the film in the moments right before, the moments of Jake struggling while Jesus taunts. The idea that is presented is one of conquering. The father not only as a nuisance but also as a haunting. A memory of that which could have been but was stolen by violence. And, yes, this small victory doesn't undo that violence, as Jake suggests in his ending monologue. But it is Jesus stating clearly that there is a power that can no longer be wrestled from him. If the trope must exist, let it fully lean into this, perhaps. Sons exorcising all the sins of the father that live within. Sure, at the end of *He Got Game,* we are to believe that there is some reconciliation of sorts. We see Jesus at Big State, after all. Jake remains in prison, as Jesus attending BSU is not proven to have happened by direct result of Jake's influence. The film ends with Jake throwing a basketball over a prison wall, only for it to land at Jesus's feet in the Big State gym. And this is fine, I suppose. Corny, as so many movies wrestling with these large dynamics tend to be. If I cannot get the victory I was rooting for, then I would prefer an exorcism, an eviction. A son, shedding his father one last time and becoming untouchable.

For anyone who grew up in a home where there was a belt, unleashed from the rings on a parent's pants, or where there might have been a switch pulled down from a tree, you know that some punishments can have an expiration date. Some of us grow too large or too accustomed to every kind of pain for our parents to physically punish us in the same way. When I started getting into enough fights with the kids on my block, and when I started losing enough fights with kids on my block, my body began to hold an understanding of pain differently. If your child comes home with a split lip or someone else's blood on their shirt, a parent might rearrange their relationship with physicality.

It is fear. The introduction of fear. And how it operated on a sliding scale for me in the household where I grew up. I don't remember when I stopped being afraid of my father, and I don't remember when he became aware that I was no longer afraid of him. After my mother died, it was just my father raising us. He was present, rarely distant. And so our resentments grew over time, slow and irrational. There's no good math to track when this happens. It doesn't happen in one day or in one argument or in one withdrawal. It happens gradually: A curfew is missed and then shrugged off. Eyes are rolled during a lecture. And yes, the threat of physical punishment barely sparks a reaction.

I think this is why the image of sons taking their fathers on in basketball endures so much for me. You can't beat the man—until you can. And then, in beating him, something new is revealed. This isn't only fictional. In *Hoop Dreams*, Arthur Agee's father comes back to the family after months of being strung out on the streets. His son plays him one on one, like the old days, growing angrier and more intense with each basket until he finishes his pops off, sending the old man packing, walking into the smoke-filled twilight, toward the dealers and the hustlers.

What I'm also saying is that there is an absence in my father never being good enough at basketball for me to feel like beating him was some kind of achievement. That there was no way for me to take advantage of whatever power my youth might have held while still a teenager, living under his roof, and underneath our shared complications—many of them exacerbated by my foolish youth. And perhaps my father knew this. That if he took to the court in any serious way, I might be there waiting, eager to prove myself. To beat him in the only way I knew I could.

The departed father is many things on-screen—but rarely a person. A vessel for a lacking imagination, or a plot device, or a breeze that upsets calm and then carries on elsewhere. And for this, I will say that if you have come expecting a story of how the fathers were emptied out of my own neighborhood, leaving exhausted mothers and endlessly wandering children, you will not find it here. There were, perhaps, too many parents in my hood. Too many grandparents. Too many aunties and uncles. This, of course, saved no one. This made us no better than anyone else, and it didn't make our institutional afflictions much different. But there were elders who wandered the tall grass alongside the basketball courts, and there were elders who tapped their feet in hard-soled shoes outside church on Sunday mornings while crews of children rode by on bikes trying not to make eye contact. There were elders on porches who lorded over the clocks and the children pretending to distract them from the time. A blessing but also a type of suffocation to curious, troublemaking youth. My pal Josh's father kept a gray 1992 Chevy Corvette parked in the driveway, covered with a black tarp. He'd pull the car out at the start of summer and drop the top on it, mostly to drive around the block slow, as a reminder for those who forgot he owned it. The entire purpose of the car was for him to flex so hard that the flex might echo for a calendar year. He'd occasionally tinker with the stereo system, playing old funk and soul at a volume that would wake a row of houses.

Once, at the end of summer, I put too much rotation on a jump shot while shooting on the rim in front of Josh's house. The ball careened off the side of the rim with purpose, spinning and bouncing its way toward the covered car. It bounced up with momentum and, even through the car's cover, knocked the side mirror so that it hung down in surrender. Before me and my boys could even have the hushed conversation about how to break the news, Josh's pops stormed out of the house, assessed the damage, glared at us, and shouted something about keeping the ball in the damn street. When someone objected with an attempt at explanation, he waved us off. *I wish you lil niggas would just go somewhere.* Without missing a beat, Josh replied *I wish you would too.*

There's a moment after witnessing someone talk back to their parents, especially if it is known to be forbidden, as it was in my hood. A collective holding of breath while a staring match unfolds. Looking back now, I think of what it is to flippantly wish a father away. But in the moment, Josh's father smirked, pulled the cover off of his car, and got in. He accelerated into the blood-red doorway between evening and night, and we stayed awake for hours, thinking he might never return.

I am yet too young to understand
that God is any respecter of persons.

—JOHN BROWN

12:00

I am convinced that gods are made out of men because men have found no other way to touch their gods. We will speak more of begging later—of desperation, of knowing what you can't have but pawing at some gilded door and hoping for an answer. There is a difference between begging and praying, although—like all differences I am interested in here—it is slight, thin as a whisper that catches someone in the moment right before they drift off to sleep. What matters is belief, I suppose. Belief in the unseen, a being who might care for you, despite their hands being full. For a great many of us, our prayers ascend, and we believe that they echo above us, somewhere, or they reach the ears of some angelic being who delivers our good word to a thoughtful god or even if we are feeling less romantic about it all, they fall into a file or a queue, and someone gets to them when they can. But the commitment to praying is the work. I was first told that prayer was a ritual, and the ritual was the reward. Anything born out of the ritual that would otherwise flow into my living was simply a bonus.

I have known elders who tell us young folks to pray only for the important things. Don't waste God's time with no nonsense. God is busy, after all. They might point to the sky on a night when the clouds have clocked out, called it a day, and let the moon and all its background dancers take center stage, and some beloved grandmother or grandfather or great-aunt will trace their fingers along some of those stars and say *You see that? God has to put each of those in the right place, every night, just for us. Don't waste no time with foolish prayers.*

I have never figured out where the line is drawn between a foolish prayer and a worthy prayer, and so I grew to believe that all of my prayers were foolish, even the ones heaved into the air in desperation, which might be the most foolish of them all. The prayers you have also maybe thrown skyward in a rushed moment of despair, pressing up against the realities that are known to be inevitable, spoken to a god you haven't thought to speak to in months or years. The kind that unfold into bargaining—you'll be better, you'll go to church sometimes. You'll stop lying as much. Please, keep the lights on for another day, and please, let the check finally come in. Please, let the name of the newly dead on the TV screen be another person and not my person, let the photo be wrong this one time, let the door open and let them walk through. Please, take the cancer away before it finishes running through the same beloved elder who once pointed at the sky and told me of your daily work, warned me to not waste your time, and here I am now, telling you what I need and telling you I need it today, I needed it yesterday, it is always almost too late but here I am again.

It is easier for some to give in and make gods out of men, some of whom might, at the very least, answer for their actions and inactions. To make gods out of the living, who walk among us, is to break the divine down into sectors: god of sports, god of finance, god of love, god of weaponry and war, god of hellish empire. But at least you know they exist. You can see them. You can watch them be punished in some way that might satisfy you, if you have been done wrong by them, and you can worship them when they've done right. There is a simpler economy to be found in the sacrilegious.

I think "savior" is a better word than "god" here. I've made saviors out of the living, because I saw no path to being saved otherwise. I've been at the mercy of those who believed themselves saviors because I told them they were, either in language or in action. I have been someone's savior and have fallen short, or fallen victim to my own glamorous cravings, my own hungers, too occupied to care for anyone else's.

And yes, sometimes these worlds, flimsy as they may be, intersect. There are those who pray for a savior and then a savior arrives, and through their arrival, that savior becomes godlike.

Home isn't a choice one makes; home is a set of circumstances. A draft lottery, too, relies on a set of circumstances, propelled by luck. Sometimes everything aligns. A child is born unto a desperate place, and the child becomes a king, and the desperate place can keep him, can protect him, can offer him a modest kingdom. But even a modest kingdom is still a kingdom. If things have gone wrong enough for a long enough time, anyone can become a god.

11:40

I never prayed as hard as I did in the two weeks before I got evicted from the first apartment I'd ever had on my own. I only remember it was 2007 because it was the middle of summer, and the Cavs had lost in LeBron's first Finals appearance, and everyone in my orbit was bouncing with the kind of optimism that requires no prayers to supplement it. They'll be back, this is only the start, there are years coming that will be even sweeter than this one, and so on.

My most hopeless years all blur together, surely as some kind of defense mechanism against memory—if it all feels like a blur, I can convince myself that it was over quickly and I hardly suffered. The only true markers I have I can attach to albums, songs coming out of cars, basketball games, the victories and disappointments of anything beyond my control.

In the two weeks I knew the eviction from my apartment was coming, I prayed every day, five times a day, the way that I was supposed to as a child. It was my first time praying regularly in almost a decade. I had to fight to remember the prayers. How to submit myself to the language, the movements. I bought a compass so that I could map out the correct way to face when praying, the holy direction. I didn't have the money to buy a Quran, so I borrowed one and tried to read from it once a day. I did all of this because I needed something. I needed to survive, and nothing else had worked, and I didn't want to know what would be on the other side of me not figuring out an answer this time, and so I placed myself at the mercy of what I believed to be an unseen savior, a savior who might have answers for the times I couldn't save myself.

How I arrived here is unspectacular. I had a job, and then I didn't. The apartment worked well for me at the time, because I didn't need much. It was situated walking distance to a Borders bookstore, and they gave me a job in the back of the shop, in the music section. During the still-thriving CD era, I got as close as I'd ever gotten to working in a record store. And because the Borders was tucked close to a suburb, people still walked in to buy music, to talk music, to ask questions about what was new, and what was coming. The pay was shit, but I got all my needs out of it. I could roll out of bed five minutes before a shift and make my way in to work with two minutes to spare. For food, I could snag whatever was left at the café at the end of the day, the pastries and premade sandwiches that would have otherwise been trashed.

But as Borders began its decline, there were those of us who

were deemed less useful. Though it was good that I had expansive music knowledge, it was a sort of bonus of the gig. No one
really *needed* someone who could wax poetic on the instrumen-
tation in a new Kings of Leon CD and how it differed from their
past output. And so I was let go. I only remember the day I was
let go because the playoffs had just started. I went home and
watched the first Cavs game of the first round, alone in my
apartment, and convinced myself that I wasn't feeling dread at
all. Or if I was feeling dread, it would quickly be replaced by a
newfound freedom. Anything I wanted to do, I could do now. It
was still the middle of April, and I had enough money for one
more month of rent, and by that time I'd have something newer
and better figured out. I was a hustler, after all. I'd come up
around hustlers. There were no circumstances that I believed I
couldn't hustle my way out of when the time came. Fuck the
noise, it was going to be a good summer. A summer where I
wouldn't have to pray my way out of any fresh terror.

11:30

I am most drawn to the concept of the witness as it presents
itself in its two primary realms, the legal and the spiritual. And
depending on where you come from or what you come up
around, you might be likely to not wanna witness a damn thing.
Find a new route when the alleyway sprouts more shadows
than you want to answer for, which is any shadow beyond your
own if you let me tell it. Me and everyone I fuck with mind our
own business, turn the volume up until it distorts the treacherous world beyond our sphere. And that isn't to say that me and
my folks won't correct some foul shit unraveling in our orbit.
Any hood worth a damn keeps the cops out by policing itself
and so surely somebody gotta get their hands a little dirty to

keep the badges and guns just beyond the gates. But I am saying I know when some shit that got nothing to do with me and
everything to do with someone else's survival is going down,
and I've got no problem not seeing what I don't need to see.
I've got no problem baptizing the mind every now and then.
What good is a witness in a country obsessed with forgetting?
But I'm talking about history now and history ain't nothing but
a whole bunch of shit a lot of witnesses don't wanna speak on.
What you learn is that even when you do your best to keep
them out, the cops are still gonna come around, and they're
still gonna hem you up on the way back from the corner store
or the basketball court and they are gonna wanna know what
you know and it is best if you don't tell them fools a damn
thing, but it is even better if you don't know a damn thing to tell
their asses in the first place. Look, all I know is that be it the
spiritual or the legal, the work of the witness is to not only be a
watcher but to evangelize, to spread the word about what was
seen. And depending on what you choose to see or not see, the
word might be the only good thing, or it might not be good at
all. For example: *Our boy coming home, he beat the case because
didn't nobody show up on the witness stand.* For example: *He
turned state's witness, and them boys left flowers on his mama's
doorstep. Nobody seen his ass since.*

11:20

When I was a boy, I would find any number of ways to get out
of saying prayers. Praying five times a day isn't an especially
heavy burden, particularly when the prayers don't last more
than six or seven minutes at the absolute most. In terms of
hard math, Muslims might actually get a deal when considering the time spent in prayer per week. My most devout Chris-

tian pals would get up early for church, get ready when it was still morning, and not make it back home until two, sometimes three hours later. My pals Mario and Brandon were Seventh-Day Adventists, and every time the sun set on Fridays, they were out of commission for twenty-four hours, usually longer, since their mom wouldn't let them come out the crib until Sunday mornings. All things considered, I didn't have it too bad when it came to the work of keeping my spirit clean. Yet I was so averse to the task of it for how it interrupted the movements of my days during summer vacation, when I'd be expected to come inside twice in the afternoon and pray, or keep an eye on the clock for the evening prayer, which arrived during the best part of evening—the sun barely starting to go down, the wind mercifully shaping itself into a cool river, lifting each hard-earned bead of sweat from your arms and filling its pockets with them before twirling into the coming night.

It was best if I lied, or pretended. If I, for example, ran the water in the bathroom and splashed water on my face, arms, and legs, to simulate cleaning myself in preparation for prayer, before closing the door and sitting silently in my room for a few minutes, hoping no one checked to make sure that I was really going through the motions of praying.

And of course it would have been easier to just actually pray. To push the act of pretending to those lengths instead of actually following through on the work of prayer might suggest that I never wanted my soul saved all that much anyway. This is where a different version of myself might express, here and now, that I'm not proud of this. That I am ashamed of what I've done and who I was. But it doesn't matter to me whether or not I lend my shame to you here, now. If there is indeed a life after this one and I must answer to someone or many someones in order to unlock its glorious bounty, there will be more than enough time for me to lay down the burden of all that which I am ashamed of. You don't get the key to that door this time. Even as I have recklessly made gods out of the living, out of the lovers, even out of enemies, I know that no one among you can lead me to the kind of promised land I'm looking for.

But I will say that as a child, I was foolish enough to not understand desperation. To not think I would ever be desperate enough to *need* to pray. It seemed like a luxury item. When I was caught faking prayer once, my father shrugged. *OK*, he said, the two letters expanding into multiple syllables, rising with an inflection of warning at the end. *But don't turn back toward Allah when you need something.* This was my only understanding of consequence—when I needed something, God would no longer be my audience.

I thought of this during the two weeks when I frantically prayed, borrowed prayer rugs and Qurans while the eviction notices were affixed to my apartment door. I thought of this as my prayers became more direct, even slightly teeming with rage. I'd begun the journey selflessly—praying for others, praying for the world, praying, broadly, for anything I cared about beyond myself. And then, with those things taken care of, I thought it could be a good time to ask for mercy. And when none came—when no jobs called back, when the money in my bank account ran out, when the checks I wrote the leasing office predictably bounced, I thought of what my father said once when I was young. And I cursed my younger self for thinking I'd never need any god, and in the numbness of the moment when I watched all of my belongings moved to the street, I thought it was most funny to imagine God this way. So many of us try to play our gods for fools. It's incredible that we think they wouldn't notice.

11:11

Tough for me to tell the difference between a prayer and a wish, though some might say a prayer is simply a wish that punches above its weight. A wish leaves the lips and depending on how it is spoken—its tone or the desire attached to it—it either gains wings or falls on the ears of the living. Though the living can certainly fulfill some wishes without an ounce of divine intervention. Someone pitches *I wish a nigga would* across a basketball court or a playground or a locker room and depending on who does or doesn't believe you being about what you say you're about, a nigga just might make that wish come true. So okay, this paper-thin difference defines itself by the cracks through which blood can exit. With enough ferocity, we are told that a prayer ends in mercy. Our wishes might not render us so lucky.

11:00

When the campaign began in 2006 and took off in 2007, WE ARE ALL WITNESSES made a home on a mural piercing the Cleveland skyline. There were T-shirts, plain and black, with the word WITNESS across the chest (and, of course, a small Nike logo below it, as to not get the motivations twisted). In a commercial, a fan stretches out their arm, the word WITNESS scrawled across it in dark ink. This was the presentation of witnessing in the biblical sense. If there were any doubt about the approach, there was a second, quieter commercial released as the Cavs set out into the Finals in 2007. In black and white, LeBron James rises toward the rim for a dunk in slow motion and then descends dramatically, just as the screen fades entirely to black, and the now-familiar slogan of WE ARE ALL WITNESSES emerges. But it is less the action and more the soundtrack that does the signaling here. The sweet, piano-soaked version of "I Shall Be Released" sung by the great Marion Williams, who once helped carry the Famous Ward Singers to fame and glory, with her voice, which maneuvered through the spirits it was summoning with complete control, a singer who made the work of gospel sound easy, and right when the language of witnessing appears on the screen, it syncs up with Marion tiptoeing through the lyrics *I . . . see . . . my . . . liiiiiight . . . come . . . shinin'* and you know she lingers on *light*, letting the vowel sound spin away and transform into an entire word on its own, and for a moment LeBron appears back on the screen, his skin wet and glowing even through the absence of color, jogging back down court at peace, his eyes closed, as if propelled on the wings of this holy song, only disrupted, once again, by that tricky Nike logo and some language beneath:

BELIEVE at nikebasketball.com

The closing is revelatory, though. The campaign was beyond simply a sneaker campaign, it was a campaign for an entire city, with a mission statement: believe what your eyes are telling you is real. There is a church to be made here, now. A church in our arena, a church in our skyline, yes, God very literally in the architecture, a church on any court where there is a ball and a player pretending to be another, better player, a church in the silence surrounding the stunned and wide-open mouth of a child who has seen what was impossible to them just mere seconds earlier. And if we are to talk of mouths,

10:59

in the King James translation of the Bible, the word "witness" appears 167 times, more than in most other translations, and when it appears, it sometimes summons the actions of the mouth.

18:16

But if he will not hear thee, then take with thee one or two more, that in the mouth of two or three witnesses every word may be established.

19:15

One witness shall not rise up against a man for any iniquity, or for any sin, in any sin that he sinneth: at the mouth of two witnesses, or at the mouth of three witnesses, shall the matter be established.

10:45

And so the holy books know what the law knows—a silent witness is no good to us. A silent witness is one who betrays the gospel of their eyes and ears. And not that Cleveland had to work very hard at getting its people to spread the gospel, but its people were more than willing. Heaven was here, and it is exactly what you'd imagine it to be if you could touch it, for a moment, before it drifts elsewhere and vanishes, like the embers of white chalk that would explode from the hands of LeBron James before Cavaliers home games, when he'd grab a handful from the scorer's table, rub his hands together, clap, and then throw the remains skyward, creating a small white cloud bursting from his fingers. Eventually, people began to mimic this even in their homes. Children watching the television, dipping their own hands in something white and powderlike, and waiting for their moment to ascend, temporarily, with their savior. Living rooms and the thick air of arenas and the skies of downtown filled with the residue of white powder, tributary clouds, hovering and then becoming another memory. This is how you know a city has started to become your city. When it moves alongside you, a dance partner who you can never out-step.

10:20

Depending on who you are or how long you've been without housing or what you've resigned yourself to, whether you define your circumstances as temporary or permanent or somewhere in between, the city can feel more like your city than it ever did when you were confined to one apartment. One walk to the grocery store, one bus ride to the office you never loved all that much but went to because the check was just good enough to keep you there.

I had to grow into this kind of optimism. Sometimes a life ruptures, and the wound that opens within your living becomes the new normal, so much that the rupture itself doesn't matter much anymore. But nothing prepared me for the immediacy of having nowhere to go. Having a place to sleep one night and then not having one the next. Even if you know it's coming, but have lied to yourself about its arrival. I pulled the eviction notices from the door for weeks and turned them over on the kitchen table. I thought that if the demands of the language weren't visible, the demands themselves would vanish. On the day I was set to be evicted I left the apartment in the morning, I walked around for hours, mostly trying to avoid the embarrassment of being present while my meager belongings were being moved to the sidewalk, while the locks were changed.

At the storage unit a block down from my old place, a kind woman behind the counter glanced tenderly at the two trash bags of items I'd dragged in behind me, and noticed the haphazard assortment of items spilling out of them. She mentioned that they were offering a special, two months free and then just twenty bucks a month after.

The unit itself was only big enough for what I'd carried, and a few select small pieces of furniture that I could haul on my own with a walk: a flimsy nightstand, the small coffee table I'd purchased at an antique store after signing my lease less than a year before. At first, I didn't consider the storage unit my new home as much as I considered it the place where I would keep my things, for free, for a couple of months, until something else made sense. I had run afoul of my family too many times to rely on them for help, and I was too ashamed to tell any of my friends of my newfound predicament, and so I figured out the math on how to fake it for a while, like nothing had changed. I had my storage unit and I had a gym membership I could still afford, which allowed me access to a shower. In the in-between time, the city became my own, the way a city can bow to anyone with nothing but time and the need to survive.

What you may learn is that there are places you can go where no one will pay attention to you if you don't cause a fuss. Sink down into a big chair at the library for a few hours, and hold a book on your lap, and if you fall asleep, no one will be bold enough to wake you up. Spend a dollar or two at the McDonald's and sit with a newspaper you swiped from the top of a trashcan, and that booth can be your booth for a little while. There is a way to blend into the architecture of a place, as long as you don't summon any chaos while you do it. Walk through a park where the weight of summer has broken the necks of the sunflowers, sent their faces moaning near the soil they burst from, and imagine that even the flowers must try to make a deal with whoever their god is, hoping for a better result than their current predicament.

I have never loved the city more than I did in those first moments of wandering, unhoused, through its gentle vacancies and rebellious cacophonies. Since it was summer, I'd have to measure out how long I could walk without becoming drenched in sweat, measure out where to stop along my aimless travels. If I walked far enough east, I could walk past the park where I learned to shoot a basketball. Past the church with the big gravel hill that my boys and I rode our bikes down, with no hands, courting violence as the reckless youth sometimes do. I could walk by my father's house, another site of eviction, one I'd surely earned many times over. I could, depending on the day, see the lights on, the car in the driveway. And I'd move on, quickly, hoping no one was glancing out of a window.

The truth of the matter is that when you have little to no other options, a city decides some things for you. This is to say that I did not intend to start sleeping in the storage unit where my meager belongings were, but on the fifth night of my being without shelter, it began to rain. Every other night I'd simply stayed awake, drinking in the silent and fluorescent glow of the city at rest, waiting until a church or a library opened where I could sneak two hours of sleep. But the rain was heavy. In Columbus, the summer storms come swift and without warning. There is often no strict continuity to them. They happen in loud bursts of light, water, and wind, a quick pounding of a drum that arrives and fades and arrives again. It is no dilemma to be caught outside in, not for the inexperienced and unprotected.

I expected to wait out the storm's intermittent percussions

inside the storage unit, but I ended up sleeping on a pile of coats, with the corner of a trash bag as a pillow. It stormed for the next three nights, and so I repeated this routine until it became my new normal. I'd retreat to the unit after the office closed and settle in for the night. I eventually got a small lamp, a cheap sleeping bag that I took from the lost and found at the gym. No one was supposed to live in these units, of course, and so I had to wake up earlier than the office workers would come in to do their sweeps of the facility. Which was fine, because that also meant that I could get to the gym early enough to get shots up on the courts, which were mostly vacant at 7 a.m.

It was strangely fulfilling to have a routine, even through what some might consider to be aimless living. No one close to me suspected that I was spending my days walking through the city, eating whatever meal I could scrape together with a couple dollars a day, and then spending my nights in a storage unit just wide enough to hold my entire body when sprawled out on its floor. But I imagine

10:00

they did suspect all of it. They had to. The greatest engine within the machinery of deception is mercy. The mercy visited upon you by those who know something is amiss but don't say shit. Who know the machinery is what is keeping you going, granting you a little bit of dignity. And the deception that mothers all other deceptions I may try to finesse past you is the one that whispers in my ear and tells me I keep all of my heartbreak in the chamber. Zip it up before going out into the world. But oh, how it overflows, even when I have prayed that it doesn't. And so I suppose I should assume there are many people to thank for their mercies. The friends who never asked the questions I didn't want to answer about the same clothes two days in a row or why a new person opened the door of my apartment when they knocked once and then never again.

But yes, also, the kind woman who once handed me a key to a storage unit I couldn't afford and who also, surely, heard me rustling around in that unit on the mornings I couldn't get out in time and who never knocked and who, when her manager came to do inspections on a morning I was tucked, trembling, in my sleeping bag, steered him in another direction, telling him *I've checked these already* outside of my door, the faint echo of her lie breathing life into my own prolonged lie. And yes, the library workers who did not shake me back to the living when I had nodded into a dream where I was free, and I mean the good kind of free, a dream no storm could snuff out. And yes, whoever saw fit to open the doors of the downtown church a little early on the mornings, and whoever saw fit to leave blankets on the pews, and whoever saw fit to play the gospel so low it became a morning lullaby, women singing about God and those who have run toward God and been lifted up beyond the wreckage, and I am thankful, too, that I did not, in that moment, stand over the cauldron of my rage. I am thankful that I simply slept, bathed in the glow of stained glass and the hues of the pastel Christs. But there was rage. I came to God once. I made a deal. I said *If you give me this, I will give you anything.* We both knew I was a liar. I suppose God is under no obligation to be merciful about our deceptions.

9:50

One way sports works is because of the fact that many of us do, in fact, survive on the miracles and mercies of others. And if you saw what I saw at the end of May, I believe you also would have not slept. You, too, would have stayed awake and run into June, breathless and certain of some divine forces at work, some divine forces that might choose to save you from your self-made chaos if you were good enough, if you spoke to them enough in their own language.

In '07, Detroit won the first two games of the Eastern Conference Finals by a combined six points. The Cavs won Game 3 by six points and then won Game 4 by four points. In the first two games, neither team broke 80 points. LeBron was dazzling in Game 3 but struggled to find consistency every other time out. And then Game 5, in a tied series, with neither team giving an inch of freedom to the other.

It isn't just that LeBron James scored the final 25 points for his team in the game, it's that in the moment, anyone could have told me that he'd scored 50 points in a row and I'd have believed them. Players take over games in any number of ways. Anyone who has watched enough ball or played enough ball has seen it before. A lucky few of us have had a sliver of a moment of taking over ourselves, hitting four jump shots to close out a pickup game, or getting up in the grill of another team's star player and shutting their water off for a quarter or a half. It isn't that taking over a game is unremarkable—it is often mighty work, in any form—it is that what LeBron James did at the end of Game 5 was something else entirely. It was like entering a portal, going from one game to an entirely unique game, almost cartoonish in nature, a game in which there was LeBron James, maneuvering through five foes and emerging victorious in almost every possession. There was a point where I and everyone around me couldn't remember a life where LeBron James hadn't scored a point. It is one thing to take over a game and another to transform time, to rearrange the minds of everyone watching.

Because of this, I'm not sure when it began. Even now, when

watching the fourth quarter of the game, it's hard to pinpoint. LeBron hits a three and then gets a steal and then drives to the rim and gets fouled. He's got seven points in the quarter. Neither team is pulling away, every bucket brings the Cavs within one or gives them a one-point lead, occasionally two, but never more than that. A late three-pointer puts the Pistons up by two with less than thirty seconds left. LeBron drives for an easy dunk. Tie game. He's got nine in the quarter now. Pistons miss a three. Overtime. LeBron drives and gets fouled, makes his free throws. LeBron drives for another easy dunk. Tayshaun Prince, a more-than-adequate defender under most circumstances, begins to look exasperated. This is where it shifted for me and my pals, watching in my cramped one-bedroom apartment, right before eviction, where I hadn't paid the rent for two months but managed to keep the lights on and the cable bill paid. After the dunk, the atmosphere shifted from *He's having a great stretch* to *I don't think anyone on this or any floor is in the same universe as he is right now.*

"Miracle" is another word for deception. Who or what can make someone believe anything that would be otherwise unbelievable. I have no money for rent, but something will come through. I go to bed hungry but will wake up in the morning, and something might fall in my lap to keep me full. A team is losing until it isn't. Until an architect of the miraculous takes over a game, and the deception becomes real. This is really happening. All of the good you believed would arrive, suddenly has. All of the bad that is coming, certainly will.

9:00

Even the act of witnessing has its limits, if it is left to its most idle definitions—the act of taking something in and even perhaps spreading the news of what was taken in. What becomes of a witness who is an audience to the unbelievable? In the very literal sense, that which pushes up against one's capacity for disbelief so intensely that it might, in its pushing, undo the certainty of witness altogether. This is the uncertain and often barren field from which miracle blooms. Yes, I saw what I saw, but I do not believe it and my not believing must mean that there is something greater at work, something I am chasing the language for, even as I watch it shrink on the horizon, like LeBron James, drinking in heavy breaths in Detroit, staring at the floor, perhaps unsure of what took hold of him and, by extension, what took hold of all of us who were witnesses to his brush with what can best be described as the supernatural or the divine, something holy enough to trick even the nonbelievers into thinking something good might come their way if they knock loudly enough at the gates, if they kneel humbly enough at the altar, if they face the holy land and close their eyes, if they hear a rustling outside of their window that sounds like someone speaking back, if they convince themselves it isn't the wind.

8:45

There is a dictionary definition of what a miracle is, and there is a biblical definition, and though the two are close enough to touch—like the interpretations of "witness"—there is a slight difference in tone, and in mission. The dictionary definition, simply:

> a surprising and welcome event that is not explicable by natural or scientific laws and is therefore considered to be the work of a divine agency

Sports unfurls a whole host of examples. See: Miracle on Ice, Minneapolis Miracle, Music City Miracle, Miracle at the Meadowlands. Acts performed by those who are human but who were, perhaps, briefly touched by the divine.

And then, biblically speaking:

The purpose of a miracle may be in the direct and immediate result of the event—e.g., deliverance from imminent danger.

See: the passage of children through the Red Sea, curing of illness, providing a wealth of provisions where there were none before.

The biblical miracle presents itself out of necessity, a look behind the curtain, the arm of the divine that reaches out to touch humanity despite what we are to understand as humanity's undeserving nature.

The work of one is to make people believers, even in moments of assumed mundanity. The work of the other is to make people believers through the evidence of their survival, even when they know they shouldn't have survived.

8:40

A consideration of miracles as performed by two men who, for a time, fooled people into believing they were gods:

8:30

That nigga Terrance lorded over the soda
machine like a hawk like Ronald McDonald
himself was paying this fool to ensure not a splash

of anything other than water made its way into the
small, unadorned cups which hovered by the drink
station, free to all who may have been short
on cash but still firmly in the clutches
of thirst which was everyone cuz it was one of those
summers & the sun is a bareknuckle brawler
that can only be held back by the clouds for so long
before it needs to get a taste of whatever your skin
can offer up as evidence of suffering or even
discomfort will do in the collection plate
of unbearable seasons & the mcdonalds at least
had AC and wouldn't care if the folks with no place
to sleep or stay would linger for a while and get cool
long as you ain't making no trouble & trouble
be in the eye of the beholder & in the eye
of the beholden & sometimes that be
a homie from the hood who got promoted
to manager a couple years after the block
dried up & the babies still had to get fed & so
you would think Terrance might respect a hustler
& perhaps he did & just didn't fuck with the hustle
all that much after all there is no hustle
that doesn't leave a victim tangled in its extensive
yarn & I do remember Terrance shouting out
I ain't getting fired for you lil niggas at the kids
from the hood killing time, hungry but with
limited cash in pocket, a crew of six
with enough cash to feed three & I am not
saying Terrance wasn't merciful I am saying
mercy has its limits & its limits are a mother
you promised you'd keep coming home to &
a child who you don't have to stare at long

before being reminded of your own face
weary & aging as it may be & so I get it & yet
I still cursed that fool as he lingered
over the soda machine on the days I wanted
something sweet to drown myself in & water alone
would never be enough but the trick
was to pretend to push the water tab
which hung down from the lemonade
dispenser like an exhausted tongue &
cover the transparent cup with your hand
while filling it with lemonade & if you were
feeling risky enough, a layer of sprite
certainly wouldn't hurt & these were the only
times I felt like I had any power at all
I am not satisfied with what I am given
I can fuck around & turn water
into anything

8:00

'06 I can hardly remember
the game itself but I remember the fan
who was getting on LeBron's ass in Detroit
the way fans sometimes do when afforded the
proximity to a player's ear & how they sometimes
do when they can tell that the player has heard them
even once if a player glances in their direction or
smirks or makes a shot & glares at them
even a little bit & I would say here & now
that the shit don't ever work depending on the
player & let the good brother spike lee tell it

reggie miller done set up shop in his nightmares
but that's not the miracle & the miracle is also
not LeBron dragging his boys to overtime
against those boys from Detroit
one year before he had to do it for real
at the doorstep of the nba finals but this
time it was just a regular season game &
a fan who had a little money in their pocket
& enough to fund whatever vice kickstarted their
courage & had the residue of that courage leaping
off the tongue with a bit of outsized passion &
that's when the game ain't really the game anymore
I guess just you and someone you wish you could beat
in a one-sided waltz & clearly wasn't nobody worried
about that fool cuz LeBron went off for 38, 7, & 8
& the Cavs walked out of Detroit with a win
but not before a small and mostly forgettable
moment where LeBron went to his courtside
enemy & extended a hand & there it was you could
see it you could see what whispered beneath
the shouts & curses & it was desire again making
a cameo at the exit of rage it is desire that arrives
for the curtain call when our tantrums
have exhausted themselves & I remember
LeBron looking his hater in the eyes & smiling
& I will say that from where I sat it appeared
to be a smile of pleasure & it appeared it
might have been a smile with an entire
unspoken scripture woven between it
your spirit was unclean & now it has
been cleansed

7:30

Swear to god it only takes about two
times running from the cops till you figure
out you're probably smarter than they're
ever gonna be or at least you actually
know the streets you actually have an
intimate relationship with its cracks &
corners & they just show up to give
niggas hell & stumble back to the suburbs
& so the fools don't stand a chance
on foot on wheels with a choir
of horses me & mine still gonna get
to a spot where we good as ghosts
& it's best not to need a reason to run
true that
but I hadn't seen the probation
officer in two months by late '06 cuz I didn't
have a gig & I hadn't paid back
what I stole & I wasn't trynna hear it
& so when the cops caught me lifting
a few sandwiches from the deli case at Kroger
& I started to run they had to know some
other shit was up & yeah those boys ain't
smart but they also don't need much
of a reason to chase a nigga & so here we go
& I ain't the fastest but I sure am
the most willing to survive in this scenario
& there are some things that just don't
show up in the body until we need them to
& when two cops turned into three & then
turned into five & then turned into

the apartment complex where I thought
I could get lost among the buildings
but couldn't because the complex
was no longer the complex it was once
& half the buildings had been torn
down for the sake of some boutiques &
I have certainly been done worse by
gentrification than I was in that moment
but needless to say I'd have cursed it
once again if I didn't have a larger dilemma
unfolding at my back & all I had going
for me was that I wasn't gonna get tired
or at least not tired of running shit
I made a life outta running from all
the things I was tired of & so
something gotta shake eventually
or so I believed as I ran into the woods
by the baseball fields where there was
a dugout & also slightly beyond that
a shed that was barely large enough to
fit a person & its door was always unlocked
& I knew both of these things
because a year earlier when after nearly
falling asleep in the field Brittany
said we should find somewhere quiet &
I knew she meant the kind of quiet
where we could be the architects
of the symphony & not leave it
to whatever devices the night had in store
with its shouts & screeches of bugs & cars
& faint arguments flooding in from the houses
alongside the baseball diamond & it was then

that we opened the shed & to our dismay
it was too small to hold both of us & therefore
certainly too small to hold both of us and our
salacious aspirations but that was then & this is now
& I knew I'd lost the cops for just long enough
those clowns wandering the trees which
I suppose all look the same if you wander
deep enough & this is how I slipped into the
shed just barely & watched through the cracks
& ate the only sandwich I hadn't abandoned
in the pursuit & watched five cops out of breath
collapsing into the grass field & shaking their heads
& there is the casting away of demons into a herd
though I can't recall which animal but maybe you can

7:00

but let's not kid ourselves
resurrection is the one that sells
the tickets it ain't every day some
motherfucker rises from whatever got them buried
& my pal who used to pull a heavy gold cross
from his neck & pay the block kids some coin
to hold on to it tight while he lit up the eastside
courts now wears a robe with a gold cross
stitched into its center & he scratches his beard
while the bells of the church thrash themselves
into a melody that finds itself in a dance between terror &
sanctifying though I guess that depends on when the last
time you spoke to god might have been & whether or not
you believe he spoke back to your ass & how long it has been
since you've thought of an eternity on fire but anyway my pal

tells me there is no real difference between resurrection and
revival 'cept that the latter can sometimes require a human
    intervention
a laying of hands upon whoever or whatever it is that needs
to be brought back among the living
but this is no time for semantics I suppose
I have seen the fingers stretched out along the forehead
of a body at rest & I have seen the body rise & I don't know
if it matters much how deeply I believed the body would
or wouldn't rise again & so I don't know for sure what language
to lend to cleveland in the spring of '05 when the playoffs were a
    kiss
away for the first time since '98 & all the dark & dead
air between the years & it only kind of mattered that they barely
    missed
cuz LeBron went for 27/7/7 that season & he still couldn't even
    legally
buy himself some shit to sip on if he wanted to & so the thing is
sometimes you lay hands on a city & sometimes the city reaches
toward you to keep itself afloat & so I ask my pal in all his gold
if it is also revival to keep the living alive a little longer & if it is
    also
resurrection if both geography & savior are granted a new life &
my pal shakes his head & says no no, you got it all wrong—no one
should place their heart in the hands of a human in hopes for
    salvation
& ok ok fine I say but then what do we make of kings

6:30

and kingdoms and things of that nature. There are those who
do love to adorn their beloveds and their heroes in the regalia

of monarchy, and I'm not immune to it. Never have been. When my homie who moved to the suburbs of Licking County got his first car with its first real license plate, he drove the old, unspectacular shell of a whip to my driveway and we rolled around in it for a few hours until we found ourselves in a parking lot at sunset with cold cans of soda perspiring through the cracks in our fingers, and I watched my old friend take out a blade and scrape the LIC off of the plate hanging down from the back of his car so that when he was done, it simply read KING COUNTY and that was that. *We all kings out here anyway* he told me, stretching an arm out and scanning it across the barren fields of the Eastside.

And I can get down with that, I suppose. Though I don't much want the responsibilities that could come with ruling over any kingdom, not even a kingdom of my own making. Shit, I barely made it through 2005 alive, and so what does that say about anyone who might look to me to be any kind of metronome for their own living?

There were times LeBron never looked all that comfortable as a king either, but the nickname fit too damn good to just let it slip through a city's fingers. In '05, *Slam* magazine put him on their cover again, this time the cover itself made to look like a playing card, a large red K at two of its corners, hovering above a diamond shape. In the center was LeBron, a burgundy-and-white robe over his shoulders but not obscuring his wine-and-gold Cavs jersey. His then-signature headband firmly affixed to the top of his forehead, giving way to a crooked crown, perfectly matching the robe. In his left hand is a sword. The look on his face can certainly be read a couple of different ways, but it looks to me like even he is a little bored with the monarchy. But what can you do. Sometimes the nickname is too perfect to do anything other than soak in it. King of Northeast

Ohio. There are prophecies about this. The ones that say you don't become a king, you are born a king and remain one for an entire lifetime, and sometimes for whatever comes after a lifetime. I don't want any parts of that either, but the stars aligned for LeBron James, and even in the early aughts, they weren't making NBA nicknames like they used to. Folks who lived through the nickname heyday of the '70s might suggest that the golden era had long died out, but the '80s and '90s did their best. Might be some fools who don't even know Magic's name ain't Magic. And speaking of Magic, the onetime second coming of Magic, Anfernee "Penny" Hardaway, didn't do too bad in the nickname department in the '90s. Penny just floats off the tongue, smooth as the man's game itself. And Penny did us all the solid of wearing the number "1" on his chest. One cent, running the one, leave you dropped off like loose change and all that. The Glove, The Worm, The Admiral, The Dream, and so on. All fine, safe to say that a lot of the good ones were taken by the time I was a kid watching NBA on NBC, but we made the most out of what was left.

Some might argue King James is not a nickname but a brand statement, which is fair, though I would say by the time LeBron came around, a nickname wasn't *always* what you were known by all of the time, what announcers called out after you've orchestrated an especially scintillating play. The nickname is sometimes what you are called by and sometimes it is whatever encases you, whatever you are born into and then carry for a lifetime, and whatever comes after.

6:00

There are few stories of actual kings that I find to be thrilling, and so I won't bore you with many except that since we are speaking of King James, there is the King James VI of Scotland (and I of England), who broke off some bread to translate the Bible into English and now the holy book wears his name like its own thin crown of gold. Who reigned during revivals of literature and art and who died of dysentery, without the same ceremony as Scotland's King James IV, who was killed at the Battle of Flodden, between England and Scotland, in September 1513, about a hundred years earlier. It can be said, of course, that it is also unceremonious for a king to be killed in battle. After all, what good is a king if they are not, at the very least, sacrificing themselves at the altar of violence that their constituents must fight, must endure.

James IV was disfigured by a parade of arrows. Disfigured as his body was, it was still put in a lead coffin and carried back to London, where it was received by Catherine of Aragon, who was married to Henry VIII. Catherine stripped the bloodied and torn coat from the body of James IV and sent it to her husband—who was off fighting in France—with a letter, suggesting that he use the blood-soaked coat as a trophy of sorts. A symbol of one small victory.

The body of James IV, though, presented a different issue. Though it rested for a time in a monastery, James IV could not be permanently buried there. He had been excommunicated from the church shortly before he died, because he broke the 1502 Truce of Perpetual Peace, negotiated between Scotland and England. The war that killed him also prevented his burial. And so he was relegated to a woodshed at the monastery. Years went by, and the corpse was forgotten entirely. So neglected that the head detached. Legend has it that workers on the ground of the monastery played soccer with the detached head of the king, until it was taken home by someone as a trophy, but a detached head is not a trophy that can last long in any reasonable home. And so it was disposed of. Dumped in a pit of stray bones at Great St. Michael's Church in London.

James IV is the interesting one. The one I return to. If I had to guess, it is because of my fascination not with his death but with his discarding. You are born a king or you are named a king, and sometimes the best thing you can do is survive whatever enemies bloom from the decorations of a ruler. There is a kingdom where you are revered, and there is a kingdom, somewhere else, where you are nothing, useful only as a corpse.

5:30

But to be fair, I didn't know anyone who wanted the head of King James I from Akron, Ohio. And if anyone did, they couldn't get through the wall of prayers and dreams erected in the Kingdom of Cleveland, turning back all those who hoped he might fail or stumble or make a fool of those who hoped to achieve something a little beyond mortality by being an audience to his greatness. Let some of my own beloved elders tell it, and prayer is the only cloak that can never be torn from the shoulders of anyone it is placed upon. And so, made from the lips of a person who loves us, we're all one good prayer from being royals, or something close.

JOHN BROWN, HUDSON AND FRANKLIN MILLS, OHIO (1800–1859)

He buried four of his children in one year. 1843. Dysentery took them, and then they became of the Ohio soil. If there is anything to throw your life in front of, it is probably freedom. Not your own, even. But death is a mode of freeing the self, I suppose. If you believe in an afterlife. If you believe that the people you love might be there, waiting, beyond the beyond. If there is anything worth killing for, it is probably whatever might unlock a chain from around someone else's neck. And still, there was one funeral for every season. It can become impossible to fear death.

SERINAH ABDURRAQIB, COLUMBUS, OHIO (FOREVER–FOREVER)

we are to believe the dead / get wings / have to get up there / one way or another / but even some of the living / levitate / have feet that never touch / the earth

5:00

As funny as it is to say, I don't remember the exact reason I ended up handcuffed in the back of a cop car in the fall of 2004. I'd been in and dodged so much trouble by that point, I think some dirt I did simply came back to catch my ass. I know the cops said they ran my plates and saw I had a warrant, and I realize that could have been true, though there's no telling what the warrant might have been for.

If it happens enough times, especially with minor enough offenses, being led back into a jail cell can become mundane and then forgettable. But I remember the first time, which I of course thought would be my last time. With the understanding that I'd be there for at least a week, if not longer, it felt strange. There are people who say they feel relief when they get caught doing dirt, like they can release the anxieties that were haunting their waking hours, they can stop looking over their shoulders or stop feeling a chill making its way through their extremities whenever a siren's lights paint over the walls of a dark room.

I was not one of those people. I believed that I was too good at doing dirt to ever get caught doing it. Then again, as bad as I was at lying to others, I was always at my worst when I was lying to myself. I wasn't good at stealing either, but I did it often. Which is how I found myself pulling on the tan uniform with FRANKLIN COUNTY CORRECTIONS on the back in cracked, black letters. Mine so old that it read FRA K I N CO NTY and I thought, for a moment, of me years earlier, in the arms of another sunset, with my homie scraping off the useless letters of a county on his license plate to remind himself that no matter the rust or the loud muffler or the window that wouldn't roll all the way down on his busted-ass whip, he was still a king as long as he was inside of it. Though, scraping down the hall in those loud-ass orange slippers, a cop on each shoulder, I felt like anything but royalty.

The first night, in a small holding cell with one other person, I settled into a top bunk and could hear the echo of correction officers yelling, hitting metal against metal, someone moaning from a place that did not signal pleasure. The person below me, a tall black man who looked about a decade older than I was, must have clocked my nervousness, the way my breath quickened as I sat up in the small bed. He chuckled, lightly, and calmly exhaled.

"Don't worry, man," he said, evenly. "Whatever they do to you, they gonna do to all of us."

I thought about this all night, after the sounds quieted and most everyone else outside seemed to be asleep. At first, I thought what he was saying was *We all got your back,* but the more I thought about it, I think he was actually saying *No one in here suffers alone,* which is close to the same thing but also decidedly not.

When we were transferred to the workhouse, another jail a few miles south of downtown, the man who was my bunkmate the night before gave me a Bible. He did this without ever giving me his name. Just handed me a book while he unpacked his things and said, "You might need this in the early days." When I refused at first, insisting that I'd be out soon, he just smirked and nodded. I didn't yet realize that he'd seen a lotta folks who believed they'd be out soon. Instead he shrugged, told me, "Even if you do get out this mufucka, you still need the word."

In the sprawling, open-concept floor of the workhouse, where everyone was locked up together and found their own corner of space, I opened the Bible and saw that words were circled all throughout, on almost every page. The same words: *body, eyes, ears, man, people, sons, children,* and then, sometimes, *witness.*

4:45

A jail cell is both kingdom and church, at times, depending on where you're doing your bid and how long your bid is. That workhouse cell was like a high school gym with all the bleachers rolled up. Nothing but space on a dusty wooden floor, crowded with the thin blue mattresses we all got shoved into our chests as we first entered through the doors. No proper cots, because there was no room. Just your blue mattress and whatever else you got approved to carry. Which, in my case, was nothing except a spare pair of white socks that I had, for some reason, been given by a guard after my first night. Some of the more savvy among us made trades, offering up whatever they had for a chance at someone else's slim mattress, so that they might double up. Inch a little bit closer to a good night's sleep if someone didn't mind sleeping directly on the hard floor. It all depended on finding someone who needed something you had more than they needed the comfort of a border between them and the ground. Separate but relentless desires can make two fools out of desperate negotiators.

I learned early to make a quiet space, and that space was my kingdom. I made sure to choose a spot I wouldn't reasonably ever have to defend. In a corner, out of the line of sight that would have allowed me to see the small television craning down from the wall, a strobe light of static shimmering over its shaky reception at all times, which led to the other folks locked in with me shouting at the screen, making their best guesses as to what might be unfolding through the glimmering gray chorus line of disruption.

I was posted up near the scant library, which mostly held Nicholas Sparks books and a couple of generic instructional books. How to start a business, how to use the internet. It was a corner that no one was especially excited about venturing to, and so it was mine. There were those who picked more enticing spaces, there were those who had been down in the workhouse for far longer than any of us in the new batch of residents, and there was a respect among the more tenured. How much space was yours to rule depended on how long you'd been in for, or who you'd fought to receive and then maintain your small kingdom. But if you didn't mind shrinking, becoming invisible in the terror of the slowly descending hours, it was good to have claim to a corner that was yours and yours alone. A king remains a king, no matter how paltry the square footage of their realm.

4:00

On my fifth day, still awaiting my court date, the face of LeBron James was on the television, pushing through the static enough to become unmistakable. It was a preseason interview, it seemed. No one knew what he was saying, and even if we did, it wouldn't matter. The minute he appeared on the screen, the loud and reckless debate unfurled. He ain't shit, or he is. Cavs ain't never gonna be shit, or they are. Two other people tucked away in a corner not far from mine quietly watched. One of them turned to me and the person next to me, pointed at the screen, where LeBron's smile fought through the gray gate laid atop it. "I played against him," the man said to us. "All through high school. Busted his ass for 30 one time."

My new companion and I looked at each other, knowingly. It doesn't take long to realize that in a place where no one knows your history, you can be anything. And so we nodded, said something affirmative but slightly dismissive. Performed our awe. Mercy, also, is how the imagination survives.

3:50

Nothing survives but the imagination in a place like this. Nothing fights its way to the surface of anguish, still breathing, like the imagination. The tunnels you can close your eyes and speed into, praying there is no exit or at least no exit that will place you back in the reality of a cracked blue mat and a meal that was gray when it arrived, turning grayer by the hour. On the other side of the walls, the stars that I cannot see are surely glinting like a gold tooth in the mouth of some dark-skinned and adored living ancestor throwing their head back and letting a laugh play a symphony across the night sky. And on the other side of the walls, someone might be holding a photo of you, someone might be wishing you weren't such a damn fool but missing you all the same. Someone might be telling a child to shoehorn you into their bedtime prayers, the way children sometimes pray, a collage of names and half-formed wishes thrown up to the sky where someone surely has to untangle the fabric of it all before handing it off to someone else. And somewhere on the other side of the walls, the stars run a tongue across the lips of night and someone is thinking of how you are surviving, speaking your name, even at a whisper, into what we will call the heavens, and praying the sound of it reaches you. And it might, if yours is an imagination that has not yet been broken by the pain in your back upon rising each morning, the fluttering and ominous lightbulbs in the showers, the men who can't sing but do anyway. The man who, not far from your kingdom, says a prayer

3:30

on the night before his court dates and then comes back the next afternoon, newly broken but still moaning the Lord's name into his palms in an attempt to put himself back together. At night, I'd hear him, softly reciting verses from the Bible by heart. I never asked what exactly he was praying for. There are places where questions are a salve, and there are places where questions are a weapon, pushed into a wound, and it's best to learn the difference between the two before you end up in some place you don't wanna be, acting a damn fool.

Instead, at night, with lights out, I would pass my waking hours resting on my back with my ball of white socks, shooting them toward the ceiling. Perfect form, middle finger last to slip off the white cotton, tight rotation, the pair of socks spinning into the black infinity, becoming small and momentarily invisible to my eyes, before arriving again, tumbling back toward my open palms. Sometimes, if you stare into darkness for long enough, anything you've ever wanted can emerge. And so there, affixed to the ceiling, backdropped by whispered prayers, there was an orange rim. A fresh net woven between its hooked mouth. A clean net, the kind I remembered from when school let out at Scottwood and the school custodians, knowing the hoopers would be out in the summer, would do the hood a solid and put fresh white nets on the rims. Long ones, too. The kind that exhaled with relief when a ball whipped through them. I'd task myself with making twenty shots, and then forty, and then eighty, or however many it took to depart from one dream and into another one. To wake, some tiny handful of hours later, the balled-up socks still in my palm, my desperate companion still with his face in his palms, a photo of a woman on the floor next to his feet.

3:00

With enough repetition, anything can become a religion. It doesn't matter if it works or not, it simply matters that a person returns.

2:30

Even before getting locked up, it was hard as hell to get a gig in this city when you were young with no experience and no paper from a college with your name on it. But if you gotta get paid, you gotta get paid. And in 2003, there were a lotta folks who borrowed money but couldn't pay that shit back and they sure enough needed to be called at all hours of the day whether they liked it or not, and so collection agencies everywhere would hire anyone who wouldn't mind fucking up someone else's day for a few hours at a time, and I wasn't really with the shit but I was with paying my little paltry rent and not having to steal in order to eat for once and so I took the damn gig. All the agencies in the city back in '03 had three-letter names, acronyms that attempted to tidy up the damage of the work itself. SRM, ARS, PYT, whatever allowed people to have to guess, for a moment, when they got the answer to *Who is this calling me?* coming across the line.

And I was shit at the job. I wasn't in it for the bonuses, the big commissions that came down if you could push someone to pay a debt with money they didn't have. If you could make them scared enough that they would tend to the immediate fear by kicking another inevitable fear further down the road, paying off one credit card with another, covering an old car payment with some borrowed cash. I was just in it for the base salary, which was also shit, but it was enough to get me to and from work in my loudly decaying car, enough to get me the basics. A mattress on the floor and a couple bowls of cereal a day.

And even then, even with the flimsy and barely present political framework of my youth, I realized that I was bad at the job in part because I could barely pay my bills. And I would spend my day trying to contact people who could barely pay their bills. And I was doing this for a paycheck that was only kind of enough. And I'd walk outside on breaks and look at my phone, and I'd have a missed call from someone calling me about money I owed. I was bad at the job, in part, because when someone told me they didn't have it, I believed them. Because I also didn't have it. And I didn't care to scrap over the phone about what we both ain't got.

All of the collection agencies looked the same. A nondescript building furnished with a bank of wall-to-wall cubicles. Sparse desks, a computer, a headset, a phone. A cavern of noise. People shouting, threatening, arguing. I was foolish then. In 2003, when I took this job, I hadn't yet seen the inside of a jail or slept on a street. I hadn't yet become entirely invisible. I spent most of my days thinking about the viciousness we visited upon people with no money. How these people were, in some ways, also my people. The people I knew and loved, and lived with.

Before I quit that job, before I couldn't square away my desire to get some pay with the realities of what it took to get that pay, I would cover my cubicle in pieces from sports magazines. Covers, or centerpieces from the magazine's insides. In the summer of 2003, after LeBron James had been drafted and was preparing to begin his NBA career in Cleveland, *Slam* magazine put him on the cover in a white Michael Jordan throwback jersey from the 1988 NBA All-Star Game. Two chains hung from LeBron's neck: a platinum cross and then, dangling lower, two dog tags. He cradled a basketball in one hand. He looked, still, like a child. Certain and eager, impenetrable cool.

I put the cover up in my cubicle. A couple days later at lunch, a small group gathered. A few of the women looked toward the cover and smiled, fawning over how good LeBron looked. "I have met him a few times," I told them, eager for a small slice of my own attention. "After basketball games, I've talked to him a couple of times . . . not for long, but yeah. . . ."

They looked at each other, knowingly. Smiled, said something that was both affirmative and dismissive.

2:10

The point, I think, is that as one life begins to ascend, another begins its descent. It's unremarkable. It happens to everyone, everywhere, even if you don't know the person who is watching your rise from a distance and cursing their own shit luck. But it doesn't always happen with a life that feels touchable, even if the touchable nature of two lives can be a myth. It wasn't long ago that I was a high school athlete in awe of a high school athlete. It wasn't that long before my desperate clocking in at a hellish job that I reached my hand through a crowd, seeking the hand of LeBron James, walking off the floor at the Coliseum in Columbus, Ohio, after Akron St. Vincent–St. Mary took down Brookhaven High School, the heroes of our beloved city. There is something about witnessing greatness before the rest of the world fully arrives to it. The witnessing can make you feel like you, too, have access to anything and everything. For a moment, it feels like no horror will ever befall you. And then, without knowing the exact origin point, you descend further from any once-possible promise. You're a spectator in an always-unfolding coronation. Watching through the fence, because you can't afford a ticket.

And speaking of tickets, my god,

2:00

bless our grandmothers who spent their last years playing the lottery and never winning. My grandmother loved her numbers, even when they didn't fall in her favor. When I was a kid and she lived with us, she'd walk down to the corner store, put her numbers in, and get a pile of scratch-offs for a little extra cash if some happened to come through. When the local television station would broadcast the lottery numbers each night, small white balls buzzing in a plastic machine and then shooting up toward an opening, she'd sit at the edge of her bed and watch. It was always the most painful when she got close. When the first two numbers, or sometimes the first three, were hers, and she'd glance down at her paper with the numbers on it and glance back up at the screen by way of confirmation that she was halfway to the miracle. And then, always, the next number would be the one that snuffed out the wish. She would, for a moment, sit dejected on the edge of the bed, or would every now and then curse at the screen, but then she'd return right back to it the next day. The dream only temporarily extinguished, returning with a newfound ferocity at each sunrise.

1:45

With enough repetition, anything can become a religion. It doesn't matter if it works or not, it simply matters if a person returns.

1:30

It is hard to watch a team you know has dedicated itself to intentional atrocity, knowing that they still have to at least try and put on a show for the dwindling crowds in the arena. Even if the crowds, themselves, are also rooting for that team to lose. The 2002–2003 Cleveland Cavaliers won one game in all of November. For the entirety of the season, the team averaged about three wins per month. It was hard to say that they were *led* by anyone, in the traditional sense. But they were highlighted by Ricky Davis, mostly a gunner off the bench to that point in his career, now thrust into a starting lineup where someone, anyone, had to take shots. And lord, Ricky never met a shot he didn't like. It didn't matter how he got his points, but best believe he was going to get them. He averaged 20 per game and also somehow managed to stumble his way into over 5 assists per, despite the fact that if you watched the games themselves, it seemed like he was shooting the rock every time he touched it, and despite the fact that the '02–'03 Cavs didn't have much in the way of talent to pass to. Big Z, Zydrunas Ilgauskas, was a steady and reliable veteran. But beyond that, the team was pieced together by the kind of guys who were still trying to cash in on their once-lucrative well of promise and potential. Or the kind of guys you would remember lighting it up in college for a while, a name you vaguely remember from a Final Four run or even a single hot shooting night in the league. Carlos Boozer and Dajuan Wagner were the rookies who sometimes inspired hope, but never *too* much. Darius Miles had come over from the young, exciting Clippers team he'd been a part of for the previous two seasons, though he didn't imbue Northeast Ohio with the same kind of exuberance that permeated Los Angeles.

But the season didn't matter. The mission was to lose, and to lose as much as possible. Tanking is an act of fascinating calculations. One must lose but still look as though one *desires* victory, even though everyone is already in on the secret. The act of tanking still gets treated as clandestine, or something that teams shouldn't outright admit to engaging in, even though we all see it. The Cavs of '02–'03 took to this task rigorously, firing John Lucas as coach, after he only won eight of the first forty-two games, and then handing the team over to his assistant, Keith Smart, who proceeded to win only nine games the rest of the way. It was all an exercise in optics. Any change is a good change when you're losing but want to make it seem like you could be winning if the chips fell in the right order.

To throw a game with intention is shameful, of course. But to alter the course of a close game to give your team a better shot at losing isn't such a deliberate shift that it might ruffle feathers, even if people know what to look for. The guy with the hot hand getting pulled from the game and staying on the bench a bit longer than expected, even when the opposing team goes on a run. The final play in a tie game clumsily drawn up, ending in one player taking a double-teamed fadeaway. A dunk careening off the back of a rim as time expires.

It was all about momentary suffering, which is only suffering if one doesn't think about the benefits of what awaits on the other side. Even if all that awaits on the other side is a *chance* at something better than what you have now. A few more lottery balls with your team's logo tossed into a machine. A little more money in your pocket than the money you spent on a ticket, scratched off with one of the last coins you have to your name.

1:15

The dreaming that happens in the in-between phase of wanting and obtaining is possibly best suited for sports, though the outcome is still reliant on the dance of numbers: what is in the loss column, what team logo rests inside of a large white numbered envelope. What number on the draft board ends up being yours. Numbers are as unpredictable as any other god, I suppose.

1:10

The specific brand of gambling on lottery tickets is the kind of thing some might consider sad or foolish until they fall into it themselves. At twenty years old, I didn't have a steady job or enough money to buy consistent meals, but I could definitely put some cash aside to blow on tickets at the corner store. I can't explain this except to say that it is seductive, to feel as though your luck might change in an instant, that you don't have to work your way through or toward anything. Just that one day, the numbers will fall in your favor, and your problems will be held under the raging waters of newfound wealth. And yes, of course, this cycle preys on the poor and on the desperate, but if you've ever been poor enough and desperate enough, there is no open mouth you won't blow a prayer into, hoping that it is blown back out, one day, wherever your darkest hour descends.

I played the same numbers every time. I won't tell you what they are, because they are my lucky numbers, which means that I might have to return to them one day, if and when everything else dries up and I find myself flush with wishes that cannot be fulfilled but are worth reaching for anyway. My lucky numbers never crawled across the bottom of the screen, but I still called them lucky, and I still called them mine. Luck isn't always about what wins and sometimes is about what you can keep close. What doesn't get you glory but what has also never done you wrong.

I never felt more free than I did in the space of time after putting my numbers in but before the winning numbers were announced. I would imagine what I would do first with six or seven figures tumbling into my bank account. I started to believe that I wasn't returning to the corner store every day for a chance to win, just for a chance to dream myself beyond my circumstances for a few hours, before succumbing, again, to the wide, sharp grin of reality.

And also, I admit, I believed that if I just lost enough—if I just kept losing and kept struggling in the face of an all-seeing and all-knowing divine entity—maybe I'd be broken off a slice of something sweet. At the end of my suffering, there might be a window, cracked just enough to gently lift the curtains like the bottom of a dress on a person you love, twirling to a song you didn't know but will never forget. The breeze through the window making a way for some unbreakable light spilling over and creating a path, just for you, beckoning.

1:00

With no emotional investment, watching the NBA draft lottery unfold can feel clinical or distant. On its face, it is a bit of a drag. An unceremonious ceremony for most of its ten or so minutes, usually delaying the tip-off to an anticipated playoff game. But in the late spring of 2003 I clocked out of my shitty collections job and I gathered some pals and found a bar in Columbus, most of its patrons adorned in some kind of Cavs regalia, making a night of it. This coming together of hope. In a way, it was beautiful to see collective wishing played out through this faulty and somewhat archaic ceremony. Though, perhaps, it was also permission-giving for me. Someone who, by that point, had lived years on the wings of small miracles coming through. A few bucks won here or there, some left-overs that someone didn't want. I wanted, then, to be a witness. A witness to a group of people beyond myself, cashing in on the big dream. The baptism, the holy mercy beyond suffering.

0:30

Once, when I watched numbers flash across a screen with a crumbled lottery ticket at my feet, a pal told me that I'd have a better chance of being struck by lightning than winning the lottery. And not only being struck by lightning once. I'd have a better chance of being struck by lightning, surviving, and being struck by lightning again. I think the laying out of this fact was meant to deter me from my reliance on lottery winnings being what turned my life around, and so I appreciated the senti-ment, but in my head, the two of us were considering different types of odds. I know of no good fortune that I haven't had to chase. The bad fortunes are going to show up whenever they want, whether you invite them or not.

0:28

With enough repetition, anything can become a religion. It doesn't matter if it works or not, it simply matters if a person returns.

0:20

In the bar I was watching in, every time an envelope was opened
and a card with a team logo other than the Cavaliers logo was
extracted from it, a collective exhale would be released, in a
single note, like a small choir seeking the collective sound during a warmup, so that they might be ready for the real riot of
noise that could arrive just around the corner. As the picks descended, the sighs would become louder, slightly more colorful, punctuated with a collage of indecipherable murmurs. My
pal Trav's leg effectively crashing into the top of the table by the
time pick seven was announced. And by the time Russ Granik
pulled Denver's card out of the envelope labeled 3, it is hard to
call the sounds emitting from the bar sighs anymore; the sighs
had turned into hopeful shouts, the murmurs had turned into
waves of percussion, hands rumbling against the bar's wood,
other eager hands pushing glasses into each other, offering up
the sound that comes before the sound of breaking, when two
glasses kiss each other's foreheads and are pulled back before
the cracking begins. There were only two envelopes left on the
table, and the team that had the same good odds for that first
pick as our guys ended up in *third,* of all places. Numbers,
those flimsy and flailing gods. Finally in our favor.

0:15

When the second envelope was opened, and the Grizzlies logo
emerged from it, the thing I remember was that most people
around me didn't cheer. Trav's foot didn't stop tapping against
the metal stand holding the table up. It was over. There was no
other math to be done. Destiny had been fulfilled, and the Cavs
had the first pick. To open the #1 envelope and pull out the

Cavs card was merely ceremonial at this point. But even Cavs owner Gordon Gund didn't celebrate until it happened. There was silence in the bar until it happened. Even the crowd at the draft lottery didn't make a sound until it happened. These are the true believers, it seems. The ones who suffer so mightily that their blessings must be confirmed in the most concrete and touchable ways. Believe me, it gets less funny the more time you spend thinking about it.

0:10

Since we are considering all manner of jokes: in a courthouse in early 2003, months before I was on what was called my last chance—the chance *before* all of my warnings ran out and I'd have to spend some time in jail—someone walked out of the probation office, their T-shirt half on and half off, a portion of the pristine excess white thrown over a shoulder, an exposed arm swinging out of a tank top with the ink *only god can judge me* in big block text, winding down the shoulder and stopping right before the elbow, and I admit, it was not funny to me then, as I trembled in the waiting room of an office where someone was going to tell me to make amends for some shit I did and then tell me how long I'd be down serving time if I didn't make the amends as quickly as I could. And I admit, when I say "funny" I mean funny as in "Isn't it funny how the assassin demands answers while holding a loaded gun inside of your open mouth?" I mean funny as in the punchline is not the grave itself but the towering mounds of dirt ready to be heaped upon the coffin.

Yes, only God can judge me, but then, what to make of the judges? The earthly rulers of lives. What to make of the people awaiting trials in a box, the families waiting for a number to

start counting down from. What to make of the people, anywhere, who can no longer tell the difference in sound between
a door opening and a door closing and only know there is no
place for them on the other side? A sentence is an arbitrary
thing. It begins and ends at the whims of its most vicious architects. Who is to say what *good behavior* is when the reward for it
is being a little more free? If I will play the game and submit
myself to a nefarious binary, I will say that I have been good. I
have never been innocent, but I have tried to be good. Even
when I robbed, I was good. It is good to survive, after all, if one
is to be sentenced to living. All I know is a door closed once,
and even when it opened, there wasn't enough light to find my
way out of the room that consumed me. Forgive me for com-
mitting to suffering. I thought it might be the answer. That if I
suffered loudly enough, for long enough, I would be owed
something from somewhere holy. And isn't it funny, also, to
imagine that the only time God judges us is after we've died?

0:02

With enough repetition anything can become a religion it
doesn't matter if it works or not it simply matters with enough
repetition anything can become a religion it doesn't matter if it
works with enough repetition anything can become

0:00

Intermission

ON THE DARKEST HEAVENS: *ABOVE THE RIM* (1994)

the   glass   illusion   fragile   as   life
             itself
beyond
             darkness   rests   another   dark
the taunts   echo   until   we wake
             gasping
into   borrowed   light
from a distance   the   glass   like any other illusion
             fragile   as a life
at the mercy   of night itself   beyond darkness   god also rests
but doesn't dream   another kind of   dark   is born
love   can't quiet   the taunts   which echo   until
             we wake   gasping into   the screams of
             borrowed   light   after the darkness   rinses
       itself clean   god wakes   again   but   doesn't bring
       the dead back

From a distance, before Nutso jumps, you notice the panes of glass. They look close, but it is an illusion. They belong to the other, distant building. Like any other illusion, the glass is fragile, reliant on what the viewer sees. Flimsy as a life at the mercy of one long stretch of night itself. I would like to think that beyond the stars, beyond the darkness itself, God also rests. God sleeps but doesn't dream. We are an audience to God's dreaming in the daylight, but through God's resting, another kind of immense and unforgiving dark is born. Love couldn't have saved Nutso. Couldn't have fastened the rim to a firmer backboard. But love also can't quiet the taunts from Shep, begging his friend to *jump, jump, jump,* which echo even as the wooden backboard crumbles and Nutso falls from the rooftop and into the dreamless night. There are sounds that haunt us until, eventually, we wake. Sweat-soaked and gasping into the newly arrived screams of harsh and borrowed morning light. Awakened to take account of what we still have after the darkness scurries off and rinses itself clean. In the morning, God wakes again and you might wish for good news through his waking. But he doesn't bring the dead back. Another illusion. The closer you get, the more you see. But it's always too late.

THIRD QUARTER

THE MERCY OF EXITS,
THE MAGIC OF FRUITLESS PLEADING

What is this
beautiful freedom
we long for, then promptly
grow bored within?

—RITA DOVE

12:00

There were years before the fences crowned with barbed wire. Years before the monochromatic manufacturing plants began to sprawl, before concrete was poured over the grass, over the brightest shouts of the yellow flowers. Before the parking lots and the cars, flooding the lots so tightly one could barely walk among them. Mostly, though, it was the time before the simplest, most mundane pleasures could be governed by fear.

In those years, when I was still young, my father would take my brother and me to a field that pushed right up against the airport. It is hard to imagine now, because of all of the aforementioned architecture designed to keep people away, or at least keep people with idle time and idle intentions away. But you could walk right up to the airport in those days. The Greenbrier housing projects were next to it, and our complex was just down the street. We'd drive most days, but if one wanted to, one could, in fact, walk straight onto the field, sit in the tall grass, lean back among the flowers, and watch the planes take off.

We'd always go at sunset, mostly on Fridays after my father got off work. It was one of the rare times with my father that demanded silence. No speaking, no music pushing the limits of stereo speakers in a car or living room. You were so close to the runways at the airport that you could feel the ground tremble when a plane was preparing to take off. That is how you knew to look up. The soil would jump, slightly, brown specks spilling over onto the brown hand pushed against the earth. And then, moments later, the reveal. From behind the airport building or a single tower interrupting the sky, a plane would emerge, the front of it tilting back, a mouth drinking in the sun's final offerings, brightness collapsing atop another, more alarming brightness. A metal machine, large and loud at first and then smaller, smaller, smaller, silent, gone.

At that age, I never thought there were people inside of the planes. I never imagined anyone leaving anywhere, or who they might be leaving behind. It all just seemed like a show, no different than the explosion of fireworks. Temporary decorations before the sky went black.

11:35

I would like to be granted an audience with the architect of longing. It isn't my first time casting this wish out into the distance, but I would like for the wish to be taken seriously this time around by whoever is in charge of such things. I don't believe the architect to be any kind of God, though I would be open to being proven wrong. I imagine, most likely, that we are dealing with one of God's lesser angels. One of the bored and mischievous ones, with too much time on their hands, who disrupted an otherwise reasonably stable emotional cocktail with their own whimsy.

If this meeting were ever to occur, I would most like to discuss the nuances of heartbreak. Heartbreak itself is a primary color. Stagnant without a series of secondary colors to activate it. Longing is an activator. Loneliness and heartbreak are not the same. I have been heartbroken and preoccupied with any number of pleasing but ultimately foolish pursuits, just as I have been lonely with a heart at least mostly intact (though it can be said that my heart, and perhaps yours, hums at the frequency of a low and ever-present breaking). But longing is the engine, dropped in and speeding me to all of my most pointless ponderings.

11:10

Would it help, here, for me to tell you that my father was a man who left one place to make a home someplace else? New Jersey, and then New York, and then Ohio. He and my mother and my two older siblings left and came to Columbus, Ohio, because that's where the adults could find jobs. Migration is sometimes a requirement, an act of survival. I never thought of my father as longing for a return to anywhere, which is, of course, what a child believes. Even while sitting beside a man who has made a ritual of silence. A man who made a ritual of looking up and watching planes take people from the place he was to any place he wasn't.

11:00

But let us dwell on heartbreak and its subplots for a moment. For example, I would like to examine the admittedly childish impulse that exists when seeing an ex-anything in the throes of a new pleasure, a pleasure that you do not have access to. One that you could not provide for them, and even the pleasure that they left you to seek. I don't mind bumping into an ex at the movies or while fumbling through the towels or toiletries at Target. In a small enough city, it happens. And with enough heartbreaks, every city can become a small enough city. We can make our small talk and keep it moving. Or depending on the circumstances, one can quietly slip a couple aisles over and remain extremely still, hoping that we weren't spotted and hoping that our ex-beloved doesn't require any of the goods in the aisle we've stumbled into.

But where I have struggled mightily is in the feeling that comes with knowing someone I loved once and maybe still love is enjoying a life with someone else. And yet! Even struggling with this and knowing very clearly that I do not wish to be the shepherd, dragging myself to my own devastation, I still! Like you, probably! (I say "probably" because while loneliness is not at all a crime, I do not wish to be alone here!) I have indeed reached for my phone! On a night when no one else will return my texts, on a night where my dull and understated flirtations have gone underappreciated and without reciprocation! And yes, I have opened Instagram and made my way to the page of a person I miss. I do this, in part, with the hope that they are missing me, wherever they are. That they have littered their Instagram stories with sad songs and dull photos of the sky. Meals for one. Walks through the doldrums of winter, leaving behind only one set of footprints.

A shaky proposition, of course. Even shakier when greeted with your old person living a new and joyful life, one that looks unfamiliar to the one you burdened them with, you fool. And yes, a new cast of characters has emerged, none of them you, all of them probably cooler, probably better-looking, most likely laughing at you in this very moment.

I am unsure why any of us would pursue this. The anxiety of scrolling through our pasts, lightly, of course, so as not to trigger any dreaded accidental liking of a weeks-old photo (or even months-old, depending on exactly how down bad you might be).

It doesn't make sense to me, even in the rare times I find myself doing it. I believe that what I'm chasing, probably, is a type of certainty. The closure beyond the closure. Preparation for what I might say if I were to ever see my old person or old people out with their new person or new people. This ache is, of course, not exclusive to the romantic relationship. I've found it harder, even, when it comes over the platonic relationship (which, when done correctly, is also a romantic relationship).

And this, I think, leads to the greater question I will pose to whatever wayward angel (if we are still to believe that it was, indeed, a wayward angel) is behind the layered concept of this specific brand of anguish. There is, sometimes, a thinning of the portal between wanting someone gone and wanting them back. I have found this to be the worst of times, I must admit. Longing in its most vicious hours, laughing its way past your lonely windows, your empty couch, the side of the bed that was not always only your side, the basketball court where you shoot alone now, get into fights alone now.

I am afraid of what getting under the hood of this moment will reveal about my own messes—the ones of my past and the ones that are surely on the horizon, as I don't learn from my repeated heartbreaks as much as I learn to catalog them, to pull them from their cases and admire them with a type of fascination for a while before locking them away again. But I imagine it much like the sweetness of seasons, if you live any-where that has seasons arriving harshly, seasons that fight their way toward the exit, kicking and shouting out one last torrent of cold or stifling humidity.

The worst of Ohio's winters often comes in their final act, and it's especially vicious because within the otherwise seem-ingly endless scroll of gray days adorned with ice and wind, there might be a day, or a few hours, of absolutely perfect weather. Spring, twirling out from behind the doldrums for a brief audition, just to check and see if it's still got it—and it does. And you might, for a moment, remember that this is what it was like. This is what it was like when it was good. Back before so many of us were emptied and left numb at the frozen and monotonous gates of winter.

I am of a particular emotional makeup, and because of this, I believe that misery doesn't *need* company as much as I believe that misery *is* company. Damn good company too, if you can get it honest enough. By this I mean that I get it. The sun dances from behind the gray, and I want the warmth. The trees are trying to fight back to life, and I root for them. But then, I think, what will become of this misery that I've held? That I've kept for myself, that I've made my own? I know my way around this. I want to keep the familiar as much as I want to run toward whatever newness arrives. I want to wallow in the memory, in the reality of what I know. What can only hurt me as much as I allow it to.

10:50

When LeBron James and the Miami Heat lost in the 2014 NBA Finals, most of my pals were ecstatic. Not just that they lost, but the manner in which they lost: 4–1, in a series that was never especially close. No one around me gave a shit about the San Antonio Spurs, the team responsible for the dispatching of LeBron and the Heat this time around. The Spurs were, at least to me and my crew, a boring squad. A squad devoid of star power and flair. But in the Finals, they were the team we were drawn to, because they were the team that could keep LeBron from the immortality of the three-peat. Keep him from winning three titles in a row, which is the number that *means* something. The first in 2012 could be minimized, washed away on an ocean of excuses. ("They were playing a young team! No experience! They should have won that! It doesn't count.") The second, in 2013, was hard-earned against the Spurs, and even the most cynical or vengeful among my crew had to tip a hat. But three in a row would be unforgivable, and so in the summer of 2014 there were Spurs fans throughout Ohio, adorned in Cavs jerseys.

Miami's collapse in the 2014 Finals didn't even have the courtesy to be spectacular. There was no dramatic flameout, not much rage spilling over into arguments on the bench. Just a team that looked entirely exhausted, seeking a quick end to an exhausting era.

This took some of the satisfaction away from those of us who were watching, hoping for LeBron James to be humbled in a very specific manner. It is one thing to lose by way of simply seeming to surrender and another to lose after pouring all of yourself into the game, only to be outdone by someone better. The Spurs were better, sure, but not at a level that reflected the outcome of the series. By Game 3, it was clear that the Heat just didn't want to be there and were content with letting themselves be run over. LeBron still got his, to be sure. Even in the blowouts of the final three games, he got his. But it was never going to be enough to overcome the broader flaws of the team, their lack of depth when compared to the Spurs, the obvious exhaustion that they were feeling toward each other, toward the game.

I can't say why it was satisfying, looking back. LeBron James had already achieved what he'd left Ohio for. What was whispering underneath The Decision—the neatly arranged television special, the button-up shirt, and the prolonged, droning, ten-minute interview before the reveal—was a far simpler reality: LeBron was leaving the Cavs because he wanted to win, and he didn't feel like he could win in Cleveland. Championships are how legacies are built and how they're measured, and you have to find your way to them however you can. It wasn't going to happen in this place. This place he'd loved, this place that embraced him, this corner of the world that defined his life.

A multitude of rejections sting in a multitude of ways. This rejection could have been looked at from two different angles. From the first, it makes sense that someone who spent the majority of their life in a place would, eventually, want to at least dip their toes into an elsewhere. That desire, of course, accelerated by what seemed to be the very real limitations of their home state. This happens, to some degree, almost everywhere. People I love have marched out of Ohio with an eye toward the coasts, toward the south. Kids I went to high school with charted paths out of this town by the time they were sixteen. That is a rejection, sure, but it's easier to live with when broken down to its simplest parts, even though the stakes and circumstances aren't legacy or a championship. It's still just young people trying to figure out where they fit.

The other way of looking at it, though, is more painful. Someone who is beholden to a place. Who loves that place, who wants to be in the place. And still, it just can't work. It has less to do with wanting to explore or take risks. It's not even a firm rejection of the place itself. It's the circumstances, which have become so unbearable that it serves someone to leave even their most familiar comforts behind.

You take what vengeance you can when you are aching from what you believe to be a betrayal that you cannot control any more than you can control the whims of a storm. Any LeBron James failure would have sufficed in that moment. But by 2014, he had already won twice. He'd already gotten what he left this place for. There was nothing for those left behind but confirmation. The knife that fills an absence. But there were always people who wanted him

10:35

back. There was no rage that could mask this, no amount of times someone could bring up the circus of The Decision, seething the entire time. I wanted him back, and I was confused by the feeling. What was wrestling underneath the pleasure in watching Miami lose in 2014 was also hope. Hope that the loss might be what brought him back to Ohio, an understanding that a return would be all it would take for him to be forgiven. Oh, how glorious it would be—the King returning to Cleveland as a winner, knowing what it takes to win a title.

Watching, and even participating in, this oscillation between harboring some residual bitterness toward LeBron, wanting him to fail, and also wanting him to come home was at some points bizarre and at other points deliciously familiar, for better or worse. Particularly the latter two motions. Not just wanting him to fail and wanting him to come home, but wanting him to fail so that he *would* come home. So that he might, through his failings, realize the error of his ways and return to familiar arms, with all forgiven, both parties eager to get back to the work of healing.

Of course this is absurd, but so much longing is steeped in absurdity. Sometimes, people want someone back just for the sake of having them, despite what both parties know and have known about their failures and how, when paired together, those shared failures were insurmountable. No, it is better to apply this type of feeling to a game. To an athlete. It is better to want someone to come back home if you, alone, cannot make them want to leave again.

10:05

If you have ever committed to a marriage that didn't last, or a years-long romantic endeavor that eventually quieted and died down, you perhaps know this exact feeling. A heart, sometimes, breaks slowly and without ceremony. I haven't been able to make sense of how or why it happens to some of us and not others. My pal who has been recklessly and relentlessly in love with his partner since they were two starry-eyed seventeen-year-olds who met at a punk show unfurls a string of advice that seems both practical and entirely overwhelming in equal measure. It's all about what you're willing to forgive, he tells me. You have to choose what to ignore every now and then, he tells me. Sure, there are things that begin to grate on you, he says. But there is beauty in even that—being so intimately familiar with the nuances of a single person that you are comfortable even with their encyclopedia of small annoyances, even as those annoyances snap at your heels for years, and then a lifetime.

On the other end of the spectrum, my pal who has never met a morning that didn't render him newly single suggests that the mind, the body, the heart, all have microscopic limits. And who are we to deny the consistent, ongoing testing of those limits? I am meant to love someone only for a small burst of time, he says to me one night, sitting on the hood of his dad's old truck. The argument, when presented this way, is that love itself is not linear, not necessarily defined by the clock or the calendar, as so many have assumed it to be.

Somewhere in between these two extremes, I find myself eager to resist falling in love and then relinquishing what little control I believed myself to have.

The dilemma for me has always been the reality that the

early moments of falling for anyone or anything are so seductive, and can rarely be captured again. They can be manufactured, but never fully sung back to life by the same effortless chorus. They appear, and then they drift away. I remember the first time I heard Nina Simone's voice, singing "Pirate Jenny," leaping out of an old and creaking record while I played on the floor as a small child. I will never be haunted in that specific way again. I may get a similar chill when Nina dismounts, spins *and / on / it / isssss / meeeeeeeee* into its own dark universe, but it will not hover like it did for me the first time. There will be no nightmares of a ship blowing a town to pieces while a black woman laughs.

Love is like this, too. What my happily committed pal is saying, I think, is that one must become content with shedding a version of oneself that one might only vaguely remember but not be able to touch again. While my other pal has accelerated this process, shedding so frequently that there is no past self that can even stick around long enough to be remembered. Just a constant scroll of new selves to revel in and then discard.

9:57

I am recalling a moment in March 2013 during a game where the Miami Heat played in Cleveland, fending off a feisty and determined Cavs team and getting a comeback win. The night itself was strange, beginning with a leak in the roof that delayed the action for nearly thirty minutes. But by the time the game ended, the leak, the score, the in-game action were all afterthoughts.

It wasn't reported much, as these things sometimes get buried as to not inspire other, similar actions, but there was a fan who ran onto the floor in Cleveland in the middle of the game.

The fan was wearing a white shirt with writing on it that looked like it was done with shoe polish, or paint, or something thicker and more distinct than permanent marker. On the front, the shirt read WE MISS YOU and on the other side 2014 COME BACK.

It was a desperate act of attention-seeking, and one where the person who ran onto the floor—as these things often go—didn't seem to know what to do once he got there. He ran close enough to James to startle him before security got ahold of him. He yelled, gestured in LeBron's direction, and pulled toward him while being dragged off of the floor.

There is a photo from this moment that I remember. LeBron James, with an almost sympathetic look, extending a hand toward the fan. Who, by that point, had a security guard's arm firmly around him. LeBron's face, in the moment, looks both sad and understanding. Like he's also known the exact velocity of this kind of longing.

9:40

There are all kinds of songs about people leaving places upon vessels of transport. Sometimes, if the singer of the song is lucky, their beloved comes back home. Sheena Easton's fella has a job. A working man. Yeah, he takes the morning train, sometimes before she can even kiss him goodbye, but it doesn't matter because when he punches the clock after his eight hours, he's right back home. Gladys Knight gets to follow some man back to Georgia when things didn't work out for him in Los Angeles, and that's not entirely sad either, I guess. You can't be a star everywhere, and when you can't be, there's always a home willing to take you back, even if you have to sneak out at midnight so that no one can call you a failure in broad daylight.

And lord, yes, there are those songs about getting in a car and driving and driving and driving. These are often the most urgent songs about exits. A person can't afford a plane ticket but can afford a couple tanks of gas, and they own just enough shit to fit in a trunk or a back seat, but not much else. Jo Dee Messina says let's flip a coin. Let fate do the work, but either way, we're gonna get gone for a little while.

But it's the planes you've got to worry about. If someone in a song is leaving on a plane, they aren't coming back. You will ache until the ache becomes so familiar, you forget to feel it at all.

9:35

The Leaving Song is the mother of a petulant, sometimes loud and unruly subgenre of song that is among my favorites: The Begging Song. It is a true but sad fact that this subgenre is most commonly dominated by men, some no-good mother-fuckers who swear they might do right this next time around if you could just / if you would just / if you could find it in your / baby please don't / and so on.

And shit, I ain't always been above being some form of that no-good motherfucker myself, but what I'm saying is that I have at least a little dignity and plus I can't sing all that well, so you won't catch me down on my knees, pleading, trying to bend a single note through the closing eye of forgiveness.

But lord knows I love to be a spectator to someone else's mess every now and then, since my own is so frequently unappealing (and relentlessly immovable), and so I do love a song where someone is doing some begging.

There are absolute titans of this subgenre. Otis, of course, who sounded pained even when he was singing about the exuberant pleasures of love. You must hear Otis Redding sing "My Girl." If you have already heard it, you must hear it again. Through the entirety of the tune, he is always just a half-step behind the drum beat. He enters this way and never completely catches up. The all-too-familiar bassline builds the doorway, the guitar runs a fresh layer of paint over the door, and then the drums rush through the entryway, all breathless and blazing. And then, lagging slightly behind them, here comes ol' Otis. This isn't a slight to the man, mind you. The whole point of these popular tunes that got passed around like the blues at a funeral is that everyone had to put their foot in it in a slightly different way, and Otis couldn't even sing a song about love without a little hint of ache, a precursor to the begging.

Let us take, for example, the chorus. The chorus of "My Girl," sung in its God-given form, is always on the upswing, one syllable flowing into an upward arc, the question that already has an answer, an answer both singer and listener know, but it still feels like a secret. The chorus, in this form, feels like being pushed on a swing until you get high enough to jump off.

Unless you are Otis, who tiptoes through that chorus like he's walking around a hardwood floor, trying to avoid stepping on glass. His "I . . . guess . . ." is tentative! His "you'd say" is a shrug! He takes the language at its most literal! As in, yeah sure man, I guess you'd say this shit, but *I* don't have to believe it. But it is the next movement, still just a touch behind the beat, when Otis sings "what . . . couldmakeme . . . feeeeeel this way" as if he is resigned to a type of doom. In this mode, the reveal that rests within the chorus is less of an excitement and more of a painful revelation. Yes, it is my girl, of course. But what if my girl is not always my girl. Otis sings the song like he is watching the door closing for the last time, the woman he loves on the other side of it. Call me a fool and call me a cynic, but I love Otis because he approaches romance in the only way that makes sense to me: love as a feather that just hasn't found the wind to carry it away yet.

There are other singers who sit at the top of this mountain of subgenre. Marvin doesn't get enough credit for how great he was at pleading, even though so many of his songs oscillated between questions and demands. He was a singer who couldn't make sense of the world, who sometimes couldn't make sense of himself, but he knew how to ask, and when asking didn't work, he knew how to shout to the high heavens. "Let's Get It On," for example, is a song where the question unravels until you realize, at the end, that nothing is being asked at all. It is a ravenous demand built from Marvin's creaking howls in the song's final act, a final act that seems like an entire universe away from the restrained conceit of the song's entry.

Our old pal James Brown could pour it on when he wanted to, though I never believed it, because even he seemed to not always believe it. I'm not saying everything on a record has to be believable, but I'm saying she ain't comin' home if you've realized you like the home more when she's not in it.

Ohio's own Mighty O'Jays are underrated beggars, underrated likely because their most prolific pleading comes in songs where they've already made some level of peace with their new-found loneliness. "Use Ta Be My Girl" is a perfect song of understated pleading, but it's the slow reveal and admission of the love that still lingers that do most of the work. Sure, if they had the chance they'd take her back, but that chance is almost certainly not coming, which is a different kind of ache entirely.

It should be made clear that begging and apologizing are two different things. They perhaps live in the same apartment building, and when done at the right temperature, they can be heard through each other's walls. Sometimes one may invite the other over, but the invitee can very easily either outstay its welcome or leave far too early. Apologizing is for the humbled; begging works best if the humility has yet to set in. This is, often, what makes begging such a unique vessel for this brand of song and—I must admit—why it makes sense that men have the most prominent hold on the genre. This can be a tender, thoughtful, self-reflective mode of tune, but so often, the begging is about both refusal and entitlement, which I suppose seems nefarious on its surface, though I am committed to seeing the usefulness in this type of refusal, at least to a point.

But even within the subgenre, there is another subgenre nested. In the basement of the begging subgenre, we get into the specifics. The begging song that revolves entirely around someone (again, usually a man) seeing a relationship nearing its end and trying to get it all back in a single exhaustive three-to-five-minute sprint. It must be noted that within these songs, there's usually some acknowledgment of how this person has failed or become neglectful or simply lost track of that elusive flame of persistence. But they can get it back, they're sure of it. If you could find it in your / if you could just give one more / if you can forget about the /

There are masters of even this. As much as I hate to summon the good brothers Boyz II Men into the room, they made quite the habit of falling to pieces within this very specific container. Rolling around on the ground, falling to their knees in the rain, fucking up coordinating silk outfits and whatnot. And I admit, I do not love most of the songs that arose from my Philadelphia brethren when they were in this mode, but they did seek to make a point, and the point was surely made, manipulative deep-voiced monologues and all.

The thing about the "come back to me before you've even

ever left" song is that it is only barely about the song itself and more about the catharsis of the song's narrator, who knows they have done wrong and is preempting whatever might be said about them around a table they are no longer present at.

My favorite tune within this cluttered basement is the Soul Children's "Don't Take My Sunshine." The only thing I share in common with our dearly departed Prince is that he and I both love this song, with its almost marathonlike anguish.

It isn't just that the man in this song is already mourning an exit; it's also that he's mourning an exit against the realities of his current circumstances. The verses are filled with the usual clichés: the sky doesn't look the same anymore, the flowers are blooming a bit later this year. In short, the vibes are off. But where the song turns is in its monologue, which is performed by a woman, the singer's beloved, who is explaining herself— why she's been off a bit and why, in turn, the relationship has suffered. She had been pulling away to get her mind together so that she can be a better partner, she explains. And also, she adds, she was concerned that our singer was becoming bored with her.

Yet, as she finishes her final sentence, our singer comes in over the top of her, screeching and moaning about how it's obvious that someone has taken his place in her life, begging her, once again, to not leave. This is where the song, the entire sub-subgenre, becomes most delicious for me. Once we, as listeners, come to understand that the songs like this aren't really ever about anything but ego, and the panic that sets in when ego is ruptured. These songs are structured almost entirely in opposition to the fear of being alone. Yes, there is a specific person who might fill a void, but I don't want to deal with the seeking.

In the end, there is something especially confounding about

drifting in this space: the space where you know you've fucked up, where you know you've done something no good or, even worse, you've been a shell of your once-loving self. The love has dwindled, and your desire to recapture it has also spiraled down the many drains and distractions of living—the mundane routines of a life, or the smile from a stranger on a subway that lingers in the mind longer than it should, or the rapidly accumulating nights where two people turn off their respective lamps and roll on their sides, away from each other, without speaking a word.

But then, when the exit is present, when it seems, in fact, like this would be a much easier path than any path to rebuilding, there is another game that begins. The hope that a person you loved or loved once but don't love in the same way fears loneliness with the same ferocity that you do. And so, sometimes, two unlucky people remain, outrunning a desire to hear their own echoes.

8:40

It was easy to be seduced into a similar sense of denial or confusion or hope or despair in the summer of 2010, as the free agency of LeBron James loomed, as people waited for him to announce if he'd be staying or going. The preemptive pleading began. A sort of fever dream of longing for an outcome that felt unlikely, but could maybe / if we were lucky / if we just prayed / please / please

8:38

What these songs and pleas hang their hopes on is the sometime reality that leaving is not permanent. That people sometimes come back. Come back to relationships, come back to cities they once left, come back to jobs they stormed out of. Sometimes people return because the pleading is effective, and sometimes they return because they have to. Like in "Midnight Train to Georgia," sometimes the dream dries up, and home beckons, where one can be relegated to the familiar limits of one's old dreams.

And sometimes people leave because they have to survive. Sometimes people leave because staying has run its course, a course littered with failures. I know what it is to leave in hopes that whatever has failed me isn't a part of my own internal makeup, that it is a place dragging me down, beckoning me toward all my worst impulses.

In the spring of 2010, the probation officer thumbed through my ever-growing file and sighed, shaking his head and nearly laughing. He leaned over a wide wooden desk, covered in pictures his children had drawn for him—the kind of art that resembles something close enough to familiar but still has a haphazardly abstract quality that can only be summoned by the whimsical exuberance of a child. Mr. Riley had been my probation officer for over four years, and by 2010 we'd frustrated each other into a type of familiarity. He was a black man who looked older than he actually was. He was only forty-four, but his beard was pristinely thick and white, like he'd pulled a cloud from the sky one day, tried it on, and liked the look. The hair atop his head wasn't so lucky. Most of it gone, save for some thinning strands on the sides that he sometimes flicked at with his long fingers while he spoke, almost as if he was checking to see if they were still there. He had a raspy voice, a smoker's voice. Language sounded like it was fighting itself out of him. He didn't laugh much because when he did laugh, he'd break into loud coughing fits that seemed painful. I often wondered if he found many things funny but simply chose to not endure the pain it would require to give in to the emotion.

Every time I got sentenced to probation and more probation and more probation, our time together was extended. I'd come to his office once a month and he'd ask me if I'd found work, often without looking up from my file. Sometimes I had work, sometimes I didn't have it. On the months I didn't have it, he'd ask how I'd been spending my time. This was a fascinating process, one that became colored with a slight concern or tenderness over the years. He once told me that he'd come to the conclusion that I wasn't a bad *person*, I was just a bad decision-maker. When I perked up a bit at this, thankful for the affirmation, he responded, "No, you don't understand. That's actually *more* concerning."

And so, on a day in the late spring of 2010, he leaned back in his chair, swiped at the wisps of thin gray on the right side of his head, and offered: *Why don't you just get out of here and try somewhere else?*, noting that my probationary period was coming to an end soon, as long as I could make it to September without any additional arrests or police interactions.

And I considered it. I had tried everything else, I thought. I went to church, sometimes. I prayed to two different gods, sometimes. I was a composer of pleading songs, in different languages, thrown up toward the unseen heavens in hopes that I could catch the ear of someone with an interest in mercy. To stay out of trouble, I'd spend idle afternoons at the library, looking at jobs in other cities on Craigslist. Jobs I wasn't qualified for but would sometimes apply for anyway, lightly enhancing my résumé to match requirements that I figured I'd never *actually* have to prove an ability to meet. I told myself that by September I'd be gone. Somewhere else. I'd leave behind the town I loved because I wasn't convinced the town loved me back anymore. *It isn't me,* I'd tell myself. *It's this place. I never had a chance.*

My license had been suspended for so long that I didn't even think about it when I handed it to the police officer who pulled me over in July 2010 on the way to my probation appointment. I'd made a turn in a window of time in which turns were illegal. The kind of thing a more passive officer would have let slide. Driving with a suspended license is barely a charge if you are someone without a record, or even a light record. I had no one in the car with me, and I obviously wasn't allowed to drive it any further, so I had to walk the last ten blocks to Mr. Riley's office. When I got there, covered in sweat, I handed him the paperwork the officer gave me—a court summons. I told him I was planning to get gone. To start a new life somewhere else. To leave and become something better than I had been.

Mr. Riley looked at the summons, shook his head, and smiled. "I ain't never gonna be done with you," he squeezed out, harsh air surrounding every syllable. And then, he muttered "goddamn" before slapping his desk and breaking into a laugh that became a collision of sharp, violent coughs, each of them sounding like an engine, desperately trying to turn over while a car sits at the border of a city, dying

8:15

to get out.

8:14

An obsession with suffering on the path to triumph is not uniquely American but does manifest itself in uniquely American ways. It's the lie we're told about what success truly "counts" and what doesn't. This, too, prioritizes a type of staying. Fighting it out where you are until where you are is the place you win, and in doing so, you endear a place to you, eternally, without interruption.

But by the end of the 2010 Cavs season, when they walked off the floor after losing to the Celtics in six games, I knew LeBron was leaving. I knew he'd had it. He'd given all he could to the hard path, and there was no reward. No rings. A city that bowed to a king with no jewelry.

7:55

I remember the immediate moments of the offseason, the looming understanding of LeBron's free agent status descending, becoming more tangible than it had been during the season. This is when the emotional negotiation that we learned from those foolish soul songs began within the hearts and minds of Cleveland sports fans. My pal who believes in the eternal nature of love, who has loved one person for almost all of his life, had no such optimistic reserves left for LeBron James and his future with the Cavs. I remember the night the Cavs lost Game 6 to the Celtics and my pal, draped in an oversized LeBron jersey, pulled it over his head, dropped it beside him on the couch, exhaled while sinking into a cushion, and muttered *Well, fuck. That's it. He's gone.*

On the other side of this, though, there were people who convinced themselves that he'd never leave. As he took meetings with several other teams in Cleveland, their response was *Well, that's just what you do when you're a free agent.* When he'd be sort of openly flirting with these ideas of building out a super team of his own, there were those who said *Great, who can we get to join him right here in Cleveland?* There were also those who leaned into the wayward and poorly sourced reports that LeBron was working to convince Toronto Raptors forward Chris Bosh to join him in Cleveland, instead of working with Bosh to figure out a landing spot for both of them beyond their current destinations.

I don't know which approach I admired more, the folks who immediately gave in to what they could sense to be true or the people who were in denial. Who, despite all signs pointing to the contrary, allowed themselves to be steered directly into a seemingly inevitable heartbreak.

I have been both of those people at points beyond this one. I have had my foot in both of those graves, sometimes both at once. There is something merciful and tender about the prolonging of heartbreak, especially when it requires lying to yourself in order to do it. That's another part of what makes those old soul songs singularly special. Because they are also about control. Not always control over *another* person, though. The people who ignored LeBron's obvious exit knew they didn't have any control over what LeBron James did or didn't do. But they were in complete control over when and how their own heartbreak arrived. And yes, when it arrives in this mode, it might come all at once and render the broken-heart holder a bit more breathless than it would if they were to take the former approach, acceptance that lets the ache through in small manageable portions. But I appreciated those Cleveland fans who, like I have in the past, let their denial lead to some torrential damage.

And then, of course, there were those who did fall to their knees. Who saw the end coming and figured they could beg a way out of it. They could perform the large unfathomable gestures that would win back their hero. And my god, would you believe there was a song. Of course there was

7:23

a damn song, or else all this talk about begging and pleading and the mechanics of how to seek salvation for whatever wrong you've done would be futile. And yes, however embarrassing you are imagining the song to be, I assure you it is even more embarrassing. It helps that the song doesn't take itself too seriously, but it's also hard to tell. It came at a time when Cleveland was unraveling in a wave of panic, throwing anything at the wall to try and get some clarity out of its seemingly apathetic king.

The song is called "We Are LeBron," and if you are, right now, counting syllables in your head, wondering if this is a riff off of "We Are the World," you have already done the required math to understand this level of desperation. Instead of chart-topping singers clustered together in a studio, this version was populated by local news anchors, politicians (including Ted Strickland, the actual governor of Ohio at the time), a TV lawyer known for his absurd commercials, an alumna of MTVs *The Real World,* among others.

When I said back there that the song doesn't take itself too seriously, what I meant to say, I think, was that it is impossible to tell how seriously the song is or isn't taking itself. Some of this is simply because of the vocal performances of the involved parties. Most of the people can't sing and don't really try. But every now and then, there is a perfectly stitched together two-part harmony between a meteorologist and a county clerk. The uneven nature of the cast itself also leads to confusion about the song's urgency.

The song is both a production and not, one of those things that many of us know all too well, built off of the notion of "of *course* I'm joking . . ." with one eye turned toward a reaction, and an "*unless . . .*" tucked underneath the tongue.

If there is something to be admired about the song, from my point of view—lover of the pleading ballad, lover of the too-late sobbing, lover of the person leaning against a makeshift wall of packed boxes, refusing to move until they can state their case just *one last time*—I must say I truly admire how shameless the lyrics of this cursed collaborative tune are. How, under many other circumstances, these types of pleas would be, at best, whispered in a prayer heard by no one but whatever divine power they were being sent up to.

Where this song turns and faces the soul songs of old is, first, in the question of need. The song, silly as it is, doesn't really offer up much in its first act other than reminding LeBron that Cleveland needs him and may not survive without him.

But the song's emotional engine relies on an expression of what could be offered, and—like in so many of these kinds of songs—what can be offered ain't much. Look, the song says with a half-shrug, no one will love you like we can. Yes, the wide world has more to offer you than we've got here. The coasts are more beautiful. There is a shortcut to glory that does not run through Northeast Ohio. But no one will love you like we love you here. How can we get you to believe that's enough? That whatever is out there, beyond this place we have loved each other, is too uncertain to trust. Even if you're bored or unhappy. Even if we don't dream in the same language anymore. We're familiar to each other, and that depth of knowing is an intimacy that can cover at least some of the sins that might otherwise tear us apart, isn't it?

The song is pathetic, sure. But all of these songs are pathetic in some way. I find very little shame in the absurdity of the pathetic when it's all a person feels like they have in their toolbox to keep close what they imagine is better than absence.

The difference between the soaring, crooning soul ballad that begs and begs and the all-star cast of Ohioans attempting to squeeze more time out of a savior is that the ballad has no real epilogue that anyone can see. Sure, sometimes we are to believe that the beloved comes back or sticks around or forgives the no-good motherfucker. But many of the songs dismount with a reliance on assumption. Even if the beloved returns, we are to believe that the no-good motherfucker has changed their ways and that there is a renewed period of happily ever after. The ones I love the most, like "Don't Take My Sunshine Away," just end with a rotation of chorus, a single man's voice stomping along the outskirts of the song with short yelps and shouts that become almost unintelligible, some version of *I don't know what I'd do if*... even as the music fades down, the voice still haunts, throwing the same word against the dwindling wall of sound. And what other outcome could there be, then, but a person giving in? This is what fools like me have been made to believe, what the movies say, what the romantics say. And so I believe that on the other side of this robust suffering, there must be a bouquet of years better than whatever years led two people to a near-demise.

7:05

And I do love a song that appears to take effort. I have little use for effortless songs, as beautiful as they can be, and as easy as it is for me to be spun into them. I sometimes resent the birds breathing out small melodic shouts from the branches outside of my window. It is a resentment I recognize as borderline evil, but I hold it nonetheless. Nothing so beautiful should arrive with such ease. The lone bird on the lone branch sings a pretty, lonely, effortless song, and no one runs to its side. Because how could they? There is no sweat on the notes. The sound is too clean to suggest that its maker has ever known pain, has ever longed for anything but a sky as clean, as empty, as blue as a perfect note from the lips of someone who has just made peace with the fact that they might die lonely.

7:00

I remember the dismantling of the mural. Along the Cleveland skyline, LeBron's two arms extended wide, a cloud of smoke billowing up from them, the player posed as if he was in a position to both give and receive a blessing, his neck craned backward the way that it might be in a church, when a preacher catches a good groove or the choir drags the sweetest part of the chorus out for a moment longer than everyone expects. The text WE ARE ALL WITNESSES hovered above LeBron's mouth, as if it was blown from his lips. And when they took the mural down, just two days after The Decision, they did it piece by piece, spread out over three days. I always thought that it could have been done in one, but drawing it out was more strategic, to play on the preexisting grief and rage of a resilient but hurting city. There was no real rhyme or reason to which parts got taken down first, it seemed. The mural was massive and had been covering the building it was on for years. By the second day, both of the sides were gone. Before the final day of work began, it was in an especially devastating state. Pretty much all that managed to remain was LeBron's torso, CLEVELAND blazing across it. The top remained until the end, one of the last things to go. The panel that read WE ARE ALL WITNESSES outlasting the image of the man himself. It endured as the last true thing. The witnesses remain, regardless of whether or not the savior shows himself.

6:54

In real life, in a relationship forged not between two people but between many people and one person, or one person and a city, there is no need to imagine the outcome. It was always going to be this way. He was always going to leave. I am a devotee of the emotional politics of place, but even I know they are flimsy. Not a requirement for anyone else to find themselves beholden to. The politics of place aren't necessarily always linked to the politics of staying as much as they are linked to the politics of *knowing*. I do dirt here because I know exactly where the dirt can be done, I know the shelter I can run toward when the dark city bathes in a silent siren's rotating lights. When I am lovesick here, I know where there is a bar with a jukebox. A place where one quarter gets you four whole songs and no one asks why you're alone, because they're alone too. There are few things more intimate than the history made when a person touches a place, runs a hand along it for decades at a time. Few things more intimate than the history made when a place touches you, too, if you are open to it. Every repeated turn toward the familiar is an act of that touching. The drive you take from one corner of the city to the next, avoiding the highways so that you might, again, reach for a memory that can only be seen from the street. Taken in at twenty-five miles per hour. Someone in the passenger if you're lucky. Someone who learns you through every past you've survived. The long way home is still a way home. I am a devotee of these politics, overly romantic as they might be. And of course I'm not immune to the desire for exits. I've said already that I once believed my salvation would be found in another place. And so I get it. What it comes down to is that some of us would rather live a long life of what some might consider failure, but do it in a place that will catch you, every time. I will take that over a triumph in a city that doesn't touch me back. One that holds my joyful shouts but returns no echo. But this is to say nothing

6:40

of fire. Nothing bearing my name has ever been burned in the streets of any city I love. On the night of The Decision, there the men were, in Cleveland, cigarettes in their mouths and lighters pressed to the bottom of LeBron James jerseys. When the lighter alone didn't do the trick, someone squeezed lighter fluid on the jersey's back. When the jersey got a good fire going, it was thrown to the ground, the 2 and the 3 burning in their own quadrants, like two separate countries collapsing at once. Miraculously, even as the flames spread, the JA in JAMES was spared, temporarily, before people began to throw more items atop the jersey. First T-shirts and then, for some reason, a pair of Adidas sneakers. Someone on the outside of the circle gradually pouring more lighter fluid on the fire while the small but growing group yelled the occasional thing about betrayal. A microphone was placed in the face of the man responsible for dousing the items in lighter fluid, who, with a voice run ragged from shouting, informed the public about his feelings on LeBron James: *He's dead to me.*

6:38

I return to the scene of the jersey burning to mention what most commonly haunts my memory about this era of Ohio heartbreak, and it is that everyone circled around the flames was white. Everyone having their smiles illuminated by the sharp orange pushing into the otherwise darkness of a late summer night was white. So many of the people with microphones pushed into their faces in the aftermath of The Decision were white, and so much of the language affixed to that moment, out of those mouths, revolved around death, around burial. Sure, some of it was simply people saying that they hoped he would never win in Miami, they hoped that he would never find that shortcut to glory that he left town to seek out. But there was an overwhelming sentiment not of people wishing LeBron James dead, but like the person at the site of the burning with an exhausted bottle of lighter fluid in his hand would say, the idea was that LeBron James was dead to them. He served a purpose—though if you let them tell it, he wasn't even good enough at that—and then he did something displeasing, and so he no longer existed. And look, yes, under another set of circumstances, I have surely been that person. I have comforted that person. I have, myself, insisted upon someone being dead to me as a coat of armor. It makes it easier to turn the picture frames on their faces, to lock the ephemera in a drawer.

And so it is possible that I'm being unfair here. But I know what I know about heartbreak, and I know what I know about this country. And so it is possible that I'm being as fair as I can possibly be.

6:30

Though I suppose fire is a type of song, too. Some might say fire is the song that arrives after all the begging has exhausted itself and after all those who reasonably asked and prayed and wept rise from their knees and make use of newly idle hands. Don't know what good it is to burn a few cheap jerseys and a pair of sneakers, but fire sho' gonna have its say, one way or another. Just let anyone who has ever stood in front of a police precinct with fingertips reeking of gasoline, wrapped around a bottle, a lighter itching in their pockets, tell it. Just let anyone taping a bomb underneath a car tell it. Just let the niggas who want their hood back one way or another tell it, but definitely don't let the gentrifiers ever tell it. And look, I'm not placing a value or morality judgment on the shit (I suppose it depends on who and what is doing the burning and what brought the burning to life), but fire is a song, fire be a whole symphony if you allow it to be. And I don't just mean its sounds, the way it disrupts the sky with a snapping of fingers—rhythmic if you catch it on the right notes (I suppose it depends on who and what is doing the burning there, too). I mean the hands, I mean its makers, I mean the things that drag people to its urgent heat, to watch and to spread its gleeful damage. The people who bring every wayward feeling they've held behind a near-bursting door and throw it in the flame. People who bring what some might plainly call sadness but what we know as the dry and fraying pages of our past lives, peeled off and accumulating in all the places we can't avoid and so let's instead say haunting. Yes, bring your hauntings down to the fire and throw them in. Bring not just the trinkets and tokens of dismantled love but bring your broken hearts, the whole damn faulty machine. There are enough new ones to go around. There are those who might say fire carries a mercy with it, which I take to mean that it doesn't prolong the anguish. In the promised land, on the other side of this sometimes-wretched scroll of miserable, spinning days, I would guess that the decorum there will suggest that we not ask each other how we died or what dying felt like, the same way that those who have been locked up don't ask people how they got there. But the living have thoughts on burning alive. Scientists say that it's the worst feeling imaginable at first. But then, nothing. The heat from the fire quickly chews through nerves, senses, renders the dying person without feeling. The dying person, they say, is transported toward a type of ecstasy. Forgive my wandering into the fantasies of no longer living, once again, but I would want to hear from someone who crossed over, who spun through the flame and ended up in the afterlife. No telling how I'll go whenever I go, but I am skeptical of anyone living who suggests that any part of dying is less painful than it seems, in the physical sense or otherwise. But I want to believe. Knowing as I do that I absolutely will one day have both legs over the fence that divides living from whatever comes after, and knowing as I do that leaping from the top of that fence might not be my choice. I would like to believe in this idea of ecstasy, or at least a moment when there is awareness of what consumes us but no physical feeling to attach it to. I respect fire like I respect any song that bends to the desire of the person who summons it. The flame is political, of course, but it is sometimes mundane, sometimes romantic, sometimes simply a necessity, and not all necessities are political but some certainly are mundane and a few damn sure are something close to romantic. And speaking of burning for a brief, candescent moment before there is nothing left to be felt, this, too, is longing. This, too, is at least one stage of heartbreak. The earliest stage, when any damage will do and it is seductive to watch some shit go up in flames, even though the burning won't bring back anything any of us miss or love. But that ain't the point. I get why the jerseys burned in Cleveland, I get why the men gathered around and sacrificed their once-beloved garments. How quickly can we get past the part where we feel everything and cross the other threshold, gasping and numb.

6:10

In Oakland in 2009, black people were asked *How could you burn down your own neighborhood* & in Cincy in '01, black people stood in front of glass, bent into a scarred web like a wounded moon, & they were asked *Why would you do this to your own* & in Bloomington in 2000, white kids turned cars over when a basketball coach got fired but no one really asked much & in Los Angeles in 1992, black folks stared into news cameras, their faces half-illuminated by the glow from burning buildings disrupting the night, & someone with a microphone asked *Why here, in this place, you live here* & in 1989 in Tampa, in 1980 in Miami, in any place where black people have been conductors to a symphony of fire, in any place where there were buildings once & then only ash, only the scent of hot wood, or brick, or paint, the question is always about how a people could do this to *their own* place & there are many answers & most of them are about how none of this shit is ours & you have mistaken being in a place for having control over it, a mistake I've made before but certainly did not make with a brick in my hand & a bandana over my face & it is harder to sell this on the evening news but the fire is a baptism, the fire says *Get gone & we can start clean* & so then what isn't your own can become your own if it is all some vast & empty burned-down nothing at the end of a long night & I know this isn't generous to the shop owners & the elders who have lived on a block for decades & wanted to die on a block that was at least close to how they remembered it, but what can I do to convince you that fire is not the villain & the person who lights a match isn't a villain & the people cheering while a building burns aren't the villains & there are villains, surely, but they aren't here, not among a people seeking deliverance & the villain is an inven-

tion, our enemies, the ones I promised we'd leave behind, those
are inventions, but they are inventions born out of a heart's

6:00

breaking. I swear to you, I would never take to the streets looking to watch something burn if my heart were not broken. If,
through its breaking, I did not need to invent an enemy. Name-
less and faceless as a brick building or a glass window. Woven
through almost every story of heartbreak, there is a villain.
Even if the name isn't spoken out loud, or even if, through a
retelling of the damage, a person smiles and reassures their
audience that *there are no hard feelings.* Tell me you haven't invented a reason to transform the beloved into the wretched, at
least one time, to yourself, in the quiet of a dark room, when
the weight of loneliness demanded you find a target, at least for
now, at the start of it all.

I have been sad and have not yet wanted to look directly into
the light of that sadness and so I have distracted myself with
the manufacturing of villainous moments from a person I
loved and certainly still love. I may never speak these imagined
moments out loud, but I cling to them. The time they accidentally broke a picture frame holding a photo of my mother as a
living, smiling, younger woman—I can, for this exercise, convince myself that this was surely a larger character flaw. They
were always so clumsy, after all. And inconsiderate, surely.
They never really listened to me when I talked about things
that interested me, right? Probably, I guess. That's bad enough.
I can't believe I wasted my time with such a selfish person, and
I am mad at them now not for leaving but for being here in the
first place.

And forgive me, but I love the pure spectacle of a people

newly in pain or newly feeling rejection. How hurt flows into rage, one body of water tumbling into another, larger body of water. The irrational nature of it all.

In the summer of 2010, amidst the burning of old fabric, I didn't know if I believed LeBron James to be a villain, but I relished watching the rationalizations of my pals, all of them, imaginations in overdrive, watching Game 5 of the Celtics series to attempt to determine exactly *when* LeBron quit on the team, when he decided he was leaving, even when there was still a series to be won. One pal of mine watched tape of the third quarter of Game 5 all through August, a quarter where LeBron went 2 for 7, and he'd mumble *That was it . . . he was trying to lose. Just wanted to get the fuck outta here sooner.*

This is a strange but necessary subplot of heartbreak. One that is easiest for me to access when I've been rejected, when I am back at the doorstep of a familiar pain. It isn't so much that if you see something enough, you begin to believe it. It's that the belief is already there, already planted and waiting to be ignited by seeing, and the seeing could be anything. One missed shot or one forgotten returned phone call or one kiss that didn't feel like the others. Yes, I have been sad and have convinced myself of anything and everything. There is a mountain between the immediacy of anguish and the far-off hopefulness of clarity, and it is easiest to convince anyone scaling its outskirts that anything they are feeling is justified. That list of things ignored in the past? All of them were weapons. If I watch the Game 5 footage long enough, I could easily convince myself that I was watching someone give up on not just a game but also a team, also a city, also a people.

And then we have an enemy. And I cannot love an enemy, at least not out loud. Out loud, I curse my enemies. I only want them back in the silent hours.

5:40

Here I am reminded of another dear friend. Who, in the midst of a jersey burning on his street, carried his old LeBron jersey out to the center of the flames and nearly threw it in but then pulled it back at the last minute, held it close to his chest, and slowly backed away from the fire. When I asked why he didn't throw it in, he shrugged.

I'll keep it in case he comes back one day.

5:32

And sometimes, when what we desire and what we see aren't enough, the manufacturing of an enemy takes work. There was the letter Cavaliers owner Dan Gilbert wrote and posted on the team website in the early hours of July 8, written entirely in Comic Sans, which made it seem at first like it was a prank, a thought that wasn't at all calmed by the bitter and vindictive messaging within it, written like an angry teenager in the immediate aftermath of a breakup, some words in all caps littered throughout—short clipped sentences making up most of the text. Much like the song pleading to keep LeBron in town, it is hard to tell how seriously or not seriously the letter should be taken, and the Comic Sans didn't help. The emotional tone of the letter is uneven, oscillating between hopeful platitudes, haphazard accusations, ominous threats, and equally ominous promises. The letter never refers to LeBron James by name, only by things like "former King" and "chosen one" and "our former hero." It makes allusions to the impact LeBron's decision would have on "our" children before pivoting to the strange proclamation that LeBron leaving is good, actually.

That his leaving finally lifts the curse from the city of Cleveland, and now LeBron himself is the holder of the curse, which meant that Miami is now the cursed city, at least until LeBron does "right" by Cleveland. (There is no clear explanation of what doing right would actually mean, and the word "right" is placed in quotation marks in the letter, which makes the dilemma even more puzzling.)

There was a single, central assertion in the letter, which emerged directly in the middle, in bold: The Cavs will win a title before LeBron James ever does. Take it to the bank, Gilbert insisted. Sure, he was teaming up with two other superstars and sure, the cupboard in Cleveland was relatively bare, but this was a promise. A promise to the uninitiated, of course. Some of us know a plea when we see one. And still, I didn't believe it to be true and no one I knew believed it to be true but isn't that the point of all of this?

5:01

The point of all the music and all the moaning? The point of all the stained knees and the suits dripping with rain? The point of all the closed fists, thrown recklessly into the exposed torso of empty and useless air? The point of all this absence and those foolish enough to howl into it? Yes, the real gift heartbreak leaves behind is the gift of the most delicious delusions. Let the mind run wild with what could be, even if it cannot actually be. Someone I love is gone, and I cannot get them back. And after I have convinced myself that I don't want them back due to their surely evil ways, what is there left to hope for except the previously untouchable miracles that I have surely earned through my suffering? I don't believe in reparations for my own sadness—until I do. The world certainly does not owe me any rewards in the aftermath of all it has put me through, assuming there is an aftermath beyond the swampy flood of suffering. But I don't mind lying to myself about what I might be owed when my number is finally called, and I ain't talking about my number being called in some heavenly formation, not this time. I'm talking about kicking down the door of some good living while I'm still alive to leap through that bountiful threshold, while I'm still alive to flash the spoils of some good living past the eyes of whoever has caused me a specific type of pain, a pain where low-stakes revenge feels not only appropriate but necessary. I am no fool and I do not roll with fools and so no one I rolled with thought Cleveland would *actually* win a championship before LeBron James, paired with two other All-Stars, would win a championship. Cleveland win an NBA title—with what? The shell of a team left behind by its once-savior? It wasn't ever about that. It was about dreaming through the brutality of leaving, of being left. What I didn't mention when we began this examination of the subtle nuances that come along with heartbreak is what is humming underneath this specific delusion: I *need* anyone who has ever hurt me to know that I am doing more than just surviving. I know after a while none of us cares anymore. The person who leaves stops checking in, the person who is left behind stops scrolling through old photos. But if we are to deal, strictly, in the myths and delusions that propel us from one heartbreak to the next, I need to imagine that somewhere, I am still not good enough for someone, for something. And the remedy—comically temporary as it may be—is to drag a loud and alarmingly bright choir into the streets to sing of whatever minor pleasures I've received on the other side of my pain.

4:55

Revenge is not the language I am looking for, then. Revenge signals something more sinister than the emotional approach I'm attempting to summon, which is somewhere in between an impenetrable self-satisfaction and an overwhelming self-consciousness, a cavern from which there is no escape, but there is an occasional beam of light stumbling through, and with it comes the shadows, which, too, are not entirely sinister in their shape-making, even the ones that remind you of what you had and then lost. I say *I want a championship* and mean I am looking for a light so consuming that it overwhelms all absence.

4:45

Some people think they should go to heaven but NOT have to die to get there is a line that makes an appearance in Dan Gilbert's letter, standing alone. Followed by a space, and another stand-alone sentence. *Sorry, but that's simply not how it works.*

4:40

And I *am* sorry, but I have a different definition of heaven and when and where heaven can be achieved, and I definitely have a different idea about the value of dying, or sacrificing oneself to reach some promised land. Look, forgive me, but if there is an easy way to get to the gates, I will take it. If there is a place beyond grieving and I do not have to grieve to reach it, I will hitch my ride to whatever train will take me there. I didn't grow up in the church but have spent enough time aligned with both religion and sports to know there is no gospel richer than the gospel of suffering, of living through large stretches devoid of pleasure for the sake of reaching some place beyond your current circumstances and feeling as though you have *truly* earned a right to be there. I have seen enough and I prefer the path of least resistance. There is a shortage of imagination when it comes to the pleasures of simplicity. I would not like to answer any questions. I would like the gates to open upon my arrival, and I would like to walk in untouched. Some people think they should gain entry to heaven without first dying, and some people decide they don't want death, and they certainly don't want whatever heaven you're offering.

A Timeout in Praise
of Legendary Ohio Aviators

VIRGINIA HAMILTON, DAYTON, OHIO (1934–2002)

I recall the cover first / tucked in the back / of a shelf / brown with age / but still luminescent / the people could fly / of course / there they were / hands on each other's shoulders / all of them, above / the clouds / as a boy I liked the animals / who pulled tricks on the fools / who thought them too small to disrupt / the divine order / but of course / it was always about the enslaved / the mercy of flight / no chains to hold / what the sky desired / freedom beyond language / on the day my mother was buried / it rained / but the sky was awash / with dark birds / their shouts wrecking / the impermanent gray / & I remember believing she was up there / ascending / beyond the dark feathers

TONI MORRISON, LORAIN, OHIO (1931–2019)

& I won't hold you / but to mention that in the story I love most / Toni Morrison says / *my mother talked about her dreams like they were real . . . she would never say "I dreamed," she would say, "you know, I thought . . ."* / I find it most precious / the things we hold / when we make it back down to earth / how upon waking / the dream might begin to slip through our fingers / & so it must be told to anyone / with a willing ear / & some time to spare / & that's how we stay / suspended / in the magic of it all

2:56

Because I was still of the villainous sort, someone slowly and inefficiently working off the sins of my many pasts, I worked at the diner near the arena downtown in the LeBron-less years. I took the job because they didn't really care much to do a background check, or at least not as much as they cared that I would show up on time, not cause any problems with the regulars, and not hover around the drink station, texting or looking things up on my phone (a problem more common than I'd think, I was told during my interview).

After desperately trying to find work and relying on odd jobs to cover some paltry rent I'd fallen into, the diner job felt like a real gift for me. It was a breakfast spot, only open from 6 a.m. until around 2 p.m., sometimes until 3 p.m. on a Saturday or Sunday, when the biggest rush of money came in. At the time, I was trying to break into writing more steadily, penning reviews of albums for local and regional papers. And I was also defined by a nightmarish schedule of living that saw me, most days, sleeping from about two in the afternoon until eight or nine at night, and then staying awake until morning, with the hours sometimes varying, depending on what there was to get into that night—who was playing a show, or what house a party was happening at.

For this, the diner gig was perfect for me. I'd jump on the earliest shifts—not the opening shift, as I found myself to be too lazy to be reasonably reliable to open up a restaurant, but the 6:30 shift, which allowed me to settle in after the hard work of opening shop was already done and allowed me to enjoy the slow trickle of regular diners who would pop in before their jobs at the newly built Arena District offices or the hockey players who would sometimes come in before heading to the arena for training.

I used to talk about "growing up poor" as if it is something that left me, no longer hovered over my life well into my twenties. A better phrase is that I grew into poverty and simply learned how to navigate it as efficiently as possible through various disasters. And because I grew into poverty, my needs, by this point, were simple and constricted. I could, for example, survive for a week on a large pot of Kraft mac and cheese, if enough supplementary items were added to it. If I didn't feel like cooking, I could set aside some cash and get one footlong from Subway every day of the week, eating half of it before falling asleep in the afternoon, and the other half after waking up in the evening.

My tips at the diner weren't paltry by any means, but they weren't immense. I was a good enough server. I never tried to be so dazzling that I didn't write shit down, which people appreciated. I could talk music or sports with pretty much anyone, and politics with the right crowd. I knew when to leave people alone and when to chat people up. It's a job of self-awareness, mostly. On good days, I'd walk home with three hundred or so dollars stuffed in my pocket, a messy arrangement of disparate bills. I'd pat my leg every block or so, checking to make sure my stash was still there. Even on bad days, I'd pull down a hundred or so, which was enough to get me from one week to the next. My credit was too bad for me to even get a bank account, so, as anyone who grew up around hustlers might, I kept my money in a shoebox under my bed. I kept some tucked under my mattress.

What didn't go to rent most commonly went to seeing shows—getting to and from shows, buying merch or zines at shows, wasting some cash at a diner for a post-show meal. But whenever I had a little extra, I'd take trips up to Cleveland to watch the post-LeBron Cavs with a few pals who, like me, found themselves fascinated by the tragic nature of the scene. The first year of the post-LeBron era was especially bleak, but also sometimes comical, if you were the type who found yourself laughing through waves of anguish, or if you were, like me, a somewhat neutral observer, overwhelmed by disbelief. Even removing a player of LeBron's caliber, it was still a little stunning to watch a team fall so sharply from grace within the same calendar year it was seen as a serious contender in the playoffs.

What this did mean, though, was that tickets were cheap. And not only were tickets cheap, but in that first year—in the post-LeBron, pre–Kyrie Irving era—there came a point where most fans stopped going to games altogether, which also meant that the security folks stopped caring. Those poor souls who, in far busier and more successful times, were charged with the task of checking tickets and guiding people to their correct seats and making sure no sneaking-around shenanigans were afoot. And I cannot say I blame them, as someone who knows all of the tricks involved with sneaking from a bad seat to a good seat, even if just for a little while.

But the mercies of a season steeped in disappointment meant that not much of anyone cared anymore, and since me and my crew would never miss out on a good hustle, we didn't mind going to the games and turning our five-dollar tickets into near-courtside seats, even if the games were an absolute calamity—hardly an identifiable sport at all and more like a rapidly unfurling circus of incidents that *might* resemble basketball, or at least the kind of clumsy streetball that gets played after all of the best players leave the court and the young folks amble out onto the concrete and try to replicate the moves they don't have the skill for just yet.

The roster itself was largely a mess of journeymen veterans, some energetic young players (who lost some of that wide-eyed energy as the losses accumulated), and some dudes who absolutely did not wanna be in Cleveland anymore. The once–All Star Mo Williams spent the offseason and early season insisting that he didn't want to be traded, and even gently criticized LeBron's exit strategy. Williams had one of the highlights of the early season, when things were still somewhat promising, hitting a game-winner in mid-November to give the Cavs a win over the Bucks. By February, he was gone, traded to the Clippers in exchange for an aging and mostly ineffective Baron Davis. (Though the trade also included a first-round pick, which ended up being Kyrie Irving. So it ain't all bad.)

There was pleasure in watching this aimless disaster of a team. Veteran castoffs who had been given up on, young players who seemed, mostly, bewildered by the pace and intensity of the games, forced to play minutes because someone had to, after all. At a certain point, it seemed anyone who could run up and down the court would do. The team won nineteen games total that season, and seven of those nineteen were won in one month, during a stretch from late October to late November. From December to February, they won four games total (which, if I recall, was the point in the season when my crew and I began to get access to our ill-gained front court accommodations).

In a season like this one, if you are going to be around, if you are going to make the most of it, you have to invent reasons to stay. Figure out a reason to stay, or to keep coming back. The trick is, if the team isn't worth rooting for, find a player to attach yourself to. A player who defines whatever you believe your own personal struggle to be, for better or worse. That's your player, the one you live and die by. Watch the box score, not the scoreboard. There's glory in the box score, if you get lucky enough. For me, the guy was Daniel Gibson. Boobie Gibson, to be exact. I do love a player with a nickname,

2:00

one so potent that it renders their God-given name irrelevant. Then again, the line between what is or isn't a so-called God-given name is flimsy, depending on how one defines their deities. And Boobie got his name from his beloved grandmother, who would lovingly tease him with the nickname, as such things begin. Boobie kept the moniker in the family until his grandmother passed away just before he went to college. And then he wanted everyone to call him Boobie. Said he felt his grandmother in the air whenever people shouted that name out. If that ain't a God-given name, then I don't know what is.

Boobie Gibson ain't the most famous Boobie to come outta Texas, but he's the only one to make the league, though even Boobie Miles would tell us there's more than one way to make it, and sometimes you make it even when you can't make it out. Boobie Gibson writes poems, sometimes. When the grief gets to be too much. Keeps the poems tucked in a shoebox under his bed. Boobie a little undersized for his proper position. Boobie don't got the height to defend two-guards but don't got the handle to run point. But he can make it work. You got it hard enough growing up, no telling what you can make fit when the measurements say otherwise. Boobie looked damn good in the '07 playoffs. Boobie lit up Detroit for 31 in a closeout game. Sent those bum-ass Pistons sobbing right back up Route 23.

The '07 Finals, too. Boobie was twenty-one years old, fighting for his life against the Spurs. Hitting shots when wasn't nobody else up for it. Boobie was the future until he wasn't. Boobie wasn't exactly the same after the ankle surgery, I guess. Boobie could shoot the lights out when he was on. Boobie wasn't always on, and then he wasn't often on. Be when he was on, he could make you believe. Boobie could go for seven threes one night and then miss nine the next. And he'd keep shooting, because he knew that's what he was there for. Without the shot, he was just another guy, destined for the end of the bench. Make enough to keep them believing in you for another night or another week.

From mid-January to mid-February, during a relentless twenty-six-game losing streak, Boobie was also slumping horrendously. Nights where he'd shoot 3 for 12, 3 for 10. I remember these games because of how puzzled he seemed to look by his own temporary ineptitude. In sports, there are few things I find more painful than watching a frustrated shooter. Someone who knows the shots should be falling, someone who hit ten in a row during warmups and came into the game feeling good, only to be betrayed by the realities of the moment under the lights. The games of good shooting became increasingly rare—a 7 for 11 shooting night sandwiched in the midst of a 4 for 12 night and then a 2 for 7 night. It got to the point where, even on the good nights, Gibson looked pained, like he knew with every made basket, expectations would return. In a hopeless season, with fans looking for optimism anywhere, even if it just meant that their once-promising young guard would live up to, at the very least, being the stunning spark plug off of the bench. An undersized microwave scorer that could ignite some level of excitement in the crowd.

If the whole idea is to project oneself onto a player and then ride through a bad season with them as your sole beacon, I gravitated toward Boobie Gibson for how heavily his perceived failures seemed to weigh on him. For the way he would stare at the rim after a particularly bad miss, like he was being told a lie from someone he trusted once. Like he was on one knee, holding the ring up to a space that only held wind, carrying someone he loved to another, better place.

And it was also the way fans reacted to his present struggles, when pressed against his past promise. Walking out of the arena, you'd hear *He's got all of the tools, I don't know why he can't figure it out* or some version of *I guess he's just not going to be who we thought he was.* And so how could I not be on his side, knowing what I know

1:40

about disappointment. About not being who you thought I was or would become. The places I've led people to, promising fountains, clear rivers, all manner of thirst-quenching possibilities, only to pull us all, once again, along an endless desert.

What I mean when I say that a villain stays a villain is that our damage remains even after we've been punished for it, and there is very little control any of us have over our own absolution. And so, sure, bury yourself in black if you choose. Let the crowd cover you in boos and extend your arms toward them. Boobie's biggest crime was that he couldn't be what people imagined him becoming, and some might say there are far worse crimes, but I believe failing the imagination of others might be the crime from which all other crimes are born, if I am using the term "crime" loosely, independent of what might get you thrown in a cell, but since we are talking about cells

1:30

there isn't much said for what to do when you get out of one, and I know this varies depending on what you were inside for and for how long, and I know this varies depending on what one wants to do once they recapture at least one small portion of their stolen freedom. But I am talking about the emotional dilemma. Have you, for example, ever had to look in the eyes of someone who was taking you in for the first time behind a pane of glass? Assessing you, for those first moments in your drab, newly monochrome uniform? And I mean someone who knew you when you were a child, if you were ever free as a child. If you had ever ridden a bike through a neighborhood's traffic and emerged unscathed, if you had ever jumped in a fight to save this person or if they had ever jumped in a fight to save you. When my brother came to visit me in jail for my first time there, back in '03, it was the only time I'd ever seen him look afraid, even though I knew he wasn't *only* afraid. He was, likely, also angry, also annoyed. But he was scared, too. He looked past me, into the container I was currently in, the tone of it cold, removed, sharp. I was only down a few days, but I could tell he was trying to do the math on how I might survive, because he knew I had been a child once, no matter what the tan jumpsuit and the uneven patches of beard fighting their way out of my hollow cheeks were whispering over the percussion of fears. He knew I was a child who once cried in the top bunk of our room when waking from nightmares, who disappeared into songs when the world closed in on me, who fought with him only because I loved him too much to have him think I was afraid, who fought with him only because I admired him too much to have him be disappointed in me. And there is no language I have, even now, for what happens to the eyes of someone you love in a moment when they are both ashamed of you and afraid for you all at once. There is something lost there, an incalculable loss. Something beyond the myth of innocence. The imagination fractures in the fraction of a moment like this. Someone believed that, no matter how bad you fucked up, there was always going to be a place they could pull you back from, or pull you back toward. Until they see you, untouchable, behind glass.

In the jail I was in, the glass was thick, and situated against the dull light in such a way that it presented an effect of infinity reflections, for both you and anyone looking at you through it. Each reflection becoming more distorted as it replicated itself. At some point, my face echoed into the face of my brother, and I do not mean this in any sense of romanticizing shared lineage. I mean literally, looking through the glass and our many reflections, I could not tell where his face ended and my face began, which is one way of saying that we were both afraid of the same thing. We both knew what I was capable of surviving and for exactly how long I was capable of surviving it. We were both ashamed, too, though our shames were different children, nurtured by different parents.

It is hard, in that moment, bending into a person you love, knowing you will never be who you once were in their mind.

And so it's like I was saying. There isn't much about what to do when you get out. But don't get it twisted,

1:05

it could always be worse. Survive enough, and there is always a darker tunnel lurking in the periphery. What I remember most, now, is that it was not easy drifting in between the two worlds: the world of not being shit and the world of trying to be worth

a little more than shit. The plan was all about simplification.
Get you a job. Not a good-ass job, not the kind that your pals
who stayed in school got. Just a good enough job. Don't need
enough for a whole crib, just enough to rent a room. Eat at least
one meal a day. Shit, you done lived on the streets, so you know
how to stretch a meal. Write at night, stay out of trouble. Keep
your hands off other people's shit. Don't lie, except to the cops
who might come to break up a party or a punk show, and even
then, let someone else do the lying first unless your number is
called early. Don't try to scale the mountain of your shame all at
once. Maybe no one will forgive you, but you're still alive and so
someone has. Find something to lose yourself in to pass whatever time you might have spent doing dirt. Stay inside. Find a
window tall enough that it doesn't cut off the sky. Pay attention
to the slow yawning of a changing season. Find a view of a tree
and watch its leaves curl in on each other, one hundred brown-
ing fists, bursting with a rage that refuses surrender, until they
do. It isn't that hard. It's easier this way. Better to get to be a
witness to the seasons and not a victim of them.

0:53

I adored those LeBron-less Cavs. That band of misfits who felt
like they were made just for me. Oh, the delightful mess of it
all. A team full of people who were floating along, attempting
to figure out their role on this impossible team that was mostly
just trying to hold serve, trying to stay in place for as long as
it could until another miracle arrived. That first LeBron-less
year was a comedy of errors for most fans, but for me, driving
up with pals from Columbus as a way to stay out of trouble
and pass some time, they were fascinating. So many nights I
saw them play, there wasn't the kind of rage or visible disgust

that can sometimes sink into teams that have grown hopeless. There wasn't satisfaction, either. It was what seemed like a realistic understanding of the circumstances, what it would take to get out of them, and knowing that whatever it would take, it wouldn't be coming this season—and probably not the next one, either. Some guys, mostly the veterans, were just playing out the back end of their careers, content to be on a roster where they were valued. The young players were eager, until they weren't. Collectively, it was a group of people showing up every day and just trying to get from one buzzer to the next. I was comforted by this, as a sort of inverse of my life. This team that was once great in a city that was once hopeful, now doomed to a future devoid of promise, beyond the promise that whatever was coming it was going to be hard. It was good, for a moment, to watch people, a place, a team, fight to come to terms with that reality and then eventually make peace with it, which is probably easier to do when the stakes are a game and not a life, or a place to sleep, or a person you love walking back through a door they walked out of. A ball goes in, or it doesn't. Though I suppose that's easy for me to say. When there was nothing to propel the Cavs fans I knew toward excitement or hope, they were propelled, largely, by a singular bitterness that lingered throughout the season and then grew as the season went on. It's like any breakup, any heartbreak. An idle engine, ever-present and humming, until boredom or exhaustion or dissatisfaction forces a foot to descend on a gas pedal.

0:32

I am probably the wrong person to get too precious about exits. I know this, even as I talk about the rage that can be summoned by an absence left by a single person who then has the nerve to go on and thrive elsewhere. I'm not the best person to walk you through this emotional labyrinth. It is here where I tell you that I have found myself indifferent to or even thankful for leaving, for much of my life. I have been left more than I have left, but on both ends of the exchange, it has always seemed like an inevitable part of living, one that I don't like to consider myself being at the mercy of. I steal a little bit of control back by knowing that I have none at all over who stays and who goes, or when they stay or go.

It bears mentioning that I come from a place people leave. Yes, when LeBron left, the reactions made enough sense to me, I suppose. But there was a part of me that felt entirely unsurprised. People leave this place. There are midwestern states that are far less discernible on a blank map, sure. Even with an understanding of direction, I am known to fuck up the order of the Dakotas. I've been known to point at a great many square-like landscapes while weakly mumbling "Nebraska?" and so I get it, we don't have it too bad. People at least claim to know that Ohio is shaped like a heart. A jagged heart. A heart with sharp edges. A heart as a weapon. That's why so many people make their way elsewhere.

At the end of high school, my crew was one of a small handful that decided to stick around, to go to one of the small colleges or the Very Big University that engulfs our city. Most everyone else charted a path out, laughed at their graduation parties when folks suggested that they'd see them when they came back to visit. Most everyone I fell in love with in this city spent nights looking at maps. Scrolling through apartment options in other cities. There was always the foregone conclusion— our affections didn't *have* to be temporary, but our proximity did. They would leave and we'd figure it out, or we wouldn't.

I am accustomed to the physical act of leaving and being left behind. I like a long, aimless road trip for how it flirts with the act of leaving but never fully commits. You get to try on the outfits of different sunrises through a car window for however long you want, and then you return to the familiar colors of where you are, where your things are, where your people are until they decide to make their exit, for good.

There are places where people make it and places where people make it out of. It seems there are far more of the latter than there are of the former. Every place has its limits—how much it can grow, what of its population it can reasonably swallow in the name of that growth. But still, there are the places people live in until they become the person who can survive somewhere better, and by 2010, too many of my friends were in different time zones. We'd promise to catch up and then never do it. We'd visit each other twice a year, and then once, and then not at all. When the heart breaks slowly, gradually, in a way that seems almost inevitable, you can barely even notice it. It happens in a small series of whispers, and then one day, there is a corner of it that sighs to pieces while you box up a photo or donate a bag of old clothes.

And this is to say nothing

0:28

of that other type of leaving. For all there is to be made about a chorus of pleading, of shouts, of insistent and entitled lovers and ex-lovers fighting amongst each other for a stitch of mercy, some way to rewind and undo the damage of past collisions— that is a privilege of knowing the leaving is not permanent. When it is permanent, the only audience for all that moaning is God, who, despite an alleged track record of miracles, has no interest in the pardoning of grief through resurrection and who, I imagine, grows weary of the unbearable questioning shouted out, piercing the middle of a night. No one likes to imagine God needing rest, but then again, it is impossible to fathom any being required to love that many people who are still living, still teeming with questions and demands. Yes, the permanence of leaving is hard to reckon with, but I suppose I love the dead, in part, because they are no longer here to ask anything of me. To be dissatisfied with who I've become. There's a mercy in that, though I would take at least some of my beloveds back across the threshold of living if I could.

I love the dead, too, because I have no choice. Because there are so many of them. Because in the spring of 2011, when the Cavs weren't winning a damn thing, I buried Cam's ashes under a sycamore tree in Cleveland, which I only knew was a sycamore tree because of how Cam would sometimes point to a tree that looked like it, and then point to a scar running across the side of his arm, curved sharply, like a wicked grin, and he'd say *Sycamore tree fucked me up when I was a kid. Fuck those things.* And so it was decided, bury him at the feet of his one true enemy, maybe he'd grow again there, grow into something bigger and taller, something too big and tall to die in this lifetime or in any next one.

I love the dead who have made fools of time—the elders who smoked two packs a day right up until the middle of their ninth decade, who survived and survived out of pure spite. Theirs a type of leaving that some might celebrate with a laugh, a shrug, a *Can you believe this fool?* pitched across a funeral service. But I, too, love the dead who decided that the world was simply not tenable for them, or who had that decided for them. Who weighed the cost of suffering with how long they'd be able to survive it, and chose the math that brought them the most peace.

I love you all, too. I am not mad at you anymore, I promise, I am past inventing you into enemies. I am sorry, I was selfish once. I wanted to feel nothing if I couldn't feel the world alongside your living selves. I am no longer cursing your names into pillows. I am no longer cursing the clothes you left in the corners of my apartments, where I let them collect dust. I love the dead because we cannot let each other down anymore. I cannot fail you. I am thankful for a leaving that is permanent. It is one thing to be haunted by a life gone and another to be haunted by a life that spins on, happily, without you.

0:25

Whether we know it to matter in the larger tapestry of our lives, or have washed it down with the accumulation of years, so many of us have left someone

0:22

or somewhere. So many of us have built a chamber of suffering for someone to lock themselves in. I have been the face in a picture frame, turned over and then eventually discarded. Though it might not be the best time for this revelation, now, as we will momentarily leave each other, it must be said that leaving is the unspectacular part of this emotional math. Once this ends, once we hit zero and we depart, you will turn a page, and I will have returned to you. Different than I am right now, but a return nonetheless. And what happens in between is where the magic trick turns on itself. And, speaking of returns *and* magic,

0:20

it was never the leaving that fascinated me as a child, beside my father in the grass, looking up at the darkening sky, the beautiful in-between of the sun, trying its best to hold on, trying its best to admire the work of its own descent before the angels of nighttime open their pockets and dot the darkness with stars.

The leaving was special enough—planes tilting upward, upward, upward, and then gone. But it was the returning that gently opened my mouth, into a sort of ever-widening crescent, the wind parading softly through the gaps left where what my mother called *my sweet little baby teeth* had once been, but then gone, another glistening and bright treasure lost to the morning. In my sleep, I'd swallowed one of the teeth. I had been playing with it the night before, pushing it back and forth with my tongue, listening to the small *click* of it, like its own metronome. In the morning, it was gone. I couldn't find it anywhere. I suppose I don't know for sure if I swallowed it in my sleep, but that is the story I've told for years, since no other story makes sense. I woke up with another one in my palm one morning, like it fell out in the middle of the night and I refused to let go. I have always desired proof of loss. Another, tumbling out in the sink during the brushing of my teeth. Finally, the most violent of removals. I spilled off of a bright red skateboard that I should have never been on, something one of the older boys in the adjacent projects let me play with. I hit my face on the curb. I was five years old, an age where pain is sometimes defined not by what you feel but by what you see. How much, and where it's coming from. In the tiny oceans of blood running along the sidewalk, there was a single white tooth. A single white rose reaching beyond a field of red.

None of this loss mattered, I was assured, because there

would be new teeth coming. These were simply casualties. The exits that come with aging.

And so, it was never the leaving. I was born into an obsession with returns. Something or someone leaves you, but you'll get something or someone back. Sometimes it's an even exchange. You kiss a person goodbye when they go away for a few days, and they come back to you the same person they were when they left. Other times, you lose a part of your childhood and something harder grows in its place. But a return is a return.

Sometimes, the sky would be calm for a bit, and the fields would be silent, and then a plane would emerge. If it was dark enough, you would first notice it by a blinking red light upsetting the black. And then the belly of it would grow larger as it got lower. Low enough for you to see the windows, some of them open. Low enough that you might think you could reach up and run a hand along the metal wings. I thought of this as its own kind of magic. For a while, I was so young and so enraptured that I'd believe the same plane that just vanished into the sky was coming right back down. It gave the people a small show, and now they were returning to the people and place they loved. It was simpler that way.

0:18

People ask if I will ever leave. I tell them I have carved out a corner of these skies and they are mine. I tell them I love this city because I can move through it while looking up the entire time. I tell them even when I'm gone, I am never gone. I am always returning from somewhere. I am always returning to someone. Some past self. Some future self. Some world that shifted, even slightly, while I was alive somewhere else.

0:14

There is the Fall Out Boy song that my pal Tyler hated. He didn't hate the whole song; he just hated a line within the song and therefore the whole song was ruined. I'd taunt him with it, turning up the song in the car and fighting him off with one hand while he tried to switch the track until we both laughed and he gave in, mocking me singing along. After his funeral, after his apartment had been cleaned out and no memory of him existed, I found a corner of the wall where I'd forgotten I'd scrawled the line he hated, hoping he'd find it someday.

Wouldn't you rather be a widow than a divorcée?

0:05

In order to return, one must first survive, and there is no telling what was survived on the pathway to some magic. It sometimes, truly, is just the one thing. The one loss that echoes into a pursuit of the impossible. A boy bleeds, but isn't destroyed. Decades later, another boy, with the wind dancing through the spaces in his teeth, sits beside his father and watches the sky, waiting for people to return.

0:00

Intermission

ON HUSTLES: *WHITE MEN CAN'T JUMP* (1992)

I can always tell which one of my friends didn't grow up around hustlers by how they look up and lock eyes with the person at the mall kiosk, who—by virtue of that enchanting eye contact— doesn't even have to wave them over. They drift into the grasp of the salesperson without even being aware of it. And that's when their money is no longer theirs. On the street in a city my pal had never been to, a woman sells her a bracelet before she even knows what's happening. Compliments her skin tone and lays the bracelet over it. Leans in to get a good look and then stands back as if she is witnessing a gateway to the promised land creaking open right there on the sidewalk.

And let me be clear: I am not opposed to hustles, and I am certainly not opposed to hustling. When I say I came up around hustlers, I mean that I know what it takes to keep the lights on and so I've rarely been in the dark. I have exchanged cash for some things I don't want to know the history of. I've spent time on both sides of the hustling coin before and certainly will for whatever time I've got left on this twirling rock. A rock that, by the way, is spinning faster now than it was before. I don't understand the science, but I know that time itself is a hustle. Spend a few days in Franklin County corrections and you might come to realize, urgently, that time is a currency. Silence is a currency. Any currency that can be interrupted can be the source of a hustle. Which brings me, again, back to intimacy—though I promise I won't linger here too long, except to say that not all hustles are intimate, but the best ones have an undercurrent of intimacy. I'm not only talking about physical or romantic intimacy, though the tongue and the song and the tips of fingers and the voice in an ear are all mighty vessels for the hustle. What I'm getting at is how the hustle requires a type of knowing. A knowing of oneself, of course. But also a reading of another, rapidly, before they can realize that you are acting upon that knowing. I am not the best hustler because I do not know myself as well as I want to, which leads to a series of ongoing self-hustles. Like setting my alarm for 7:30 when I've already crossed well beyond the midnight hour, immersed in the glow of my phone. But it's the promise I think I'm chasing. Like my dear pal, looking at a bracelet reflecting off the sunlight, dancing on her skin.

White Men Can't Jump dissects the hustle solely as a game of optics. Billy Hoyle used to hoop in college but now makes a living hustling streetballers. He's white, wears baggy shirts and a backward hat to the courts populated by black players who are taller, fitter, dressed for the game. But, most importantly, he's white. Sidney Deane is Billy's initial, primary target. Sidney is talented, loud, boastful, approaching a caricature of a '90s streetball archetype. Depending on the viewer, one might relish the moment when Billy beats Sidney twice in their first encounter. The second time, revealing himself, whispering, "I've hustled a hell of a lot better players than you" in Sidney's ear before Sidney misses a jump shot.

For all of its other moving parts, *White Men Can't Jump* relies on teasing out the part of a hustle that I am most fascinated by in real life. The part that relies on looking, and how a person responds to that looking. There are many ways people tell on themselves, one of them being how they choose to react based solely off of what their eyes tell them, and how that connects to what they inherently believe. In the film, we are to understand that Billy's hustle is effective because the black players are incapable of seeing who he is, and by the time he has been fully rendered, it is too late. The Sidney/Billy pairing works because of this—on every court, Sidney convincing two opponents to saddle him with Billy as a teammate, Sidney sinking into the performance of begging to not have to play with the white chump who looks like he can't make a shot, and so on.

The theme of optics and perception appears again in the plotline of Gloria Clemente, Billy's girlfriend, often fed up with his reckless behavior, which has them on the run from people he owes a gambling debt to. While Billy and Sidney clear money off the courts of the city, Gloria studies to go on *Jeopardy!,* where she eventually makes it and nestles herself in between two white men. She gets a question wrong, and then gets one right. The thickness of her accent envelops the answer "What is Mount Vesuvius?" but the judges give it to her. She then goes on a run of correct answers, hitting her stride with "foods that begin with the letter Q." When she gets into an exceptionally good groove, one of the white men throws up his hands, not angry but exasperated. She has come into focus for him in that moment.

Much of *White Men Can't Jump*'s playing with racial dynamics loses my interest when it moves away from the way appearance can be used to hustle and into attempting to unravel cultural differences. White people listen to music but don't hear it, etc. Billy's inability to dunk isn't all that fascinating (the title of the film shows its hand, after all), but his desire to prove to Sidney that he can dunk is, this desire so overwhelming that Billy wagers $2,500 on it, only to miss three times. One thing about a hustle is that if you are in too deep for too long, it is possible that you might gain a misunderstanding of your limits. If you make a life around the rush that exists at the end of the trick, it can be easy to lose yourself in that feeling, in how people must see you, walking off on the shoulders of your victories.

Once, I did a reading in rural Wisconsin. I have this vintage Allman Brothers sweatshirt that I like, essentially just the cover of their album *Eat a Peach* blown up to an almost overwhelming size. *Eat a Peach* isn't my favorite Allman Brothers album, but it has some of my favorite Allman Brothers songs on it. I wore the sweatshirt to the reading, and during the Q&A, an older white man asked about the sweatshirt. Rather, he asked about the person wearing the sweatshirt. "Is that an Allman Brothers sweatshirt you have on?" was the first part. And then, pulling the curtain back, "What's the deal with you wearing it?" And, though I promise not to linger here too long either, I know the move, even when people believe that they're nudging gently. The people, always white, who want to quiz me on "certain" music and then feel flustered when I don't oblige. The people, always white, who insist that I rework an articulation of appreciation for a musician to fit their own understanding. I take this and come to the conclusion, once again, that hustling is easiest when you are in a room people don't believe you belong in. All you have to do is show up and refuse to give the people what they want.

But, of course, Billy dunks at the end of the movie. A game-winning dunk. A triumphant dunk. I don't think this scene has ever been surprising, even as I think back on it today. Billy becomes the person a viewer might have wanted him to be the whole time. This is the part of the movie that turns on a familiar axis. Whether or not it is openly admitted, it appears, often, that there is a hunger for a white, American-born basketball star in the NBA. Among the media, among some basketball fans. And I don't mean just a good player. I mean a great player. It is the Great White Hope syndrome, baked so firmly into the DNA of American culture that there are people unaware of when they're bowing to it. When a white player emerges who might fit this mold, words like "swagger" start getting bandied about.

I've been thinking through this a lot, not just because the NBA finds itself firmly in the midst of this cycle again, thanks to the play of Tyler Herro of the Miami Heat. This one small and specific piece of the larger machinery of an American hustle requires an elevation and a prioritization of whiteness. To set the trivial nature of basketball and its great white hopes aside, I have noticed people talking about empathy again. "Radical" empathy, I believe it is called from time to time, though I'm not entirely sure what that means. I'm supposing it means overcoming the threat of personal harm for the sake of niceness. Niceness, too, is a hustle, though I will have to approach that another time, when there aren't tanks lining the downtown of the city I live in, awaiting armed fascists who might seek to break into the statehouse or who might seek to yell on a sidewalk, or who might seek something in between those two extremes.

On any day in a violent country, a politician might say "This is not what America is." As the aforementioned tanks poured into town, my city's mayor stood behind a podium and said, "This country is better than what we're seeing today." The hustle is that everyone talks about the "today" as a single day that materialized, untethered, with no connection to any history before it or any history that will come after it. As if a moment is not within a braid of moments that defines a place. As if a place is not defined, at least in part, by how eagerly and comfortably it retreats to violence as a type of language. To make a myth of a country is a misguided extension of kindness, but it is also a hustle. People who believe so richly in the inherent goodness of whiteness that they believe empathy alone will grow the hearts of fascists are both hustlers and easily hustled. Trapped within the mouth of a predator, a true hustler will talk about the glow of the predator's teeth as soft, romantic lighting. I suppose I now have to take back what I said about not being opposed to hustles. The stakes were different then. I thought we were here together, simply talking about Billy Hoyle. And then about the ways that optics can fool the willing, and how America is almost always willing. I would apologize for us ending up here, but I've already told you: I'm a bad hustler. I don't even trust myself.

FOURTH QUARTER

CITY AS ITS FALSE SELF

One of the four Royal Stars is watching over me.

Yeah, I'm blessed in these times of nervous weather.

—YONA HARVEY

12:00

If you can believe it, I swear, this story ends the way you have seen it end before, summoned by the long desperate stares of a daydream or, at the end of a film, credits crawling over a landscape, soundtracked by a song you heard pouring from a speaker and then a beloved elder's mouth in the years before the words of it danced off of your own tongue. This story is not only an ode to hustlers, though we do praise the hustler here, and nostalgia might be the most relentless hustler of them all. And I do not choose to think about what that makes me, faithful wielder of its immense arsenal of weapons, but nonetheless, here I am.

This story ends the way you might write it if you were writing it for a child, still young enough to be faithful in their pursuit of a possibility so florescent, anyone older might call it feverish, something to be read out loud while night closes in on a bedroom, with a small person breathing in your arms, for that brief moment of wonder that might exist when we enter the world of youth and remember ourselves as young.

If you can believe it, this is a story that ends in a city garlanded with flowers. Golden clouds of smoke puffing into its summer sky, wrestling with the humid air blown in from the lake, a cursed lake, though not today, for the end of this story also brings with it the end of all curses. For a quick series of scenes, all spells are broken, everyone has repented and all is forgiven. From above, it is hard to tell the difference between cars and people. From high enough above, it is hard to tell the difference between people and the street itself. It isn't so much that people have taken *over* the street; it is that people have become the roads, become the grass, become the trees, even.

But the story truly ends in the aftermath of this scene. After a city has exhausted itself with celebration and wound back down into silence. In the opened but restrained jaws of night, confetti still blows in the wind and sticks to the glass windows of shops. There are still homemade signs littering the pavement outside of an arena or along a path downtown. Chunky and uneven letters written with marker on white posterboard, or haphazard but joyful illustrations thrown together in the moments before rushing out of a house. A city is rarely silent, of course. But for the sake of this story's ending as neatly as the romantics might imagine it, I will not yet mention how steadily a place can breathe alongside its forgotten residents, how there are people at the margins of any city who fight for their lives amidst the towering mass of overgrowth. There will be time for that, I promise, but I would like for us to collectively imagine this ending as sweet. When I say that nostalgia is a hustle and we are the hustlers, placing an audience at the mercy of its tools, I mean that we must figure out, together, what we are willing to lie about for the sake of a clean memory.

The story ends with no sinners, because it must. Everyone is washed clean. A city holds its breath for decades, waiting for something good to descend, and then it does. This, I believe, means that everything resets, and so does everyone within the container of this glorious happening. To enter the church of triumph, everyone must be absolved, and so everyone is. The pistols vanish from the waistbands of cops, from the sock drawers of dealers. What you thought to be blood, dried on the concrete of the park, is instead handprints left by children who pressed their hands into dark paint and left behind a symbol of their living. Yes, living, the children are alive, even the ones thought to be dead. Even the ones who were on the news, even the ones some of us marched in the streets for and broke glass windows for and threw ourselves into police shields for.

In the end of this story, there are tattoos that vanish from the skin of those who got the names of the gone-too-soon inked on them, because no one is gone too soon. Yes, if we are to cure ourselves of curses, let us cure ourselves of all the curses tonight, let the lake cough its thick fog upon the people and let them be unmoved by the sweat. What is sweat but decoration, jewelry upon the extended arms beckoning people toward a revival?

In the end, we will make use of the lake after all. The guns have been swallowed by the water. The handcuffs and cop cars have been washed away. The bullets, too. I remember when Biggie was driven through the streets of Bed-Stuy, his body in a hearse dragging down his beloved block and people dancing atop cars and rattling the fences of a check cashing spot and falling to their knees, and I remember the cops. I remember them dragging people into the cages in the backs of their cars and crashing down on people with nightsticks, and I remember one young black person shouting *Why, why, this is supposed to be for us* and if we are to begin at the ending, then the ending must be for us, and the ending must be righteous, even if much of what we know to be righteous is tinted, slightly, with lies.

And there are few lies that seduce like a city, silent after being gripped by a long-held joy. I walked the streets of Cleveland that night. I say "night" and you will know that I mean the time that is morning, by definition, but still feels like night to those who haven't slept, who twirl between the veil of days as it grows thinner, blows gently to the side to reveal one light's surrendering to another's. Those of us who crawl in those hours searching to prolong a miracle. I have seen some of you there, I am sure of it. We have maybe locked eyes, ravenous for the residue of some hours-old joy. The hours when some of us have kissed willing strangers, or been the strangers willing to be kissed. The hours when some of us have promised someone else that we would stay awake to see the first moments of the sunset, only to fall asleep and be jarred awake by the harsh alarm of light, screaming through a window. I have called these silent hours, yes. But a silence begging to be disrupted by some stumbles toward a yet-to-be-seen magic hour.

And I was among the few awake and stumbling in Cleveland in the deepest wee hours after the party. The kind of party where someone looks at the toll taken on a place, waves a dismissive hand, and says they'll get to the mess the next day. What I remember is that it felt like nothing could ever harm me. That nothing here had ever harmed anyone. I am not especially easy to fool, but I am a romantic, which I suppose means that at the right hour, I am everyone's fool. And I allowed myself to fall into the arms of a city that was not my city but felt, in that moment, like it could be. Like I wanted it to be. I watched the streetlights dance off of my already glowing arms, still slick with sweat. Glitter had affixed itself to small patches of my skin, though I don't know from where. (Though, with glitter, isn't that so often the way of its arrival? It comes, and it stays, its origin point a blur of a memory, no matter how recent.)

It is easy to feel like you own a city in this moment, but the city still owns you. And this is how the story ends. I believed a city invincible, and so I believed myself invincible in it. I believed my people to be invincible. I believed there would be no evil to befall anyone I loved within this city's borders, because I believed there would be no evil, not anymore. Not after we'd shouted toward the sky in the name of an inevitable championship. One that felt like ours—even the "we" who never called this place home, never mourned in the name of the team that was being celebrated. I was there, running through a silent city that I had built into my own fantasy. A dream, the type you might dream if you were explaining it to a child. No one suffers, no one prays for anywhere but where they are. No one is hungry, a city is full of its own opulence, its own radiant vision of finally, gracefully, becoming a winner.

You and I know this isn't true. I knew this then, too. I knew this walking through downtown Cleveland, passing a bit of coin to the unhoused man underneath a building's awning who nodded toward Quicken Loans Arena and mumbled *Ain't this some shit?* and I didn't know what the "this" was, but I still nodded, and said *Yeah, you right* because whatever it was, I knew he was right.

There are things we know about cities—the ones we live in, the ones we visit, the ones that seem like ours during the right run of hours. But this story ends in an act of forgetting. At least for now, in this moment. Which, I must tell you, is almost over. It was a delight to drink from this dream, but know, the bottom of the glass, tilted to our mouths, is visible enough to offer a reflection. Hold whatever sweetness you can in your mouth for a little longer. Ignore the glass, dropped to the floor, fractured into an army of shards. This is how we begin the other story.

11:35

The phrase *Ball don't lie* is one way of saying *You get what you deserve*. You, who knows what you've done but still might hope to benefit from some reward for your misdeeds, even (or especially) the ones of microscopic proportions. In a professional basketball game, lorded over by officials in their black and whites, someone drives to the rim and throws up an out-of-control layup, contorting their body, tumbling into a defender leaning back with their arms straight up, leaning back. The offensive player flails and shouts, and a ref calls a foul, despite minimal contact. The defensive player, the opposing team, the opposing coach all shout toward the sky in disbelief, get in the ref's ear, to no avail. The driving player smirks. This is where the trick turns. The player gets two free throws. Misses the first. Someone at home, someone on the floor, someone in the stands shouts *Ball don't lie!* Which is to say *That's what you get for that bullshit.* Which is to say *You ain't slick.*

The slang is borderless. It doesn't require a ball or a shot or someone with a whistle, enforcing the boundaries of violence. In the streets, the ball still don't lie, but there are boundaries. A motherfucker does the wrong kind of dirt. Gunshots scream through a playground where children throw a basketball at a rim. An elder's house gets run up in. The architect of these deeds might live, untouched, longer than you believe they deserve to. But believe, they will be touched. You keep the cops out by giving them no reason to come around. The code of a place is so rigid, no one who runs afoul of it can get away for long. We don't fear sirens and badges here. We don't fear each other, either. But if you do the wrong kind of dirt, there is plenty to fear. Ball don't lie, and yet,

11:20

nothing lies like a city. A place that holds, within it, a container of our memories. Even if they aren't the good memories. A city is a vessel. A mirror for our past selves. And so it gets away with its lying, sometimes. I lie to myself about the places I love, even when I don't want to. Even when the places I love don't look like the places I love anymore. You look into the mirror and the mirror laughs, asks what good the reflection is if everything has turned to dust. And still, I forgive, and forgive, and forgive. I call this loyalty because I have to. There is no consequence I can inflict, there is no shot spinning off of a rim to reconcile both the lying and the acceptance of it. And so a place defines itself by its brightest moments, the best of who makes it out. The trophies that march through its downtowns, the children chasing them, reaching up to see the reflections of their hands in the gold.

11:15

Celebrating a championship on the home floor of an opponent is not the way it is supposed to go, but I imagine if you are the team that just won the championship, you will take whatever you can get. And besides, in the throes of our brightest, loudest celebration or anguish, anyplace can be anywhere. A city lies and makes liars out of the living. It's why all of those songs work. Yes, someone is boarding a midnight train taking them back home to Georgia, but the Georgia is anywhere. Georgia is the place you aren't in the moment, but hope to be soon. I first heard "California Dreamin'" before I knew where California was. When I barely knew what it looked like on a map. But I wanted to go there. It's a vicious trick. The *there* wasn't California at all. The *there* was a feeling. One that I found walking through the dirt path behind the basketball courts in my neighborhood, overgrown with trees so tall that someone small enough could vanish, entirely. A young enough person with a wild enough imagination could disappear, and through that

disappearance, they could be anywhere. That stretch of extrava-
gant branches was my California, I dreamt it until I could fall
into it again. It isn't always lying to make the city you miss out
of the city you're in. And besides, a trophy reflects what you
want it to. There is confetti falling down in your honor, somewhere. Someone is running their fingers through their own
hair and marveling at the incandescence tumbling downward
from atop their own head. And still,

11:05

there are those who might ache for the fans, watching someone
else celebrate on their home floor. And I suppose deep within
myself, there is a small flame of sympathy set alight for those
poor souls. The ones who stay and watch the presentation of a
trophy because they don't want to leave just yet. The ones who
are committed to the witnessing of history, even if they find
themselves on the wrong side of it. Those are the people who
didn't see this coming, and I will bow to whatever history books
write that part clearly.

But a city, miles away, opens its arms and prepares for damage. The people within the city vibrate with nerves while the
lake sings its humid song over a night that has been rendered
thick with anticipation. If you are to ever see it written or hear
it spoken, do not believe that no one saw this coming. And I
don't mean at the edge of Game 7, when the fourth-quarter
clock was ticking down in that way anyone who has cheered for
the impossible knows a clock can tick down—each second feeling like the quarter of a game unto itself. Do not believe that no
one saw this coming even at the end of Game 4, twenty-one
thousand slinking out of Quicken Loans Arena with a 3–1 cloud
hanging over their heads.

10:50

I don't know how to explain this to anyone who hasn't spent a large portion of their life betting on losing teams, betting on a city people foolishly consider to be a losing city. I cannot explain this to anyone who hasn't stumbled their way into some undeniable beauty only to set it on fire at their arrival because they felt too close to that which they weren't sure they deserved. I cannot explain this to anyone who hasn't prayed in a church for something they weren't entirely sure God gave a fuck about. The trivial, selfish pearls of survival, the things that don't entirely help anyone else but might drag someone from one moment of living to the next. Even if those things don't arrive. It's just the certainty that they were prayed for, the opportunity to have someone to shake a fist at when they don't come to fruition. I probably cannot explain this to anyone who extends their arms with entitlement or expectations when a blessing descends on them, anyone who doesn't watch the rare but joyous spoils of their living through the cracks in their fingers. Anyone who doesn't cautiously drink from the well of abundance, trembling slightly at the fear of what might be on the other side of any celebration.

But if you have fallen, an effervescent victim, into a state of dreaming, then let us begin there. If you have, in that state, been seduced so thoroughly, you might, within the pleasureful pockets of the dream itself, have finally abandoned your skepticism and given in to the idea that this dreaming is something beyond dreaming entirely. That it is, in fact, a new life. The fact that you cannot remember how you got here is only confirmation. This is where you are now, and have always been. From the infinite fields, the ground opens and blooms the favorite flower of anyone you love and miss. The words of a childhood song you'd buried tumble from the sky, first a mess of sound and then, yes, actual language, which begs its way onto your tongue, only to leap directly off, into the bluest water you slip your bare feet into, surprised by its warmth. And yes, I am rebuilding the interior of a dream that I had once, its beauty still stitched into a quilt that slips gradually from the shoulders of my memory. But imagine this as your dream. Any dream you have fallen into and loved. One where you are a child, one where you are an elder. One where your hands are massaging what will become bread, your fingers brushing another person's fingers, and you may look, but cannot make out a face before waking.

I can explain this to you if you have had any dream where you are without pain and then been pulled back awake, into a body that sometimes creaks under the weight of its own stiffness, into a world with caskets and voices you can hardly remember.

The seconds after coming to terms with what you thought to be real and what is real are rarely more alarming to me than they are in this mode. There is a video that breaks my heart that you have perhaps seen. A raccoon, overjoyed with the gift of cotton candy, takes its bounty to the water, to wash the food off before consuming it. The raccoon, of course, does not know what any viewer knows. That the ball of sugar will be overtaken by the entry into the water and dissolve into nothing. When this happens, the raccoon becomes frantic and puzzled, feeling around the puddle of water, seeking what was lost, only to be greeted by its own reflection.

The moments immediately after waking from a rapturous state of elsewhere can be the harshest mirror. One in which you reach for what you just knew your life to be, even as the concrete memory of it slips away with each passing second. And still, the remnants of that sweetness dance along the periphery of a sometimes painful living. And so do you then regret the dreaming itself? Or do you return to sleep each night, hoping to get back to that same place, knowing how impossible that might be?

I hope you get it now. So that I can explain to you that there were always people

10:42

who saw this coming. Who expected this, even if it was to their own detriment. In the early summer of 2016, my pals from Cleveland who lived elsewhere would make sometimes long drives to pile themselves into a downtown bar on the days the NBA Finals games were happening in California. They would skip out on work or leave loved ones behind, not to go to a game itself but to be around people who were also immersed in their same brand of tentative but necessary dreaming. It certainly didn't help that this NBA Finals was a rematch of the NBA Finals from just one year earlier, in which the Cavs began competitive, taking both of the first games to overtime and winning one, and then taking a 2–1 lead before surrendering three games in a row, two of them not especially close and the final game, though thrilling in its final moments, never much in doubt. And still, people showed up in Cleveland, in the arena, outside of the arena. People in their homes in Cleveland sat on the edges of beds or couches. Cleveland is a city that is overwhelmed by a desire to believe in something beyond what people outside of the place have ascribed to it. This is illuminated in many corners of the city and its people, but the way I've known it best is through its sports fans, who have infiltrated my life, much to my pleasure, even if that pleasure is a bit self-serving, allowing me to both playfully revel in their misery and be somewhat in awe of their resilience. No matter the year, the person who has done my taxes for most of my adult life taps the deliciously tacky Cleveland Browns decorative license plate hanging beside his desk and mumbles *This is the year. Super Bowl, we're going. Already got it locked into my calendar.* He says this every spring, even when the Browns finished with three or four wins the year before. I roll with children of the '90s, who watched the team now known as the Cleveland Guardians have the kind of success that brought them to the edge of a title, but never directly to it. The Guardians, who were one inning away from a World Series win in 1997, who made the playoffs with some consistency and some stunning moments, but never pulled off a single series good enough to triumph. There's something about that kind of losing, the kind of losing where you are close enough to touch and taste the finality of being sole victors, but never actually holding it. That can drain a fan base in a way that might feel similar to perpetual losing—in a way that might make one crave the familiar eras of hopelessness. At least in the bleak times, there's an honesty about the reality of everyone's circumstances. The excitement that opens a season, when there are no wins or losses in anyone's columns, and the excitement that fades as a record becomes weighed down with L's, but with that weight comes a new hope: There's always next year. This moment is lost, but soon there will be another season, another blank slate. Possibility awaits. If you can believe in it long enough, destiny rotates, tilts its wild and colorful feathers toward everyone eventually.

10:31

It is easiest to measure the distance between where I am and where I want to be in miles, in minutes. It is unfair to measure such distance in heartbreak, in loneliness. In how long it takes to stop staring at a photo of old friends, the absence that you might occupy around a table. Distance doesn't lie, even if time does. The distance from my apartment in New Haven, Connecticut, to my old neighborhood in Columbus, Ohio, was 640 miles if I took the route with tolls. It was 622 miles if I took the route without tolls. Less expensive, but more tedious. But that's distance. It says nothing of time. The drive, when mapped out on a weekday morning, should take about nine hours and forty minutes, regardless of which route is chosen. But desire is an accelerant. Or, time slows when a landscape doesn't change. Like in Pennsylvania, where one might mark time by the dead. A deer who, it seems, almost made it safely to the median's waiting grass, stretched out now on the side of the highway, its hooves brushing the green. Defining the distance between where it is and where it wanted to be.

In 2016, I was in Connecticut because I had to be there. Someone I loved was there. Someone I'd promised to love until I was dead, which by the summer of 2016, my second full year away from home, seemed like it could come any second.

I knew not to measure the distance between my new home and my old one by time, because I knew the drive well. The elastic nature of it. I made it often, made up excuses to make it. A friend was doing a poetry gig that I just *had* to see. Another friend's dog died, and they absolutely needed me home, right now. I could make the nine-and-a-half-hour drive in just under eight hours some days. Other days, I could make it in nine hours that felt like fifteen hours. The drive back felt quick as the exhale of a half breath. No matter how I tried to extend it, how many rest stops I walked through, how many trees off the side of the road I stopped to admire. I would start my car and already be back. Away from the home I wanted but couldn't have. Returned to the home I had but didn't want.

10:18

Time is the latest enemy. Yes, I charge time with being the greatest liar of them all, at least for now. I watched the dying moments of Game 7 of the 2016 NBA Finals in some Connecticut sports bar surrounded by strangers, and the fourth quarter felt like five lifetimes, all of them hard on the heart, even if one had no direct rooting interest.

In sports, the clock can oscillate between the minutes feeling eternal and then rapidly tumbling away at a pace that cannot be grasped by anyone who might reach for a few precious seconds that they wish to get back even while they dissolve. While watching the clock during basketball games, I most love the moment when the end of a game turns itself from minutes to seconds. I like to see the anatomy of a minute, the fractions of a second peeling themselves away. Fractions that we do not get treated to when the countdown clock is still concerned with the slower math of minutes. But once we dive into the suddenness of seconds, there is an urgency that begins as a hum and grows into a scream.

When Kyrie Irving first starts a slow dribble to the center of the court, the clock is at the very end of its dance with minutes, reading 1:03. By the time Kyrie gets in front of Stephen Curry, the time tilts over, we are into the urgent moments now, the clock at 59 seconds and starting its breathless sprint to some resolution. And then, the shot.

There is no good way to say this now. There is no way that I can think that will have me come across here as honest, but I swear to you, the shot looked good from the moment Kyrie let it go. Despite the people around me who held their breath, the man shouting a prolonged *nooooo* from the back of the room as the ball made its way toward the rim. A journey which gave into the cliché—it was long and tedious. In order to get the shot over Curry's hand, belated as it was to arrive, Irving shot what can best be described as a haphazard rainbow. The kind of shot that sends the ball well out of the camera's frame, depending on the angle. And so it remains a mystery for a split second, until it begins its descent. And when it did, the shot looked good to me. It looked like it would fall through, and I may have been trapped in my own delusions in that moment, since it had been so long since any shot had slipped through the bottom end of the net, so long since the rim itself had fallen to its knees and welcomed in that sweet song. I could be remembering this wrong, and I was just as stunned by the audacity of it all as everyone else. It is easy to say this now, after revelry has gripped a city, gleefully wrecked by confetti raining down from the tops of buildings. But I swear, I saw the ball's descent, back into the camera's frame, and would you believe me if I said now that it felt a little bit like destiny?

10:02

The Cavs were a team of destiny once, before this. Cleveland was a city of destiny once. In the mid-seventies. It was the '75–'76 season, forty years before LeBron James walked off of an airplane with a trophy under his arm and then above his head, and the sixth season of professional basketball in Cleveland. And it is not the point of destiny and triumph, but I do love the aesthetics of it all, and one look at the names up and down the roster of the '75–'76 Cavaliers offers a series of delights, even in one of the golden eras of NBA names and nicknames. Yeah, okay, there was a Slick in Seattle, some motherfucker in New Orleans who was so bad he wore his nickname on the back of his jersey like it was the name his mama gave him—"Pistol," just out there in the open. There was a Kermit in Los Angeles! A Tiny in Kansas City! A World B. Free throwing up jump shots that damn near kissed the rafters in Philly. And yes, Jumpin' Jim barely played in Buffalo, but the man's hair sure was laid and the name still looks damn good on a roster. But the Cavs had all that and more! On just one team! There was a Campy! A Bingo! A Bunny! A little spark plug named Foots who claimed to be six feet tall on paper but Lord knows the page and the eye be tellin' two different stories. Those Cavs had *three* dudes named Jim, and forgive me but it is never not a slight surprise to me that all three of them were black! And forgive me once again, though I have probably already stretched your limits of forgiveness, but Jim Cleamons is the one I love most, because he played at Linden-McKinley High School right here in Columbus, Ohio, before going off and winning all those rings on the bench coaching the Chicago Bulls.

These lavishly named Cavaliers played their games in the Richfield Coliseum, which had opened just a year earlier, and seated over 20,000 at full capacity for basketball games, an upgrade of about 10,000 from the Cleveland Arena, which the Coliseum had replaced. It was one of the first indoor sporting arenas to contain luxury boxes. It was situated south of Cleveland, positioned at the intersection of Interstates 77 and 271 and in the shadow of the Ohio Turnpike. This positioning was strategic, designed to benefit from the "urban sprawl" that was taking over Northeast Ohio in the early to mid-'70s, more of the once-concentrated population sprawling further outward, causing a situation where over five million Ohioans lived within an hour's drive to the Coliseum.

But it didn't matter. Once those Cavs got rolling, crowds would sell out the Coliseum well before tip-off, sending a seismic tremble through the arena as they stomped their feet and chanted "We want the Cavs" repeatedly, well before the team made its way out for their layup drills. The chalkboards in the locker room would shake. The Coliseum was a fortress.

The season itself was miraculous, but even within the vastness of a miracle, there are singular miracles, the way that a perfect facet of a diamond peeks out when placed underneath the right lighting. There was another shot, late in another Game 7, that would make a liar out of linear time. And would you believe it, another Northeast Ohio kid on this Cavs team summoned some magic, before LeBron was even an idea. Dick Snyder, born in North Canton, pride of Hoover High School, found himself with the ball in his hands, with nine seconds left in Game 7 of the Eastern Conference Semifinals against the Washington Bullets and an 85–85 score.

And it is astonishing that we've made it this far, dancing on the outskirts of two Game 7 scenes already without my mentioning how in love I am with the finality of a Game 7. Rather, the control one might have over the finality. Turning away from the ominous finger beckoning from beneath a black cloak and making your own exit, on your own time. I love a Game 7 because I have, from many high-up and far-off windows, seen a sunset that I have wished I could bottle. There have been inevitable nighttimes that I have wanted to keep behind a door, a door that I would push my back against, even in the midst of darkness thrashing on the other side, just for another moment or another hour with that flamboyant and dramatic marching band of color blaring against the sky's canvas. The blaring horns of oranges and yellows and the faint, but always present, keys of purples and reds twirling underneath. And the conductor of all that glorious racket, the sun itself, twirling toward vanishing until all that remain are the colors, their fluorescence growing faint in preparation for being washed away by that familiar and vicious darkness. I have even run out of ways to talk about beauty, which is surely a sin, but it is also how I know that I have witnessed that which dismantles a capacity for language, renders any attempts foolish. If you know this feeling like I know this feeling, welcome to the church of silence and awe. Our mouths are open, but nothing spills out. Our backs against a trembling door, praying to cut the veil of night into small scattered pieces. If you know this feeling as I have known this feeling, if you have wanted to hold the moment before an inevitable ending in your own hands and stretch it to near distortion, you also love a Game 7. Someone has to go home, and yet no one wants to. The party was good, but it has to end for someone, even if the sweetness of a stranger's kiss still spins along the lips of a person who will never see that stranger again. They have to exit through the door of their own fantasies and never return.

9:48

In sports movies, each second lasts longer than it should. It's a trick of building anticipation, asking a viewer to suspend disbelief as the camera cuts to the clock, back to the slow-motion shot of a player with a ball in their hand, running toward an open space or ascending toward a hoop. We know better but are willing to be fooled for what the act of being fooled can add to the experience. I mention this to say that rarely does a moment like this happen in a real-life game for me. A moment that feels so slow that it seems as if I am not actually in control of my own watching of it. I watch the Dick Snyder shot like this. The small window of eight seconds it takes for the shot to happen, it happens in small acts, or movements, the way a play or a dance might. In the first act, Snyder catches an inbound pass from Jim Cleamons. Five seconds left. In the second act, Snyder gently fakes a pass to his right, causing the defender to open up his body just enough. Of the many things I love about basketball, I most love to consider it as a duel of angles. A defender and an opponent locked together in a lightless chamber, both seeking a window, cracked and begging for them to slide through. And there, in the moment where Snyder's left side was opened up, just a small sigh of light tumbling out, he sprinted toward it, leaving his defender two steps behind and even catching the other Bullets players in the paint slightly off guard and scrambling.

And then, in the final act, the shot itself. The shot itself feels more spectacular to me than it is. I've built a fascination through repetition, like when you repeat a single word so many times that the word itself begins to mean both nothing and everything, a treasure chest of colliding sounds.

9:36

Snyder shoots a floater over the outstretched arm of a defender. It hits the backboard and goes in, and the Cavs win the series.

Wait, let's try this again.

9:35

Snyder takes off from one foot right above the dotted circle. He jumps, yes, but it is unfair to say that he is *in the air*. He appears to be in the midst of a type of controlled flailing, like a young bird, dropped out of its nest from the beak of a mother, demanding that it learn to fly. Snyder's legs kick out awkwardly as he flings his arm past a defender, who has foolishly arrived too late. The ball is almost secondary—

Okay, let's pause here and try again.

9:34

This is where everything slows down, the way it might if the scene were stitched together by an overzealous director. The ball is not secondary. Of course it isn't. I have simply fallen again for the romantics of the body's movements. The ball moves in slow motion. I know exactly when and where to force the scene into stillness. There is a moment when the ball hangs in air, before it kisses the sweetest spot of the backboard—the spot that anyone who has shot a basketball enough knows, the spot that breathes the ball in before blowing it, gently, through the net. Before that, the ball is frozen in the miniature heaven of Richfield, and if you can freeze the frame just right, if you can catch it at the exact moment the ball begins to ascend— which I can, which I have, and since we are talking about set- ting suns and their downward tumble anyway—you will see the dull orange orb pressed against the blue paint of the side- line. If you were to watch this enough times, if you were to stare at just this moment for long enough, it might appear to you as a sort of distorted sunset. A sunset from someone else's past, told to you in a story once, fighting its way to the top of your memory, all over again. And of course, of course it is an optical illusion of sorts. The ball is actually far higher than the blue-tinted sideline, but then again, every sunset you've ever seen is a trick. Most of the beauty I have surrendered myself to is tucking some far less delicious honesty beneath its magic, and so why not this? This moment when, even if you didn't know the ball was going to go in, you might marvel at what is on the other side of the ball's brief affair with the blue. It's like I was saying. I love a Game 7. The sun sets for someone, and the sky remains a parade of colors for someone else.

9:27

The Cavs wouldn't win another division title until 2007. They'd get to another conference finals in the '91–'92 season.

9:26

But that's the thing: you aren't supposed to look behind you if what's in front of you is already good. Even if you think, for a moment, that some part of whatever is behind you might be better. Do not tamper with the engine of the heart, rusted as it is but still running. It knows what it knows, it hums well enough to have carried you to this morning, and with luck, it might carry you to another one. If there is a heaven, I suppose there we can weep over the scrapbook of our lives while we wait for the living to climb the constellations. But not now, is what I'm told. Nostalgia is only for the brokenhearted. For the displeased or disaffected, the ones who need to look to the past to give meaning to their present. I'm told there is nothing in my childhood that will save me from what's coming whenever what's coming arrives. The old devils may resemble the new devils if you're not careful. Cuffs, cells, and caskets. Someone I loved left me because they said I couldn't envision the future, and therefore they couldn't envision a future with me. Their leaving mothered longing, which mothered looking backward, again, to a time before now. I say I was happier in the past because the pain of the past is a relic. I speak of it but no longer feel it. I do not know what pain is coming, but I know it is coming.

9:18

It is another example of time and distance misaligning. It has been ____ years since I lost someone, but it feels like ____ because I need it to.

9:17

But what we know to be true, by now, is that I have no shame in looking over my shoulder. And I have no shame in taking you with me, reader. To take your hand and run it over the wooden picture frame, inside of which I can convince you that my mother is living. I can convince you that I survived well, even when I survived hard. I can convince you there's nothing to be afraid of. Love alone is not enough, and yet the love of people I buried helped carry me here. And so I do not fear death, the only thing promised. The steady breath I have felt growing heavier with each year I survive again and again.

9:12

The anatomy of a chasedown block relies on fear. It's woven together by what you refuse to see coming, even if you know that it might be barreling toward you. This, of course, is a byproduct of what has been drilled into a life, well before a stage as large and as high-stakes as a Game 7 in the NBA Finals. In any sport where one can be chased, one of the first things they teach you is don't look behind you. In any corner of living where one might end up being chased, the message is the same. It doesn't make much of a difference, after all. Besides, if you come up in a neighborhood where you know every tendril, every alleyway springing forth from a mundane grid of street and sidewalk, every detour into a cluster of trees, you aren't really ever looking over your shoulder anyway. Know your landscape better than the devious tourists—the cops, fools from the other side of town. If you never *have* to look over your shoulder while footsteps lay down an uneven percussion some-where at your back, you get used to it.

But there's a science to it too, according to any coach I ever had (not that I trust *all* of those motherfuckers with science, in hindsight, but for the sake of this, let's say I do). To look back, to give in to the place where fear and curiosity intersect, is to sacrifice the ground you've gained. It slows you down, just enough, and also informs your would-be captor that you are thinking about them more than you're thinking about escape or glory or the open rim. The chase, like the chasedown block, isn't *only* about who is afraid and who isn't, but fear is always what hums underneath.

9:03

To be fair to Andre Iguodala, he didn't do anything wrong. He grabbed the rebound and sprinted into a fast break. It *looked* like a two-on-one advantage, and so he and Stephen Curry did what you should do: a quick exchange of passes to get the sin-gle defender off-balance. There was no time to look back, even if Iguodala had wanted to.

9:00

Game 7 of the 2016 NBA Finals was tied with two minutes left, 89–89. To make matters even more dire, there had been a scoring drought. Neither team had been able to put the ball in the basket for what felt like an eternity. This wasn't entirely due to sloppy play as much as it was due to the kind of cautious intensity that fatigue brings on. By that moment, the two teams had managed to score a meager 27 points combined in the entire fourth quarter. In the third quarter, the Cavs alone had scored 33. But it was late, what some might call winning time. Every movement has to be calculated. The game becomes more about granular math under five minutes with a title on the line. The scene before the chasedown block is almost as definitive as the block itself, or at least the two cannot be divorced from each other. Both teams heaving up shots that ended up short, careening off the front or the side of the rim. The Warriors home crowd intermittently attempting to nudge their squad forward, flooding the arena with the then-familiar chant of *Wa-rrrrrrri-oooooors*, which—if you have never been blessed with hearing the chant—sounds unmistakably like the way David Patrick Kelly bends the word through the clinking of bottles in the film *The Warriors*, his, of course, a taunt and this one, rattling Oracle Arena, also a taunt, of sorts. Or, at least, it serves the purpose of shaking an opponent the same way a taunt might.

8:45

Though another delight in the chasedown block is the delight of the witness, who can see the potential future coming for someone who can't see it for themselves. Yes, there are those who insist that looking back does not serve you, but it might serve you to not live in denial of what is coming, in the most literal sense. A chasedown block provides the witness with a window beyond the present. Something that is certainly coming that they have no control over. But the stakes are not as high as death, which is where the pleasure comes in. And it was all supposed to be over by now anyway.

8:20

The Cavs were supposed to be simply another roadblock on the Warriors' path to a continued coronation. They made history, lost only nine games in the regular season. But that was behind them. In the past. Not worth looking back at. Besides, let me tell it and I don't care about anyone's regular season unless there's some jewelry swinging from the neck of it. It is hard work to lose only nine games. Harder work still to lift a trophy.

7:15

It's that the victim can't see what's coming, but the distant witness can.

7:09

When the memories of some have faded to the point of malleability, as they have already, there might be those who speak of this play and say that LeBron James came out of *nowhere*. I have said that myself, countless times. But he's there—from the point the rebound is grabbed at the start of the play, he begins to accelerate down the sideline and then, once Iguodala gets the bounce pass from Curry, he accelerates even beyond the speed he was already operating at. This is where the eyes might be tricked into believing that he was *nowhere* until he was very much somewhere. A chasedown block is as much about timing and math as it is about an audacious belief in the self, is as much about a hope and a prayer, and in the case of LeBron James, taking off from the top of the dotted line with under two minutes left in the NBA Finals, it was as much about knowing that nothing else had been working. The game, for a little while, had turned away from who could or couldn't score and turned firmly to who would let the other team score, which is the same dilemma, but not. Not if you've been there. Not if you've been in any fight where you can tell the difference between wanting to win and simply not wanting to fall down.

But I watched Game 7 in a tiny bar in Connecticut, a place I lived, far away from a place I missed. And it was the block that defined the night for me because it was the block that pulled no immediate response out of the watching crowd, the way that it takes a moment to find sound or language while walking through the fog of witness, when that which is being witnessed is too large for sound or language in its immediate aftermath. I watched Game 7 in a bar in Connecticut and what I actually meant to say was that I lived within the moments of relative silence after that chasedown block, just the few seconds while everyone processed what they'd seen before the shouts of disbelief began. A few seconds wide enough to make a home in. A place where it was clear who was still throwing punches and who was just hanging on, trying not to fall down.

6:50

The difference between what you know and what you can see coming might rest on one small thing. A death that is inconsequential to you, but monumental to the place you are. In the spring of 1976, with Cleveland still riding high off of their Miracle Team, John Scalish died at sixty-three, unceremoniously, during heart surgery. There are no photos from his funeral. His eulogy and his obituary were both plain, dry delivery of the facts. This person lived, and now they are no longer living. There was a small story run in the Cleveland *Plain Dealer*, tucked in the bottom of the obituary section. He lived in relative obscurity, and so he died in relative obscurity. His health had been declining for years. Cancer had slowly battered him, weakening his heart. Still, he went about his business, despite being cocooned in constant pain, and despite his arteries hardening as the years wore on. It was a bypass surgery that did him in. Doctors warned him of the risks involved with the surgery— someone in his preexisting condition likely couldn't survive it—but doctors also told him that if he didn't at least try the surgery, he'd have only a few weeks to live. I find myself shaken, once again, by how much of our living comes down to luck, or a prayer, if you are a praying person. But here, I will call it luck. The sound of a coin hitting the ground and a shadow hovering over it, while one door locks and another creaks open.

It was his business, however, that made his a death that could not come without consequence. Scalish was the last great don of the Cleveland Mafia. Despite what the lack of public decoration adorning his death might have suggested, he was one of the defining figures in the movements of Northeast Ohio. He helped to push the Cleveland operations into Las Vegas casinos and California hotels, expanding the enterprise beyond the city itself while still keeping a stronghold on his hometown. I suppose it's called the underworld for a reason, but let us not pretend that the movements of the so-called underworld don't feed directly into a city's beating heart. Scalish outlived enemies and peers and legends of the Cleveland crime ecosystem, many of whom made more thunderous exits. A hail of bullets dancing off the walls of a barbershop, or a lone bullet greeting someone leaving their own home, a passenger slumping out of a car's newly opened door.

Scalish found his own, quieter exit. A bad heart in a hospital bed. Like men I've known, like men you might have known. Men who worked mundane jobs for so many years that they'd lost track of the time altogether. I am not sure what it is that fascinates me about the death of Scalish, or the many people like him—people who live salacious and high-stakes lives, awash with power and control, being forced to surrender to the heart. Not the bullet or the knife or the rope in a prison cell.

Because Scalish had been at the head of the Cleveland Family for thirty-two years, his death left an opening and left many people who had been hungry for power with an opportunity to reach for it, all at once. Through that reaching, a type of hell descended on the city, its primary architects being Irish mobster (and also, it must be mentioned, government informant) Danny Greene and James Licavoli, who was the successor to Scalish. What happened in their battle and all that surrounded it is fascinating, if only because one of the things Scalish fought so fiercely for in his life was his commitment to keeping the dealings of the mob secret. He understood that his business was a discreet business, and the longer it stayed that way, the more people could stay alive and stay out of jail, which meant that more money could be made. What Greene and Licavoli brought upon Cleveland and its surrounding areas was anything but discreet. It was loud, it echoed and tapped into the fear of an exuberant city, balancing its joy and hope with newfound terror.

6:45

In 1976, thirty-six bombs went off in Cleveland. The news dubbed it "Bomb City, USA."

Bombing itself wasn't new—the car bomb had long been one of the methods used to dispose of enemies. It left no evidence, but it was also loud, drew attention, and wasn't especially easy to execute. Pulling a trigger or even drawing a knife across a throat took less work, but also didn't always send a message. And in Cleveland in 1976, power would be achieved by the sending of messages. So the city was alight with bombs through the summer and into the fall. Cars being transformed into hills of jagged and glowing metal, whatever bodies were inside of them sometimes rendered unrecognizable, depending on the immediacy of the explosion.

All of this happened out in the open, in broad daylight. The mob was becoming populated with younger, more reckless enforcers. When a city is rattled by explosions, in an infinite cycle of retaliation so vicious it can hardly be remembered what its starting point or end goal is, even those who aren't targets become targets. A person walking next to a car that goes up in flames could become collateral if the explosion does enough damage. Fear screams through a city and rearranges its DNA.

The bomb relies on the trick we have turned over in our palms here, many times already. It relies on the fact that a person cannot see it coming. At least not the person who might most want to see it coming. Even if you know yourself to be a target, you will never know *exactly* when the flash of hot light will come for you. I like to think that I would choose to embrace this lack of knowing. At first I would frantically check my car or underneath my porch in the mornings. And then I would have to give in to the fact that what was out to get me might eventually catch me. Understanding what could come for you and being able to see it coming are two separate parts of the same machine, but I know what would allow me to put a key into an ignition without closing my eyes and holding my breath.

6:39

It's that the victim can't see what's coming, but the distant witness can.

6:38

But then, what of devotion? The kind of devotion it might take, for example, to extend your open palm so that someone you love or are otherwise beholden to might drop their car keys into your hand. The kind of devotion it might take, for example, to start a car that is not your car in a time and place where the car itself is a weapon and therefore the key nudged into the ignition is an extension of that weapon. What it might take for you to drive around a block a couple of times knowing that someone, somewhere not far from where your palms sweat against a steering wheel's leather, might be holding a small device with a single red button. And I know, this isn't entirely romantic, I know that fear can also be one of devotion's many mothers.

But someone you have grown to love is more afraid than you are, and maybe you take their keys from them, pull them out of a hand without mentioning the hand's shaking. I would like to consider the ways we all march to our sometimes-boring deaths without understanding what it is to be so devoted to someone or something that you might be compelled to speed up that march so that they can continue their own. I am not here to consider what is good or what is bad but simply to consider what is sometimes necessary, even if I don't have the heart for it. I only have the heart for far inferior devotions. So does everyone I love. There probably just aren't enough people who want us dead.

6:18

While Cleveland and its surrounding areas went up in smoke, the Cavaliers played through an up-and-down season, losing only six fewer games, but ending up fourth in a significantly more competitive division. They lost in the first round of the playoffs to the Washington Bullets, in a revenge series of sorts. But attendance rose at Richfield. If there was anxiety about the city, it felt like the arena was a place to lift some of that weight. And the team wasn't bad, after all. In the early fall of 1977, there was hope, a new season with the team's primary core still in place. There was enough buzz around the team to at least dim the horrors that hovered over the area.

On October 6, 1977, less than two weeks before the NBA season began, Danny Greene left a routine dental appointment in Lyndhurst, Ohio. As he approached his car, the car parked next to his exploded. Greene had evaded assassination attempts for years, even ducking a bombing attempt just two years earlier. You can believe in what might come for you and still not see it. Not while walking out of an unassuming office building on an unassuming afternoon, perhaps running a tongue over your newly cleaned teeth. Greene had been switching cars for months, hoping to throw off those trying to bomb him. Until, of course, the target was no longer his car. It was him, and there were those who would take his dead body any way they could get it. In the photos of the scene from above, one car's trunk is popped open, and the car to its left is entirely mangled—its top bent and blown off, its entire passenger side melted due to the heat, pushed in slightly. In between the two is Greene's body, stiffly twisted on the ground.

I believe that a city is required to have many jobs, and the cities I love fail at most of them. One of a city's requirements—one that I know well—is the requirement to hold multiple anxieties at once, multiple stakes attached to those anxieties. And so this is how it goes. A bomb rattles a city sidewalk, and inside of an arena people drum their feet against the bleachers with such intensity that the locker room walls shake. A widow dons a black veil and tries not to cry in front of her children, and a fan watches the lights go out on a season for the last time, feels their throat begin to swell. And who am I to do whatever emotional math it might take to square all of that? It ain't my gig. No matter what you've heard, I know cities better than I know anything. I know a city is a container for heartbreak. That's what it holds better than anything else. Sometimes the heartbreaks come in blood. Sometimes they refresh when the fall comes, when a stadium turns its lights back on.

6:05

So to survive, a city's people sometimes lie their way through the labyrinth of grief. Depending on the city, depending on the season. I may join people in their lies, in their wandering. I am not immune to the whispers that pour from my own open mouth and make their way into another unsatisfying night, even when I wish they wouldn't. Those things, the bad things, the sad things, the screeching horrors, the sharp and aimless hours, the silent hours after another funeral. Those don't happen here. Or, they do. But not like they happen in the places that aren't here. The good things don't happen here either. Confetti doesn't somersault seemingly from the heavens to nestle itself into a child's hair for hours. We don't lose *all* the time here, but we certainly don't win. That happens in other places, but not here. Running into a land of no expectations isn't quite pleasureful, but it also isn't disturbing the hum of heartbreak, eager to be inflamed by foolish hope.

I have lied to myself to keep loving a city, to keep myself fixed in the place I am because I'm afraid I know the truth about America, that nowhere is forgiving, and so the unforgiving familiar is better than anywhere else. I've heard all of the lies, too. Have smiled and nodded and shrugged them away. Yeah, we fight here. We'll light some shit on fire and march in these streets, but it's always in the name of some *other* niggas, not anyone here who the cops done rolled up on and left bleeding in the street. Yeah, we could take this motherfucker apart brick by brick, but then we'd have more bricks than hands willing to rebuild anything, and ain't that the way of it. We don't know what we'd do with ourselves if we won here. It is romantic to be cursed, to feel like the world has it out for just you. That there is a deity bored enough to disrupt your ecstasy. We had a good run, but it's not like any of us know what we'd do with a sky turned to gold. A child, shaking their head and filling a carpet with an entire solar system of wishing.

A Timeout in Praise
of Legendary Ohio Aviators

SCOTT MESCUDI, CLEVELAND, OHIO (1984–)

Man on the moon   man floating elsewhere   the mixtape cover   a helmet   and

rainbows   the homie says   *yeah I'm high* while blowing tendrils of smoke   into

the air   & he means to say   I am beyond here   I see the otherwise   inconceivable

and wouldn't you like   to know   when you might die   and how the

shit   goes down   I believed it   when Cudi said   he sees ghosts   not all

haunting   is of an evil sort   sometimes it's love   sometimes the people who never

wanted   to leave   find a way to stay   the hoodie at the concert reads

Thank god I see ghosts   and I know   yes   praise the lord   we should all

be   so   lucky

GUION BLUFORD, WESTLAKE, OHIO (1942–)

He rode the *Challenger* up beyond the stars in '83, three years
before the shuttle went up in smoke. First black person to cross
the threshold between this world & the next one if we're talking
literal. Some of us believe ourselves born in space, descended
to an unpleasant earth, & for the mission in '83, the *Challenger*
took off at night & returned at night & one must imagine that
in the midst of the uninterrupted black, Guy Bluford found a
window & found a city from above where the lights were on &
even if it wasn't his city, he missed it & so it became his city &

to the moon, we are as inconsequential as the stars themselves. Supporting actors at best. Unless you are the first link between your earthly ancestors & the place they descended from. Unless you can push a hand out into the fathomless black & feel pulled home in two directions.

5:45

The morning of Game 5 of the 2016 NBA Finals, I packed up my car and started the drive from New Haven, Connecticut, back to Columbus, Ohio. I didn't need to go home, but I invented a reason. This ongoing practice of invention and exit was certainly unfair to my partner at the time, who had gotten a gig teaching in Connecticut, which sent us there in 2014. But it was a negotiation, I told both of us—I thought of each trip home as a cleansing practice. A baptism, something that allowed me to reenter Connecticut blessed and renewed until the sins of longing returned.

On that day, I left a little bit later than I had intended to. It was June 13, and the Cavs were headed out to Oracle Arena, down 3–1. The game didn't start until 9 p.m., and I figured as long as I left by 11 a.m., I could make it and meet up with a crew to watch what I believed would be the death rattle of the 2016 Cleveland Cavaliers. I'd predicted to my pals that they'd make it interesting in the first half before losing their grip on the rope, as they had in Game 4. They had been embarrassed in Oracle to that point, coming apart at the end of Game 1 and then losing Game 2 by 33 points. Even though they returned the favor of the 30-point beatdown in Game 3, the trip back to Oracle for Game 5 seemed like a formality to me, though my Cleveland pals were hearing none of it. It's all about momentum, they'd tell me, waving a dismissive hand to cleanse the air of my pungent pessimism. You win one game, and then another game, and then anything can happen. Teams had recovered from 3–1

deficits in the playoffs. The Warriors had just done it in the
2016 Western Conference Finals. But it had never happened in
the NBA Finals. Teams would get close but fall short. The 1951
Knicks pushed the Rochester Royals to seven games after trail-
ing 3–0 in the series, but the Royals closed the door in Game 7.
Same with the 1966 Lakers, who came back from 3–1, only to
lose to the Celtics by two points in Game 7. The math is as
much emotional as it is physical, I would try to convince my
tentatively optimistic Cleveland Crew, all of them setting the
table for disappointment but still leaving a chair open for even
the most unlikely jubilation. It's not just the toll of pulling
yourselves back from the brink for three games in a row, it's
also trying not to give in to whatever voice reminds you that
you're not supposed to still be here. That it should, reasonably,
all be over. The wrong bounce or the wrong end of a run chew-
ing through the otherwise uninterrupted defiance and mutter-
ing in even just one ear that it's over, it's time to go home. No
one expected you to claw back anyway.

It might be better, I'd suggest, to uncork the misery early.
But this surprises no one. I prefer being accelerated to the front
row of my undoing. Spare me the slow march.

5:20

Though I had been seduced back under the familiar covers of
Ohio for far more trivial reasons than basketball, this time I
didn't make the trip home only to watch a game on a TV in a
pal's living room. On June 6, 2016, Columbus police murdered
twenty-three-year-old Henry Green. Green was a victim of the
city's newly minted Summer Safety Initiative, brought to life by
the mayor, encouraging police to target "hot spots," places in
the city deemed to be at risk for crime.

The murder happened in the early not-quite-summer that hovers over central Ohio. The days are longer and gripped by an extension of twilight, but whatever real freedom summer can contain for anyone not beholden to the schedule of school hasn't been determined yet. At 6:30 p.m., Green was walking back to his aunt's house with his friend, Christian Rutledge. A white SUV with tinted windows swerved in their direction, and two white men jumped out. Plainclothes cops. Jumpout boys. Wearing shorts and T-shirts and pointing guns. Rutledge heard one of the men shout *You gonna pull a gun on me, motherfucker?* before firing. Rutledge ran; Green was hit seven times. He was taken to the hospital. His parents were not allowed to see his body. There was blood on the sidewalk where he was given CPR, where people would place lit candles in the days to come. In the immediate aftermath of this kind of violence and the tremors of grief that encase this kind of violence, there are logistics of healing that escape the grander designs of burial, of taking meals to a family's doorstep. How does a person's blood get washed away from a sidewalk on a block they lived and loved in, on a block where they waved to neighbors, carried groceries home? What of an early and humid summer where the clouds sit, overburdened with rain they refuse to release?

Whatever is left behind dries and turns a dark crimson, the wayward light from candles flickering over what remains—a strange kind of memorial, a strange kind of haunting. I got home, and before going to the store and then to watch the game, I went to the street where Henry Green was murdered. It was a street I knew, a street near where I'd played ball before, hustled on basketball courts before, near places where I'd slept when I had nowhere to sleep. When I got there, I had nothing to clean the ground with, and if I did, I'm not sure it would have been the most appropriate step for me to do such a thing. But I remember what was left

5:19

of the blood and I remember the light from a candle hovering over it as the sun began to set and I remember staring down at my shoes and I remember feeling like the concrete was opening up and I know this to be nothing but rage I know this to be what comes after swinging wild punches at the air and imagining the faces of your worst demons the cops the politicians who call the places you love war zones the helicopters that won't let you sleep that claw through the walls and wake up elders and children and goddamn I remember at my feet that blood-stained concrete just split right in half and opened up and I want a whole city underground if it does not love my people I want to bury the new condo developments instead of my people I want to bury the craft breweries and the barcades and the mixed-use helltowers instead of my people I want the statues melted down I want the mothers of murdered children to do it I want the heat to rise from a statue's vanishing and last for ten summers I don't want apologies anymore no not this time I want the mayor to walk through a place he called a war zone at night I want people to get real honest with themselves about what war actually is I want the schools to have heat I want the schools to have air I want the riot gear thrown in the river the river that was blue when I was a boy but now leaves brown streaks as it runs away from the city I want the brown river to carry the riot gear to some other hell and I want the babies to stop passing out in school do you hear me I want a whole city under the ground some days but I at least want the rain I at least want something to wash the blood away so that

no one who loved him has to and somewhere beyond the blood
what I don't remember is

5:00

when I learned not to run from the cops and I don't remember when I first ignored that advice. But I always laugh in
movies when there are people running from cops, who stop
abruptly, fear in their eyes, when they hear a gun cock, or hear
a shot fired in the air. If there is a usefulness in being able to
see what's coming, it comes when one feels like one has at least
a little control over what the outcome might be.

But we're talking cops—motherfuckers you *know* are cops.
Who roll up in the blue and whites or at least roll up on you
wearing the uniform of treacherous empire. Easy to spot and
easy to plan around.

Henry Green was murdered by what looked like two plain
dudes hopping out of an SUV with blacked-out windows.
There's a difference when one gets rolled up on that way. Running might be in the cards, sure, but you might stay fixed to the
ground just long enough to see what's going on, even if it seems
like it might be what does you in. This is, in part, what makes
the jumpout boys exceedingly nefarious, operating in neighborhoods using tactics that have a very specific translation and
more of reaction that shifts, ever so slightly, from how someone
might react to sirens, to a badge. The officers that pulled up on
Green were supposed to be acting as surveillance in the neighborhood, calling in a cruiser if anything looked suspicious. This
stuck with me when I first heard the story in Connecticut. I
don't trust anyone who isn't from where I'm from, who doesn't
live where I live, to report anything as "suspicious" or "not suspicious," and yet this is the ecosystem that I've known and had

to rely on, that people I love are subjected to. Tourists wandering through areas they don't have any connection to, speculating on people they couldn't care less about. Life and death, determined by the haphazard tourism of people who believe they are eternally at war with everyone but themselves.

4:38

The game was an extra perk, a chance to decompress with some homies who were at least feeling a fraction of my rage. There were protests popping off for Henry Green in the coming days, and it felt important for me to be there. It was secondary, I thought, that I might get to watch the Cavs end their title run back home in Ohio. It felt good not only because I could do it with friends but because it allowed for a kind of refocusing. Black people in Columbus had stared down the realities of police violence before and had risen up against it to various degrees, but this moment felt different.

I had found myself in Ferguson in the late summer of 2014. Some black folks I knew went because they were curious, some because they were angry. I was more angry than curious, but knew that I didn't want to sit at home and watch from afar. It was the first time I'd seen, up close, what happens when people peel back a portion of a city's mask, and it was the first time I'd seen, up close, how a city fights back to continue to keep its façade poorly concealed. I had never before been in front of a wall of smoke so thick, my own two hands vanished when I pushed them forward, so thick that I lost my newfound friends in the smoke between us. I'd never held a stranger's face in my hands and flushed out their eyes after the tear gas had seeped in and they writhed in fear, insisting that they couldn't see, that they might never see again.

Less than a year later, I watched the Baltimore uprisings from livestreams in my sloppy, makeshift home office in my Connecticut apartment, staying up until two or three in the morning, anxiously tracking the movements of protesters and the tanks and choppers and gun barrels pointed at them. One night I watched as a lone protester shouted directions to their peers through a bullhorn. A tank slowly emerged in front of them, pulling up and blocking the camera. When the tank moved on, the protester had vanished, as if they had been swallowed by the machine itself. I remember blinking hard, thinking that I'd imagined it. In the chat on the side of the livestream, a scroll of concerned comments unfurled, all asking if everyone had seen what I, too, had seen. I didn't sleep until hours later, the sun coming up, when the protester confirmed that they were safely home.

Columbus had yet to have a moment that mirrored this one, in part because of those magnificent lies that some in cities tell themselves. That these things don't happen here, don't happen to us. Yeah, our cops aren't great, but they ain't just killing folks in the street (even before Henry Green's murder, this was, of course, untrue—from 2013 to 2016, Columbus police shot twenty-eight people, twenty-one of them black).

And so I came home, riding the waves of grief, rage, and now, in my own hometown, a small bit of curiosity. I wondered, foolishly, perhaps, if this would be what it took to dislodge a city from its comforts, rattle people at least somewhat permanently out of the self-made mythology of a clean and holy place, a place not like those other places that burn on the news, that fill their streets with riot cops, that make widows out of entire communities, that leave blood to grow dark on the concrete. I came home an optimist, or perhaps I came home a fool, but I came home. I wanted to run to the doors of the police station with whoever else would join me. I wanted to arrive, breathless with rage. I wanted to look toward anyone who was still on the fence, still wrapped in the arms of mythological comfort. I wanted everyone to know. There hasn't been a city built yet that is incapable of burning down.

4:00

When people ask how protests went, they sometimes ask the question as if the protest is something that can be won or lost, as if enough fear can be struck into the hearts and minds of empire and its ruthless agents. A city can turn upside down if enough streets get blocked off and the cops surrender their gas and guns for an hour or two. If they pull back their horses. But that ain't winning shit. You win for a quarter, maybe even a half, but the game is the game. After we flooded the steps of the police station in the name of Henry Green, CPD killed Julius Tate just two years later, and then flowers lined a fence on Mt. Vernon Ave. And then candles flickered in the twilight as people marched. And then fewer people marched. 2020 was awash with bullets from the guns of cops. Casey Goodson, shot in the back five times, entering his own damn home. Andre Hill, murdered in a friend's garage right before Christmas. And still people take to the streets. March past the high-rises and the new condos and some of us get dragged into the back of cop cars and sprayed in the face with gas and held down underneath a boot. And there are those who might think just escaping is winning, just making it home alive is winning, leaving with your body mostly intact is a type of winning. And I hear that, but those of us who want more with our victories are not foolish. Those of us who see the potential for a promised land, even if we have resigned ourselves to the fact that we might not be alive to bask in it.

3:45

You might delight in the underdog story, as I have before and certainly will again. You might, even now, be reveling in what you know of LeBron James and the Cavs, what you know of a city that had been called a losing city so long that there were those who had started to believe it. You might love the underdog story for the same reasons I have come to love it. The reality that sometimes, even when there is no way out, a way can be found. Or the sweetness that comes with laughing one's way through a parade of silenced doubters, those foolish enough to declare their own victories well before the final bell. Even when I pretend to not care who does or doesn't believe in me, there is a part of me that will always want to know the people who deserve to be witness to my most raucous celebration. Those who deserve to be witness to my long and slow savoring of a moment they didn't want to come, even if I'm not sure how I got there myself.

Even when I am not an underdog in the least, even when everyone believes in me or, at worst, no one gives a fuck about my movements either way, I can convince myself that I am an underdog. The same shit that had Jalen Rose in Chris Webber's grill, popping off during a game they were winning in a season they were dominating. Don't let a motherfucker see you sweat, even for a little bit.

And I'm from Ohio, which means everyone I roll with from this godforsaken state dreams themselves an underdog. Me and my whole crew embrace this flyover shit. The narrative that might say we only matter during election years, and even then we gotta lie about who we really are just to get the country to give a damn. Fuck is a swing state that swallows the residents at its most vicious margins. But I'll embrace that lie too if it means I gotta fight my way up and out of something, even if that something is pulled from the depths of my imagination, a mirage of an opponent, like shadowboxing, dancing in the backyard while the sun pulls your dark shadow taller along the concrete.

And I am from Columbus, which means I am from a hood not far from where Buster Douglas trained. Not far from Windsor Terrace, not far from where he brought a basketball state title back to Linden-McKinley High in '77.

Buster Douglas is here, upon a page I have architected, once again. Because we are talking about Ohio, and we are talking about who makes it out alive and who doesn't. And I still cannot get the mouthpiece of Mike Tyson skipping across the canvas out of my head. I still think about the moment when, instead of rising, Tyson fumbled for his departed mouthpiece, foolishly trying to clench it with his gloved hand while referee Octavio Meyran counted, kneeling alongside Tyson almost tenderly, holding each ascending number as close as he could to the eyes of Tyson, whose eyes wandered, fixating on the white crescent that had flown from his mouth. I still think about Douglas, in disbelief, arms raised like he'd seen in the movies. I still think about my own home in disbelief. Me, at seven years old, with school the next morning, given the gift of a late bedtime like all of the other Columbus kids I knew, even if none of our parents *actually* believed Douglas would win the fight. Some believing that the mercy of a later bedtime might actually just become an early bedtime if our guy Buster didn't make it out of Round One. The optimism of a child's mind knows no boundaries, which is the first taste of how one becomes obsessed with the underdog. When they don't outgrow the simplest realities of a circumstance. Maybe he'll just hit him hard one good time, and he'll fall down. And that's it.

Don't shit else matter if you come from where we come from and you get to hold a belt over your head. Get to bring it back to the hood and let the kids run their hands over it. There is some mercy in being an underdog and then thriving beyond anyone's wildest dreams of what you were capable of. I know Buster Douglas got his ass kicked by Holyfield, but no one I know gives a fuck about that. The history of an underdog can be distilled down to their brightest moment and then held on to forever.

And this is why, in Ohio, so few people I know turned away from the Cleveland Cavaliers, even when it looked bleak at the end of Game 4, when it seemed like this would be another disappointment. But what if it wasn't? What if it is most comfortable against the ropes? The bruised and weary fighter grinning in the face of the juggernaut, too arrogant to realize that it was always a trap.

3:38

What I believe to be true, and what absolutely must be true here is that if you are a champion once, you are a champion always. No one can strip you of this. If you are a champion for a day or even for a few moonlit hours, you get to call yourself a champion, no matter how long you hold on to the belt, no matter if your fingers only graze the trophy as it gets passed along to the next victor. History might not ascribe the same gravity to every champion who has ever won anything, but history is hell on so many of us, and I am feeling generous, today and always. I have felt like a champion before, even having won nothing but the desire to be alive in a day I woke up not wanting to be alive in. I deserve something for that, even if it is a parade of my own making. An invention, which is all the spoils of winning are anyway. Breathtaking inventions, to be sure. But inventions, nonetheless.

3:20

Yes, praise be to the underdogs and those who worship in the church of slim chances. I haven't fully let go of the childlike simplicity that pulls me away from the odds and whispers to my most cynical corners that anyone, anywhere can win. But I have seen a city go up in smoke and then go up in smoke again. I have seen the cops walk, go home to their families while sobs and shouts tremble the floors of a classroom. I have seen mayors pour money into military-grade weapons while public school students sweat in the fall and freeze in the winters.

I don't mean to pull us back from our delights and triumphs, but while standing inches from a police officer's face during a protest for Henry Green, I knew that one of us was more afraid than the other. And even with that math in my favor, I was the one, between the two of us, who didn't have a gun to reach for. Who didn't have an army at their back.

Forgive me for instantly stripping away the romantics of the underdog that I have so generously laid out, but I let my skepticism sink in to even the meaningless corners. The corners that I know can be determined by a good or bad shooting night or the right punch to the weakest part of a jaw.

And yet, I know what I know. Sometimes the people who are supposed to win end up winning. The bad people, the worst people, the people who shouldn't have any control, and yet they do. Whoever has the gun on their hip and a badge on their chest wins. Whoever can murder an unarmed person and walk home to their family wins. Whatever murderer can get a photo of themselves smiling in their police academy photo on the front page of a paper is the person who wins, and these are certainly not our underdogs. Whoever can sign a bill, whoever can abandon their office or their home when protesters arrive at their doorstep. Whoever can do harm and then become a ghost when it is time to answer for the harm done. These are the winners. Yes, whoever wires a bomb to a car wins, even if only temporarily. Whoever spins a city into panic, explosions punctuating the daytime hours. They win, until they are on the wrong end of a car's ignition, coughing its way toward an eruption of orange heat.

This obsession, this continued pursuit of the right underdog to believe in—it arrives to me so easily because I know who wins, most often. I know this, and I still run out into the streets, thinking it might stop them or at least prolong their inevitable victory parade. That's the trick. Stealing back one game here or there. Make it home alive. Extend the series.

3:18

Years after he beat Tyson, Buster Douglas was asked in an interview when he knew he'd won, and Douglas said it was the pursuit of the mouthpiece that gave it away. *Any time you know you only got ten seconds to get up, you ain't gonna worry about anything but just getting up first.*

3:00

There is one scene I remember from Game 2 of the '16 Finals, when the game got exceedingly out of hand. At the end of the third quarter, Klay Thompson hit a three-pointer to put the Warriors up by 20. It was unspectacular, a three-pointer from the top of the key. But it wasn't the shot itself as much as it was

LeBron James, who stared at the rim after the basketball slipped seamlessly through the net. The way LeBron, deflated, flicked the ball behind his back to his teammate waiting to inbound, and then dutifully dragged himself down the court for the quarter's closing moments.

The deflation is small but familiar to anyone who has run up against an immovable monument and thrown their fists into it, only to watch it crack but never tumble. It isn't just the disbelief but the moment right after, when his body realigns itself to the reality of needing to get back to work, needing to figure out how to hold back the flood for however long he can before it overtakes him.

It isn't the same, I know. The stakes of a basketball game and the stakes of a city's survival may look the same from a distance, draped in a romantic enough cloak. But they aren't the same. And still, in this interior moment of a game, LeBron James seemed to be realizing what it was to run up against an immovable monument for what feels like an eternity, only to see it still in the same spot it was before you began thrashing into it. Not hoping to topple it entirely but hoping at least to crack the foundation. I have been at the threshold of that specific anguish before, watching my reflection jumble itself in riot shields and feeling my shirt cling to the sweat on my back. It is an immense feeling. I tell myself it must be temporary. There are times when some of us must have a shorter memory than what our bodies hold.

2:55

Any time you know you only got ten seconds to get up, you ain't gonna worry about anything but just getting up first.

2:45

When I was Tamir's age, or younger, I made the shape of a gun with my hands. My middle and index finger extended across a parking lot, my thumb in the air. I did this many times, before I was the age Tamir was when he was murdered or slightly younger. But I remember the first time I did it was because I wanted someone to feel afraid. Or because I'd imagined that I wanted someone dead, barely knowing what the stakes of death actually were. I hadn't buried my mother yet, I hadn't buried any of the friends who would come after her, who would run into a nighttime that they could not run out of.

I remember this vividly, I suppose, because it was the first time I wanted someone dead. Which, at that age, meant to me that I wanted someone gone and knew of no other way to get someone gone, not when they are a classmate, not when they run the same blocks as you. The person I decided was my target didn't know they were my target. We were on opposite basketball courts. He stood, dribbling at the edge of the court where we'd fought just one week earlier. A fight I probably lost, by any metric that involves blood or bruise. We'd been friends once, or at least we'd come to a kind of agreement to sometimes joyfully enjoy each other's presence because proximity would not allow for anything else.

It is hard to explain what becomes of rage when someone does not love you as you want them to. When someone who you want to love you instead throws a fist. My hands alone were not vicious enough to be weapons, so I fashioned them into one. Trembling, pointing across the playground without a thought in my head except making him into a ghost.

2:30

When I was even younger than the age Tamir was when he was murdered, my parents refused all manner of toy guns. They were not allowed to enter the home or even be in the orbit of the home. This extended, even, to the imagination. Anything can be a weapon if a person points it as one with ill intentions might. A roll of paper towels, a pencil, a small enough book. My parents were not only against their children having toy guns but also against their children fantasizing about holding guns, repurposing the otherwise mundane materials of the home into vessels for even imagined violence.

Some of this was softened in the first summer of the Super Soaker, which flooded my block in the early '90s, water gun fights breaking out in the midst of basketball games, older dudes on the street doing wholesomely mimicked drive-by shootings, rolling down the block slowly and letting a tinted window descend before sticking their Super Soakers out and drenching some unsuspecting fool. The Super Soaker was the perfect tool to circumvent the anxiety my parents had about toy guns. The majority of them were adorned in bright, often colliding colors. Neon and fluorescent and too large and clumsy to be mistaken for anything beyond what they were.

But down the street, one of our pals had a water gun that looked like the real thing. Not only black, but it also gave off a shine that could be mistaken for metal when the sun lay across it at the right hour. He insisted that this added to the thrill of the water gun fight. The split second when he pulled it out and his opponents might freeze before looking close enough to see the orange tip at the end of the barrel, signaling to them that it was a toy.

In the early days of spring break one year, when it was still slightly too cold to subject each other to the aftermath of the water gun fights, my pal let me borrow his black water pistol. I snuck it into my house and slept with it under my pillow some nights. Kept it tucked in a junk drawer other days. I had no real use for it. I wanted, mostly, to see myself with it in the mirror. This is the part of the movie where the cautionary tale about black youth begins. The boy, barely ten years old, pointing a gun that could be real at a mirror and spraying a stream of water onto the glass. The moment where—like Bishop in *Juice*—the weapon itself runs the risk of becoming who you are. Folding into your identity like a darkness crawling up the arm that points it.

I thought my parents fools at the time for giving in to what I thought was this idea, when I imagined that the only reason they wanted to keep us away from toy guns was due to how the toy gun might unearth some violent tendencies that had been dormant. I didn't understand them enough. I never did. I remember watching the water run down the mirror and watching the distorted version of myself appear in the descending droplets, each of them housing a unique, smaller reflection. I was, in this moment, my own child army, untouchable in the face of anyone praying for my undoing, even myself.

There is no logic I can offer as to why children were, and are, still drawn to toy guns beyond the exhilaration. Dressing oneself up in the aesthetics of danger while not falling in love with its more treacherous outcomes. Children deserve mischief, even ill-advised mischief. When we were too young, too small to get on the courts with the older players in my neighborhood, and when we grew weary of chasing after wayward balls that had spun off of the rim, we had to build a world for ourselves—one that mirrored the world we were already subjected to. One that had heroes, one that had instruments of horror and people willing to use them. And then, when the moon knocked and porch lights came on, we could go back to our homes, breathless and still alive.

2:20

The spectacular isn't all that unfolds in a matter of unstoppable seconds

there is more than a ball pirouetting through an arena's sky navigating a course toward destiny have you considered how quickly a heart can stop

2:19

beating how quickly blood can sprint from a wound there is no clock that turns back so quickly that life might be gifted to the dead there is no resurrection from the panicked ticking that haunts the already-eager fingers on triggers and I am talking real triggers the bullet travels faster than the speed

2:18

of sound and so what to make then of the cop who pulls up in a car and maybe shouts but maybe doesn't but definitely fires

2:17

a bullet that arrives before the sound of his voice what to make of this besides someone who wanted someone else dead some-one who made up their mind who did not in doing so imagine the casket or the mother crying atop it the sound of dirt being placed upon a child's grave travels faster than the bullet but cannot stop it

2:16

no matter the symphony of moaning no matter the weight of the earth no matter.

2:13

Tamir Rice did more than just die in a park in Cleveland. I promised myself that if a black person died here, in these pages, I would remind myself—and perhaps remind you—that they lived a life where they did more than just die, more than just march themselves into headlines and endless discourse. In photos, Tamir's smile is slightly crooked, sometimes uncertain. In the photo that most commonly circulated after his murder, he's smiling with tight lips, looking like he's resting at the border between a smile and outright laughter, as if in the moment someone was coaxing him into the smile with a joke that finally landed. I have been, and remain, steeped in gratitude for Tamir's mother, Samaria Rice, how she has refused to let her son's legacy be only that of a child who was murdered. And still. The burdens that are placed on grieving parents, specifically black mothers, to continue to do this, to refuse to let their children vanish after those children are consumed by the many-armed violences of the state.

Shortly after his murder, there were stories of Tamir making pottery and crocheting small gifts for his mother. And lord, it is a tough line to walk, to not want to be seduced by this. Pouring someone's full self out for the world to see in a time when they are only seen as someone who died and deserved it. It's the most vicious trick, trying to dull the edge of the knife that keeps pressing into your grief, your rage, your despair.

But there was something that felt uniquely special about this, even more than the fact that Tamir hooped, that he was nice at ball, more athletic than his most direct peers. After marches, after vigils, after the anger I felt scrolling through comment sections and articles about Tamir's death (though never about his life) I found calm in returning to the image of him, focused, working with his hands to make something special for someone he loved.

2:12

The night that Tamir Rice was murdered, the Cavs played a home game. It was early in the 2014–2015 season, in the first season of LeBron's return to Ohio after he became a champion in Miami. They lost to the Raptors, 110–93. They fell to 5–7 on the year, and the fickle nature of sports fans began to tumble through the parade of excitement over LeBron's return. There were those who thought James had lost a step, that he wasn't up for his Cleveland Cavaliers 2.0 era. I only vaguely remember the game itself. It was background noise that night as I frantically attempted to find out more about Tamir Rice, murdered just hours before tip-off. I remember one moment, though. I remember one of the announcers mentioning a tragedy in the city, but the tragedy itself was never named. It was just spoken into the air, and then, like that, there was a fast break. There was a layup or a dunk or a foul. It is unclear to me, even now, how death can become a footnote. I have seen the names vanish, I have grasped for them in the wind. I suppose it begins with people understanding that something is a tragedy but not knowing exactly why.

2:09

The person who called the police on Tamir Rice mentioned that the gun was probably fake, that the boy pointing it at the park in Cleveland just a few days before Thanksgiving in 2014 was probably a child. But the information wasn't passed on to the officers who were dispatched to the scene. I don't believe this changes anything, and it is only something I return to because the initial caller, even in their assertion that Tamir was a child, did it with tentativeness, something that echoed through the aftermath of Tamir's murder.

Friends, we are far removed from our initial talk of enemies, and talk of how the past self can blur into the present. But when I say I don't remember myself or some of my loved ones as children, what I mean to say is that their faces now are the faces I love the most. I mean to say that I am intentionally blurring a past where I might not have loved you the way that I do now. That may be a somewhat foolish politic, but it is one that I am rooted in, a far cry from our enemies, who seem to measure childhood through a lens of who does and doesn't deserve to have one. A childhood of both the ecstatic and the frightening, teeming with joys and mistakes.

In the midst of mourning Tamir and marching for Tamir, I grew weary of any conversation that returned to and landed on his appearance. How he looked, if he was *big for his age*. No one bandying these debates around ever really specified what rested on the other side of them: what it might mean if he *were,* in fact, "big for his age." I suppose the reality is that no one had to say what many of us already knew. People were looking for a way out, a way to feel all right about the murder. Sure, it looked bad, but if he was large enough or dangerous enough, then what could anyone be expected to do, really?

I found myself recalling Darren Wilson, the police officer who killed Michael Brown in 2014. Part of his defense was that he believed Michael Brown to be a demon. Wilson actually said this: "I felt like a five-year-old holding on to Hulk Hogan."

And like that, Wilson became the child. Brown became superhuman, monstrous, thunderously raining down havoc upon a city. With Tamir Rice, similar thoughts were thrown about. People would discuss his height and weight down to the inches and pounds. It never seemed to cross their minds that what was on the table in the discussion was never how large Tamir actually was or wasn't, but how large and dangerous he was in the eyes of a police officer with a gun pointed at him. And that, of course, becomes malleable when filtered through the state and its desire to absolve itself of violence. So many police officers with guns on their hips or in their hands insist that they are afraid, depending on who the perpetrator is. They insist that they, themselves, feel small in the face of danger. Like Darren Wilson, invoking his five-year-old self to make sense of why he had to murder the massive, hulking black teenager who otherwise, surely, would have killed him.

This weaving in and out of childhood is a convenient weapon, one not afforded to everyone. Friends, we are not far removed from our talk of enemies. Not far removed from the moment when I tried, and failed, to reach for the images of my boyish self. The childhood selves of the many people I love. Not far removed from you, perhaps, looking in the mirror and trying to imagine your own self without the gallery of age exhibiting itself upon your now too-familiar structures. I let us off the hook too early there. I turned us away from that moment of somewhat hazardous thought before I could pull some clarity from the mess. But it isn't only about how we appear, friends. It isn't only about memory; it isn't only about the sounds that carry us back to a younger elsewhere or the fireflies or the joyful humidity of a summer with no rules.

Innocence is the key that unlocks the box holding all of the aesthetics within. Or at least the perception of innocence. I am not sure when childhood was first coded as innocent, but it has often struck me that to be able to understand childhood as a window curtained by monolithic innocence takes a very specific kind of commitment to mythology, one that I haven't been able to touch. I don't believe in innocence, which is another weapon of convenience. I am not sure what it means to pursue or even be stagnantly held by so-called innocence in a vicious ecosystem of living and of having to survive. But, okay, if I am to give in and briefly commit myself to upholding the lie of innocence for this exercise, I will also say that in the corner of the world I came up in, wasn't no one concerned with staying all that pure. Wouldn't matter if they were anyway. It strikes me now that a part of why I cannot retreat comfortably back to any era when I *looked* like a child is because there were so many years when I wasn't a child to the people around me. The teachers, who said I spoke *too grown* or the cops chasing me and my boys down for shoplifting a candy bar, the older homies on the bus or in the halls who would try to accelerate me and my crew into what they—still children themselves—imagined as adulthood.

No, I have no use for innocence beyond the dead. The dead are innocent, departed from the treachery of the world. Even if what comes after this life is an eternal mass of darkness, one the dead don't realize they're wading in, even that affords them an innocence. An escape from what has taken some of us a lifetime to survive.

And with this, I ask you now: Who among us has conflated the myth of innocence with the reality of goodness? With who does or doesn't deserve to live? Let us cut through the bullshit and say what we know. None of this, right now, is about who does or doesn't *look* like a child. It is about what the idea of a child embodies and how easily the American imagination can be seduced by what it believes a child to be. Many of us came into the world screaming and then spent our living enduring the world's shouting back. There might have been innocence once, before our eyes adjusted, before our memories took shape. Back when our parents whispered in our ears as we drifted off to sleep.

But I remember when I could run on my own. I remember when I first realized I could steal from a place and not get caught if I was quick enough. I remember when I understood that I was a bad liar—but a committed one. I remember when I held a water gun, painted black, to my own reflection and imagined someone else.

1:45

This is not the city it was when we began, or should I say, when we ended. This is the other rendering, the one that holds the truth underneath the tongue that lies. City of towering terrors and twilight triumphs, city of cuffs and cells, city of a lake's taunting curses, city of *I swear, God, just this one time,* city of one time, sirens and tires screaming along the concrete while sneakers scatter down alleyways, city of explosions, city of a trembling hand reaching for car keys, city of trembling hands locked into each other in arenas made momentarily silent by a ball's descent, city of diamonds too, for a night, running across the lips of the desperate, city of the desperate, city of losers if you let the fools from somewhere else tell it, and they can't tell anyone shit anymore, city of ghosts (what city isn't?), city that outlasts death, city that chases down what you owe even after the burial, *pay me what you owe me* city, city of floods, flooded streets, flows, flowers for the living (if they earn them), city of *did you see the corpses dancing or am I losing my*—city of children who could be men who could be kings, I suppose, if the lord wills, city of lords who might not will, city of finding out even if you ain't fuckin' around all that much, city of glass—glass houses, glass spirits, the soul weighed in glass shows the carrier doesn't have much longer, but then again, none of us does, city of atrocious mirrors, city of good nights and bad lighting, yes, city of the *cavalier,* which is both to be a defender of a king and also to show inadequate concern for the living, depending on which definition in the dictionary your finger lands upon. And this is the best trick of all: how I demand that each word unravels into a spool of disparate meanings, definitions, revelations even. I sit at the border of a city and pull the small threads that have frayed at its edges, eager to see which one will undo the pristine fabric. Yes, precious vessel of metal and water, I see you for who you are now, and you have always seen me. Let's keep each other's secrets a little longer.

1:15

When it comes down to it, I will remember the Nike commercial more than I will remember anything else.

I was newly living in Connecticut when the 2014–2015 NBA season began, LeBron's first season back home in Cleveland after his run in Miami. His first season since all had been forgiven. The sins of The Decision and the ensuing years had been washed away. There was excitement around Cleveland basketball again, a loud buzz I felt from my apartment in a Connecticut suburb, where I lived in a high-rise building on the water, a towering gray structure that nudged up against Long Island Sound. There was a long boardwalk where the older folks would play shuffleboard in the middle of the week-day, and sometimes, if it was warm enough, a hot dog cart would come out, or some kid looking for a quick buck would drag a cooler of haphazardly arranged sodas along the wooden planks, shouting out prices that seemed to change with the wind, depending on what the day's potential victims looked like.

My then-partner and I chose the apartment because it seemed like throwing ourselves directly into a place that was decidedly not like the landlocked place we left and loved. I had never woken up to the sound of water before, and I remember the first few nights of sleep, I had dreams that I was drowning. I'd wake up gasping, the sound of the waves trickling into the dark of the bedroom, cackling with laughter.

But we were also the youngest people in the building by a wide margin, something we didn't anticipate. The area catered to retirees or elders seeking some beachside calm in whatever years they had left. The interior of the building was cloaked in a type of calm. The walls were a sort of gray-blue, some hall-ways had floral print wallpaper haphazardly applied to some panels to briefly interrupt the gray-blue, but then the color would simply arrive again a couple of doors down. But the peo-ple were nice, I told myself. When I went to the small gym in the lobby of the building during my lunch hour, the older woman who rode the stationary bike at that same time every day would look at the door with gleeful expectation as I walked in. Half out of breath, she would ask me about the dog she would sometimes see me walking. She would ask if I missed Ohio less this week than I did the last week, and I would lie.

There was nothing that made me miss Ohio less in the first

months of that first year. Some of this I attributed to the simple emotional doldrums of a large life shift and the unfamiliarity of my new space. But some of it was that I left thinking that I'd one day get to come back. That Connecticut wouldn't work out for me or my partner, and we'd just decide to leave. And so, even my settling in was done with an imaginary countdown clock hovering above the hallways, above the boardwalk, above the violently lashing waves leaping with ferocity as if they were attempting to pull down the early autumn sky.

This felt heavier in part because of the excitement that gripped Ohio in the months before LeBron James officially suited up for the Cavs again and the dreams of championships to follow. Not only was LeBron back, but he was back with a team that could actually *win*. Not like before, when he was play-ing with what some would consider to be a parade of role play-ers, at best. On opening night I got texts from pals who made that familiar pilgrimage to Cleveland or pals who were already there. One friend gave me a play-by-play rundown of her at-tempt to get tickets for a fair price from a scalper outside. And then, for those of us watching on television, we saw the Nike commercial.

I have a healthy skepticism of anyone trying to sell me any-thing, and so I do have my limits, I do have curtains I will close when even the loudest pawing at that window commences. And yet I cannot describe this commercial to anyone without pausing a moment, at least attempting to resist tears. There is no logic to this, really. I didn't grow up in Cleveland, and my relationship to the Cavaliers is more geographical than hyper-emotional. Sneaker lover I may be, yes, but there is no Nike shoe that has ever pushed me to the brink of weeping.

But here is what I know.

1:10

That I was alone in an apartment, and I wished I were some-where else. I know that the sun had started to retreat earlier, and with more pace. The kind of moment that tricks you into leaving the lights off for longer than you would have just a week ago, and so I remember it was dark. It was dark without my knowing, the room lit by my own desire for a thrill—to see an arena that reminded me of home, to see a player who defined a time and a place that I wanted to gallop toward but could not. The commercial itself, while still special, might not be as spec-tacular to me under different circumstances. If I were in Ohio, in a friend's basement, surrounded by my people and their peo-ple, the world might not have stopped.

It is a black-and-white scene. In the commercial, the an-nouncer, finishing the starting lineup, calls LeBron James to the center of the floor. When James gets there, the team hud-dles around him while he begins a speech. Something about how whatever must be done has to be done for Cleveland. How the city has been waiting for this moment, and so the team has no choice but to rise to the occasion. Yes, the sometimes-flimsy barrier that exists between a team and a place is disrupted here, torn down right in the first fifteen seconds of the clip, and that is the first and most vicious seduction.

When the team pulls in for a tighter huddle, putting their arms around each other, a person emerges from the stands. One at first, and then a small handful of others, and then a wave of others. All of them joining the huddle, putting their arms around each other. From inside of the arena, fans crowd the tunnel, march through the overpass leading inside the arena, pulled toward the already-growing huddle, seeking any-one to put an arm around. Outside of the arena, people crowd under trees and reach out for a nearby shoulder. Small children rush to the edges of buildings overlooking Quicken Loans Arena and the crowd that has mysteriously grown outside of it, all of them linked together, arms around each other. LeBron isn't finished with his speech, though his voice has grown quieter as the arena has gone silent but for the swelling drone of prolonged keys writhing under the scene. Everything the team does has to be for the city, LeBron says. It's a question of debt. The city has been waiting for so long, surely the Cavs owe them. In a different context, these platitudes might not even register, might summon a yawn for even the most easily enthused by sports cliché. But while he speaks, the city's people grow around the language. They crowd the alleyways and spread into the downtown. They line the docks of the river. They are on rooftops, crowding bridges, gazing from windows.

In the magic of the commercial, they can all hear LeBron, though his voice has numbed to a near-whisper inside of the arena. Fans outside nod along with his voice. They lean in and furrow their brows, affixing looks of determination to their faces. And yes, this might be the point where you understand— or can at least be swayed into believing—that what is being discussed here is destiny. Finally, the pin is out of the grenade. LeBron James, making clear what was already assumed. Not just *I came home to win* but *We will win together.* My god, the greatest lies are told in the name of sports, in the name of teams and cities and the people in them. People who do march from the docks to the doors of an arena. People who do save up some coin to get seats in the highest corner of the rafters, closer to the kingdom of heaven than he who would be named King. The greatest lies are told in the name of what people believe they can reach out and touch. How the idea of winning in a place where no one believes you to be a winner can summon the heart to leap from the edge of a cliff, praying to land in a sea of outstretched hands. There are worse lies than this, ones that I'm less prone to be seduced by in a moment of weakness, in a moment of dreaming.

And in the commercial, the people are still marching, the boy with a shock of curly hair, grinning wide from his father's shoulders. The people exiting their cars and following the traveling masses. LeBron, laying out the instructions: *Hard work on three, together on six.*

And with the first *hard work* echoing through the Cleveland streets, a small flock of birds startles and trickles away from the top of the Guardians Bridge. By the second rotation of *hard work/together,* the people are swaying now, their arms still slung around each other's shoulders, but all of them locked in a rhythmic exchange, a collective metronome. And the children. Yes, those still-living children I promised you once, before we arrived here, before we had to wade through the real bullets and the real bombs, before we had to drag ourselves past the real funerals and the real fires. I am sorry I kept us away from our miracles for so long, but the living black children in this commercial are gleefully slapping the glass windows on a school bus that drives by slowly. Their smiles and small hands visible only for a gasp of a scene, but long enough for its sweetness to echo. And by now, the people in the streets have given up on waiting for numbers or instruction, have even forsaken the calm rhythm they'd once built among each other. They simply shout *together* in rushed and breathless unison, no longer swaying but leaping from side to side, so loud that it summons reinforcements who do most certainly arrive, black boys trekking up hills and a congregation pouring out the doors of a church. This is it, the hopeful city and its many dreamers. The barrier between team and city and its people, already trembling under the weight of all of this, finally dissolves.

And if you can believe it, there is more. The moment that, even now, sends me over an edge that I would turn away from if I could, but I cannot. Not with what I know of how this ends. Not with what you know, either. I say "this" and mean the world outside of this two-minute commercial, selling less of a product and more of a universe of boundless pleasure, which is easy to do when there is not yet a real game to be won or lost. Praise the fantasies that can spring to life while all potential for agony rests.

When LeBron James puts up his fist, the team joins him. The team being everyone, the entire city. A unified ascension of closed fists and single index fingers. It happens in waves. First inside the arena and then out. A toddler's small fist jerks up in an attempt to meet the fist of their mother. People attempt stoicism with their fists pushing into the sky but can't help but be overtaken by looks of self-satisfaction.

It was taking in this closing moment, watching for the first time in my apartment in Connecticut, that I realized that I had, at some point during this two minutes, entirely descended from my seat on the couch and ended up on the floor, leaning against the couch. There is the feeling of knowing and understanding that you have been crying but not fully grasping the velocity with which the crying has overtaken you until you realize that you are, in fact, gasping in the darkness—a darkness that feels new but has always been there. In these moments, the darkness is a mirror, too. In it, I remembered that somewhere, in a place I loved and missed, there were people, their hands toward the sky, witnessing what they'd convinced themselves they'd never see again. And I was alone, lying to myself about that place, those people, how soon I could return. When two lies collide, it is the aftermath of the damage that unravels us. Like walking on the gray floor of storm clouds until the sky pulls apart, becomes an unblemished blue. A miracle for those below, but for you, an ending.

1:05

I am not as ashamed as I once was to admit that there is also envy here. When LeBron came home, all I understood in the moment was that he could return and I couldn't. He could come back to a place that needed him, and I needed that place but could not even remember my most beloved parts of it some days, when I would walk on the Long Island Sound boardwalk and dodge the soda hustlers.

I would say that we end as we began, but in reality, we end as we have already ended. The city is baptized by its own people, its own makers. The city is washed in the waters spinning off its most committed disciples. The night air gorges itself on their self-made song. And we, who watch from afar, decide that this is beyond a temporary mirage, even if we know the city well. A team can have this effect on a place, but Cleveland lives and dies by sometimes misguided hopes, lives and dies by the mirage. I have fallen for this again, despite cursing myself, knowing what I have fallen for. It shouldn't be this easy to undo terror. Shouldn't be this easy to undo the percussion of ghosts that rattles the wind of any place, shouldn't be this easy to stand anywhere and not think of who might be buried underneath your feet.

I've told you before: nostalgia is a relentless hustler. Relies on how bad anyone wants to retrieve a feeling, or even an idea of a feeling. And so I can say I remember when I saw people embracing, and it did confirm whatever myths I'd built around how any of us love or live or survive in a place that tries to tear people at the margins to pieces.

But a more honest understanding of this is that all of our living can so easily be turned into decoration. We can become the flowers lining the sidewalks where people sleep and are stepped over. We can become the golden smoke winding over the lake, the cannons and the confetti coughed from their mouths. We lend our living to fantasies, sometimes without even knowing we're doing it. Never too far removed from being in the palm of a city's imagination, while someone far away whispers *Isn't this the most beautiful thing you've ever seen?*

1:00

And this is what sends me back to the wonder of children. The children on the buses in Cleveland in a black-and-white commercial for sneakers, the children who make guns with their fingers and peek behind corners, heaving with anticipation. Within the caverns of awe and wonder that exist in a child's mind, a city is bald. A neighborhood is a city. A packed living room is a city. No kings or queens that can't be touched. No kings or queens whose voices you cannot wake up to in your own home. Endings can be more romantic, but beginnings are the only honest thing.

I began once. My city was honest because I could see all of it from my window and didn't want to imagine anything I couldn't see.

In the hood I came up in, the landscape was known best by whatever function it served, even if that function wasn't its primary one. This, another form of honesty. The church with the tall concrete hill that neighborhood kids would ride down in the pursuit of danger. The church was inconsequential. We

never prayed there, never met any members of the congregation. It was a place to ride our bikes.

Scottwood Elementary School was certainly an elementary
school, though no one on my block went there, and we didn't
really know anyone who went there. It was across the street
from my house, and so it's where my bus stop was. I'd walk
through the school on the way home, sometimes intersecting
with kids who went there, playing in the grass. And still, it
barely seemed like a school at all.

Scottwood was a basketball court. It was one of the most
prominent basketball courts on the Eastside, and so it didn't
matter much that the courts sat in the shadow of a building
that could have been anything. Sure, it was a school during the
days, during the winters when it was too cold to go outside or
properly grip a ball. But on spring evenings, and all summer
long, Scottwood was so overloaded with talent on its court that
the school became invisible. It was a true testament to one uni-
versal truth that I believe in: a good court is not defined by
infrastructure but by who shows up to play on it.

And there were no games like those games. To be an audience to that impossible miracle. This many good players in a
radius of a mile or less. Running games from noon until 8 or 9
p.m., and sometimes, if the ball was good enough and the parents hadn't yet come to the porches yelling the names of their
children, some folks would pull cars up on the blacktop and
kick on their headlights just so the games could keep going.

I haven't found many things I love as much as I love the sound
of a basketball game in a park going down to its tense and silent
closing moments with a sky just beyond sunset. Players on the
court too worn down to even talk shit anymore. Nothing but
breath and the echo of flimsy metal, bending as a ball spins off
the rim, signaling a game that, mercifully, won't end just yet.

Parents who came to the park swearing that they'd drag their children home now at the edge of the blacktop, as in awe as everyone else, becoming children again themselves, praising the heavy legs that leave the shots flat, praising the fouls that don't get called through a forest of swinging hands, praising the rebounds that slip through fingers and the passes that don't twirl off the hands with the same joyous shouts that they did just a few hours earlier. It didn't matter much to any of us that Scottwood was also a place where kids sometimes went to school. It was a mecca, a proving ground, a place where you could be a star even if you rode the bench for your high school or even if you got kicked off the team. In the right neighborhood, the right park suggests all glory is within reach for everyone who wants it.

And the miracle is also the places where a chance at glory blooms. The full court at Scottwood was cracked and uneven, but it was clean. Smaller than a regulation full court at any gym, but enough to comfortably fit ten people. The court was surrounded by a playground, tetherball poles with nothing hanging from them, a fluorescent map of the United States, haphazardly drawn and colored in by schoolchildren. A wasteland of jagged metal structures, the type that one might look at now and wonder how these were ever built with children in mind. The kind of structures that don't really have names or look like anything, and so—much like the park itself—the structures took on the name of whatever function they served. Those things over there? The things that are *kind of* monkey bars but also certainly not? Those make a good bench if you aren't too worried about climbing and you want a good view of whatever the court has to offer, or if a couple hustlers slide a few dollars in your pocket and tell you to watch for the blue and whites until a deal is done.

There were actually three rims at Scottwood.

0:55

Even in the utopian universe of the park, there was a hierarchy. The full court, which sat at the center of the park. And then, off near the back, beyond the never-used baseball field and near the school's exit, was a single rim lording over a single, small half court. This rim was never adorned with a net—even at the start of summer, when the fresh nets were put on the other two rims, this old one was left naked, adorned only in the rust that had accumulated over the years. But this rim was where the kids played. The younger siblings, the cousins, the friends of friends, all of us too small or otherwise not yet ready to play on the full court with the older kids but still in love with the game enough to want to fire the ball toward an unkempt halo of rust.

To pass the time, we'd take turns trying to beat an imaginary clock. Someone would throw a ball in the air and start counting down from five, or ten, depending on how far out the ball was thrown. And it was just you

0:45

against time, and nothing else. And all that mattered was that you made the shot, before your crew howled out the noise that was supposed to sound like the buzzer at the end of a game, but

0:44

most often sounded like a flock of birds, strangled by clouds, and screeching on their descent to earth. And yes, it was best if the shot slipped through the rim but it could be argued that there was also magic

0:43

in the shots that missed, at least for how that missing would invite the orchestra of laughter, high-pitched and uneven but still sweet. The axis upon which success and pleasure tilts is flimsy, and some days I would have rather failed but been in awe of the rapturous joy I got to fold into with my crew, boys who were not yet big enough or good enough to play on a court where the games mattered, and so we made our own game,

0:42

one where we could be small and inconsequential gods, architects of the miraculous. Miss enough shots and when one falls, time slows, and bliss becomes elastic. We would hold our follow-throughs, our fingers extended and frozen toward the sky, though not like Mike. We loved MJ, but there were Michael Jordans on our block. There were Michael Jordans walking among us. Jordans four houses down, Jordans at the bus stop. If I haven't made it clear yet, this is all about the good fortune of who gets to make it out of somewhere and who doesn't. Who survives and how. But let it be known that some of us

0:30

never once dreamed of leaving. Never thought about making it out of any place as glorious as this. Tell me if you have ever built a heaven out of nothing, and then tell me what it would take for you to look for a new one somewhere else. The people who circle this heaven from the outside wouldn't know this. Might think that everyone is trying to make it somewhere else, through ball, through music. That's another myth. Crack rock or jump shot. Courts and cages and caskets. Everyone getting out one way or another, or so some might say. Some with no imagination, who speed through the hood, who speculate about sneakers ornamenting telephone poles. Who read stories of gunshots dragging serenity from the arms of nighttime. Some who imagine a place with no fathers, who—relying on that myth—believe mothers and grandmothers incapable of the type of ferocious affection that might pull a child back from any ledge they run toward. I never wanted to be anywhere other than where I was, my two feet planted on concrete that was breaking, but satisfied to still be of use. I never wanted to stray far from the shitty speakers weighing down old trunks, the symphony of bass and rattling metal, the smoke that drifts from an open window, an arm swinging from it, a wrist dangling out the side, a gold bracelet on that wrist, the sunlight running its fingers along the links, the shine of it, echoing for blocks. My people are here, and my people built the here in their image, and at least for a few precious years, there was nowhere to make it out of. We built the impossible utopia. You can't see the fence, but it's there. It'll keep you out, too, if you don't come correct. The gangs were never our enemies, but the people who look upon where we stay and see gangs in every gathering certainly were our enemies. But I ain't never gonna complain about who don't come around. If that's what it takes, then yes,

0:25

gang everywhere. A gang of stars mobs the infinite, cloudless black. A gang of black blooms infinite through a mob of dripping light, which reflects off of the sweat mobbing the skin of the black kids who should be home but are instead ganged up on the dying summer, the night itself sweating out a gang of shouts that swallow the gang of sirens, the echo of a ball fired off of a back-board mobs the silence, which was hardly ever silence around here anyway. A whole gang of porches and mobs of good folk set atop them, a gang of shoes or bare feet stomping the old wood, beckoning a mob of dust to fly skyward before settling right back down where it was, where it has always been, the homie leans back in the grass while a gang of fireflies decorate the absence above our heads and he says *I'ma have me a gang of kids, and my kids gonna have a gang of kids, and we ain't never leaving. We gonna own a whole block of houses, right here in the hood.*

0:20

Understand this: some of our dreams were never your dreams, and will never be. When we were young, so many people I loved just wanted to live forever, where we were. And so yes, if you are scared, stay scared. Stay far enough away from where our kinfolk rest so that a city won't get any ideas. They will burn down or build over a neighborhood for nothing. Doesn't matter how many stars are built or born on a cramped court, doesn't matter who gets a court or a community center named after them. But trust: there are more of us, always. Whole gang of us. Some of us carved our names into trees, into the wet concrete of new sidewalks. Some of us took small knives to metal and wrote our names into the death traps of the playground. And so we stay, one way or another. We never make it out, and we never disappear. Permanence is the greatest stunt of them all.

0:16

When Brian Wilson completed the song "God Only Knows," he spoke of the impulse to fade the song out on a loop of the chorus, suggesting that it creates a sort of infinity spiral. A world where the song is still going on, always, somewhere. And you, the listener, are still in it, as you were at the time of listening. A dream with no exit. There is a universe, always, where you are joyfully encased in the endless return of chorus, and you might age there, but let's say you don't. Let's say you and the chorus both lock into a type of eternity, a forever of wondering *God only knows what I'd be without you,* an eternity of praising the fact that you'll never have to find out.

0:10

And it is both beautiful and heartbreaking to imagine this, that we go on living while a past version of ourselves remains locked, peacefully, in a euphoric dream. What I have been asking, the door I have been pawing at this entire time, is for a reimagining of eternity. A reversal, perhaps. Not that our happiest, freest selves are fastened to a dream, while we exit and return to the living world. But that our exit is where the dreaming begins, and our real, actual living is the place where we remain at our most joyous, time moving forward by small inches, each of us growing only seconds older with each passing year. Come as close as you must to understand how much I need to believe in this, even if you do not believe in it with me. It has maybe all been a dream.

0:09

And not just the suffering. Not just the cold floors of county jails or storage sheds. Not just the fights and funerals. Not just the pills I never took, the ones I poured down drains or threw out of open car windows while speeding down a highway, sobbing into the fluorescent shades being drawn over the sky. But even the joy has been a dream. The confetti blown around the lake after a city has won a championship might have been just rain, after all, lashing across my face. All the sweetness of my survival, all the unearned pleasures, I have possibly been dreaming all of it. Which would explain your faces,

0:08

my beloveds. Why I cannot remember them as they were when we were young. When I try, the features arrive in a jumbled haze, even as I look closely now, at someone I have loved for years, I am reaching back toward how I knew them once and finding air, sometimes cradling a laugh that sounds like it could be a child's laugh. The mind can only hold so many faces. I see parts of the people I loved as a child everywhere, but never their entire, younger selves. We might still be alive back there, on the beautiful and bowing branch of youth. No one has been buried. No one has learned to load a gun. No one knows the price of anything that might sell good in any season. The weapon that might be your undoing hasn't been invented yet. It could be true

0:05

that I am still living in the kingdom of a ball descending from the sky while I stand on an unevenly painted foul line, waiting with my arms open. The friends I believe I will always love, forever counting down, a series of falling numbers, but the clock never reaching the end.

0:04

0:03

0:02

0:01

LEBRON JAMES, AKRON, OHIO (1984–)

Believes home is wherever / you land / wherever holds you / after you take flight / it is better this way / you cannot be a king / to everyone / you cannot be a king / forever / no ruler is un- killable / but goddamn / praise be / the executioners / have yet to find a weapon / that will do the trick

HANIF ABDURRAQIB, COLUMBUS, OHIO (1983–)

Never dies in his dreams / in his dreams he is infinite / has wings / feathers that block the sun / and yet / in the real / living world / the kid has seen every apocalypse / before it arrives / has been the architect of a few bad ones / still wants to be alive / most days / been resurrected so many damn times / no one is surprised / by the magic trick / anymore

Acknowledgments

This book exists in great part due to an intersection of belief and labor. My own belief uplifted by those who labored to the finish line alongside me, and I am overwhelmed with gratitude for all of these folks. Alia Hanna Habib, Sophie Pugh-Sellers, and all of the good folks at Gernert. A full team of generous hands and minds at Random House: my editors Ben Greenberg and Maya Millett, who figured out the math of another book with me. I am endlessly grateful for your support. Maria Braeckel and Ayelet Durantt, who have made sure these books live a good, long life. The team who did work to get to the end result of this book's stunning cover: Greg Mollica, Tyler Comrie, Matt Eich, and Pia Peterson Haggarty. Evan Camfield, who offered thoughtful copyedits in the home stretch. And everyone else who worked on bringing this to life: Greg Kubie, Abdi Omer, Windy Dorresteyn, Marni Folkman, Jordan Hill Forney, Tom Perry, and Erica Gonzalez.

I've been lucky to build an expansive community of writers who are more friends than professional peers, and I have amassed endless gratitude for all of them. Would especially like to send thanks to the Lyrics N' Layups group chat, which began as a silly way for writers to talk about sports, but has endured and grown into something far beyond.

My dear friends in Columbus, who have seen me through to this point, and whatever points may come after. Meaghan, Sam,

Stephanie, Madison, Mia, my earliest mentors, Scott Woods and William Evans. The organizers in Columbus, who help bridge the gap between the city as its false self and the city as its true(r) self. An honor to be a witness to, and participant in, your work.

Gratitude to the people who put the nets up at all the parks on the Eastside before those old '90s summers. Gratitude to the people who swept the glass off the courts. Who painted the lines.

This book is dedicated to the memories of MarShawn McCarrel, Amber Evans, Bill Hurley, Gina Blaurock, and Rubén Castilla Herrera.

Index

James, LeBron (*cont'd*):
  in the imagination, 150–51
  jerseys of, burned, 197–98, 200,
    204
  as King James, 138–39, 141
  as a legendary Ohio aviator,
    321
  with Miami Heat, 174–75, 177,
    180
  miracles performed, 132–33
  Slam magazine cover, 155
  "Together" Nike commercial,
    304–8
  vanity of, 34
  "We Are All Witnesses" Nike
    campaign, 119–20, 195
James IV, 140–41
James VI, 140
jersey burning, 197–98, 200, 204
jobs, 153–55, 213–14, 222
Johnson, Magic, 139
Johnson Park Middle School, 96–97
Jordan, Michael, 15–19, 76, 79, 313
Josh, 76, 95, 106
Joyce, Dru, 61
judgment, 163–64
Juice (film), 293

Kelly, David Patrick, 262
King, Jimmy, 10–13
kings, 137–41, 150
Kings of Leon, 115
Knight, Gladys, 180
knowing, 232
kufis, 21

language
  black hair as, 8–9
  of hands, 11, 32, 34

handshakes as, 4–5
  for loneliness, 24
  shit-talking, 12–13
Lavender, Andrew, 44–45, 53, 54
Lavender, Anthony, 53
Lavender, Antwain, 53, 54
leaving, 223–25, 227–30
Leaving Songs, 180–81, 186–87
Lee, Spike, 100
Leslie, 24–28
"Let's Get It On" (song), 183
libraries
  jail, 150
  as a place to rest, 123
Licavoli, James, 266
Lil' Kim, 63
Linden-McKinley High School, 254,
    286
lineage, 53–55
loneliness, 24, 170, 172
longing, 170–71, 177
looking, 232–36
looking back, 260–61
Lorenzo, 98–99
Los Angeles Clippers, 158, 216
Los Angeles Lakers, 278
losing, 247–50
loss, 74, 90–91, 259–60
lottery tickets, 156, 158–60, 161
love
  architecture of affection, 3
  for basketball, 28–30
  for the black bald head, 6–8, 24
  convenience mistaken for, 25
  for the dead, 226–27
  desire to not be lonely mistaken
    for, 24
  for the Fab Five, lack of, 20
  falling in, 178–79

sacrifices, 29, 51

San Antonio Spurs, 174–75, 218

saviors, 112–13

Scalish, John, 264–66

Scottwood Elementary School, 72,
76, 96–98, 152–53, 310–15

seasons, 173–74

Shakur, Tupac, 63

shit-talking, 12–13

shootings, 42, 278–84, 292,
294–95, 298

silence, 36

Simone, Nina, 179

"Skylark" (song), 56

Slam (periodical), 138, 155

Smart, Keith, 158

Snyder, Dick, 255, 256–57

soldiers, athletes calling themselves,
64–65

Soul Children, 185

Sports Illustrated, 10, 86

St. Michael's Church, 141

Strickland, Ted, 192

stunting, 73–74

suburbs, 58–60, 64

suffering, 189, 208, 227

Super Soaker water gun, 292

survival, 230, 260, 270–71

"Survival of the Fittest" (song),
56

Tate, Julius, 284

Terrance, 130–32

Thompson, Klay, 289–90

"Together" Nike commercial, 301,
304–8

Toronto Raptors, 191, 296

Trav, 162

Travis, Romeo, 61

Truce of Perpetual Peace, 140

Turner brothers, 53–54

Tyler, 35, 230

Tyson, Mike, 286, 289

underdogs, 43–44, 285–87, 288–89

University of Michigan, 10–13, 15

"Use Ta Be My Girl" (song), 183

Uzi Alley, 55

Value City Arena, 41, 49

vanity, 34, 73

villains, 201–3, 219

violence
enforcing boundaries of, 244
as language, 236
neighborhood, 55–56
police, 278–82, 288, 292,
294–95, 298
romanticized in sports, 64–65

Wagner, Dajuan, 158

The War Report (Capone-N-Noreaga
album), 57

war zones
aesthetics of, 63–65
the hood described as, 55–57,
280

The Warriors (film), 262

Washington Bullets, 255, 269

water guns, 292–93

"We Are All Witnesses" Nike
campaign, 119–20, 195

"We Are LeBron" (song), 192–95

"We Are the World" (song), 192

weapons, 291–94

Weaver, Estaban, 83–87, 89

Webber, Chris, 11–13, 15, 19–20, 285

West High School, 75–76

About the Author

HANIF ABDURRAQIB is a poet, essayist, and cultural critic from Columbus, Ohio. His most recent book, *A Little Devil in America*, was the winner of the Carnegie Medal and the Gordon Burn Prize, and a finalist for the National Book Award. His first full-length poetry collection, *The Crown Ain't Worth Much*, was named a finalist for the Eric Hoffer Book Award and nominated for a Hurston/Wright Legacy Award. His first collection of essays, *They Can't Kill Us Until They Kill Us*, was named one of the books of the year by NPR, *Esquire*, BuzzFeed, *O: The Oprah Magazine*, *Pitchfork*, and the *Chicago Tribune*, among others. *Go Ahead in the Rain: Notes to A Tribe Called Quest* was a *New York Times* bestseller and a National Book Critics Circle Award and Kirkus Prize finalist and was longlisted for the National Book Award. His second collection of poems, *A Fortune for Your Disaster*, won the Lenore Marshall Prize. He is a graduate of Beechcroft High School.

About the Type

This book was set in Scala, a typeface designed by Martin Majoor in 1991. It was originally designed for a music company in the Netherlands and then was published by the international type house FSI FontShop. Its distinctive extended serifs add to the articulation of the letterforms to make it a very readable typeface.